Reluctant Adversaries
Canada and the People's Republic of China, 1949–1970

When the People's Republic of China was established in 1949, the Canadian government refused to recognize it as a legitimate state. Over the next twenty years, Canada's policy toward China centred on the Nationalist Chinese government in Taiwan, keeping one eye always on the much larger and lesser known republic in whose shadow Nationalist China struggled to survive.

Paul M. Evans and B. Michael Frolic have collected ten original essays on Canada's relations with the larger China between 1949 and 1971, when Canada officially recognized the PRC. An introduction by Evans sets the context. The first group of essays explores specific aspects of policy throughout these years, such as the delicate questions of recognition by Canada and by the United Nations, and the role of the United States in Sino-Canadian relations. The next group of essays discusses the role of individual players: Lester Pearson, Pierre Trudeau, and Alvin Hamilton. Finally, three essays chart the course of recognition of the PRC by the Trudeau government, the effect of recognition on one community of Chinese Canadians, and the impact on relations with Nationalist China.

Together these pieces provide essential insight into the complex process of developing official links with a new nation, and the implications of such action, both at home and in the international arena.

PAUL M. EVANS and B. MICHAEL FROLIC are professors of Political Science at York University.

Reluctant Adversaries:
Canada and the People's Republic of China, 1949–1970

Paul M. Evans and B. Michael Frolic
Editors

UNIVERSITY OF TORONTO PRESS
TORONTO BUFFALO LONDON

© University of Toronto Press 1991
Toronto Buffalo London
Printed in Canada

ISBN 0-8020-5896-5 (cloth)
ISBN 0-8020-6852-9 (paper)

Canadian Cataloguing in Publication Data

Main entry under title:

Reluctant adversaries: Canada and the People's
Republic of China, 1949-1970

Papers presented at a conference held in May 1985
in Montebello, Quebec.
Includes index.
ISBN 0-8020-5896-5 (bound) ISBN 0-8020-6852-9 (pbk.)

1. Canada – Foreign relations – China – Congresses.
2. China – Foreign relations – Canada – Congresses.
3. Canada – Foreign relations – 1945– – Congresses.
I. Evans, Paul M. 1951– II. Frolic, B. Michael 1937–

FC251.C5R45 1991   327.71051   C91-093235-3
F1029.5.C5R45 1991

The publication of this volume has been assisted by a grant from the University of Toronto–York University Joint Centre for Asia Pacific Studies and by a grant to the University of Toronto Press from Hollinger Inc.

For John Wendell Holmes (1910–1988), diplomat, scholar, and the invisible presence behind this volume.

Contents

Acknowledgments ix
Preface xi

Paul M. Evans, Introduction: Solving Our Cold War China Problem 3

SECTION I Origins

1 *Peter M. Mitchell*, The Missionary Connection 17

SECTION II The Policy Problems

2 *Stephen Beecroft*, Canadian Policy towards China, 1949–1957: The Recognition Problem 43

3 *Don Page*, The Representation of China in the United Nations: Canadian Perspectives and Initiatives, 1949–1971 73

4 *Norman St Amour*, Sino-Canadian Relations, 1963–1968: The American Factor 106

SECTION III The Policy Makers

5 *John English*, Lester Pearson and China 133

6 *Brian Evans*, Ronning and Recognition: Years of Frustration 148

viii   Contents

    7 *Patrick Kyba*, Alvin Hamilton and Sino-Canadian Relations   168

SECTION IV   Recognizing the People's Republic of China

    8 *B. Michael Frolic*, The Trudeau Initiative   189

    9 *Janet Lum*, Recognition and the Toronto Chinese Community   217

  10 *Arthur Andrew*, 'A Reasonable Period of Time': Canada's De-recognition of Nationalist China   241

Contributors   253
Index   255

Acknowledgments

We are grateful to the Social Sciences and Humanities Research Council of Canada for funding the editors' research and the Montebello Conference. In addition, the Department of External Affairs provided a supplementary grant for the conference and generous assistance in facilitating access to the department's documentary record. We especially appreciated the efforts of Arthur Blanchette and Dacre Cole.

The book benefited from the comments of two anonymous readers assigned by the University of Toronto Press and Arthur Menzies who commented on an earlier draft.

The editors and authors are of course responsible for the interpretations and facts offered herein.

Preface

For three days in May 1985, amidst the quiet beauty of the Chateau Montebello in Montebello, Quebec, a group of thirty-five examined the sources and conduct of Canadian China policy since 1949. The group included several historians and political scientists who were engaged in original research on Sino-Canadian relations, most of them using recently declassified Canadian documents. Our objective was to subject their ideas to direct scrutiny by some of the principal actors in the events that they were attempting to recount and explain. It was gratifying that the process of exchange and criticism went as smoothly and creatively as it did.

Participants came from either universities or government. The scholars presented papers and served as discussants. Those from government, including both politicians and civil servants, functioned principally as discussants, though two (Jack Maybee and Arthur Andrew) also wrote papers. Two former secretaries of state for external affairs, the Honourable Paul Martin and the Honourable Mitchell Sharp, and a former minister of agriculture, the Honourable Alvin Hamilton, made active contributions. We also benefited from the participation of the first four Canadian ambassadors to the People's Republic of China (PRC). Of the sixteen papers prepared and presented, ten are published in this volume based on their thematic focus, originality, and concentration on the period up to the establishment of formal diplomatic relations with the PRC in 1970.

The Montebello Conference developed from a project launched three years earlier on 'Image and Policy in Sino-Canadian Relations' directed by the two editors of this volume and funded by the Social Sciences and Humanities Research Council of Canada. A central purpose of the project was to identify and make accessible as much material as possible on Canadian thinking and policy towards the PRC. We have used this material in some of our own writings and are pleased that several other scholars were already working along parallel lines or were attracted to the subject by the availability of original documentation.

Daphne Gottlieb Taras and Bonnie Elster deserve special thanks for their impeccable management of logistics and hospitality for the conference.

Concerning the transliteration of Chinese names, we have decided to use the Wade-Giles system as far as possible. Although the pin yin system is now more common, Wade-Giles was most frequently used during the period that the authors examine in this volume.

RELUCTANT ADVERSARIES

Paul M. Evans

Introduction: Solving Our Cold War China Problem

The twin subjects of this volume are the sources and content of Canadian policy towards China in the years between the establishment of the People's Republic of China (PRC) in 1949 and its recognition by the government of Canada. For most of those twenty-one years, China was above all a diplomatic problem that seemed to defy solution. Very few Canadian officials privately or publicly endorsed the wisdom of the military containment and political and economic isolation of the Communist government of Mao Tse-tung. And very few felt warmly about the Nationalist government of the Republic of China. Yet on the central diplomatic and strategic issues pertaining to China – especially on recognition and U.N. representation – the policies Ottawa pursued followed Washington's lead.

The diplomatic record gives rise to several questions. What were the dominant Canadian conceptions of Nationalist and Communist China, and how did they influence Canadian thinking and action? How was China policy formulated? How did it fit with the broader objectives of post-war internationalism? How much room did Canada have for an independent approach to China? More directly, in what ways did American actions and attitudes affect the decisions made by successive Canadian governments? Was China policy really about China?

China and Asia have never been Canada's major preoccupations. But Canadians did spend a great deal of time worrying about their Cold War China policy. Occasional sceptics have challenged the effort that went into the issue. 'The fact is,' one American commentator observed in 1974, 'that Canada is not of overwhelming importance in the scheme of things, except to Canadians.' Earlier, in 1966, another American stated to a Toronto audience, then wrestling with the recognition problem, that Canada should forgo an agonizing policy review and simply flip a coin for all the difference it would make on the world scene.[1]

John Holmes's modest rejoinder that Canadian policy is 'a poor thing but our own' reinforces the sentiment that at least Canadians take Canada seriously, China policy included. There is no doubt that the China question posed a difficult set of choices which brought to the surface ideological divisions in the Canadian polity and some of the contradictions embedded in the post-war objectives and strategies of Canadian diplomacy. But these choices also reveal a great deal about the international environment and fundamental attitudes which conditioned the actions of many other governments.

There is a big difference between a focus on 'policy,' which is the realm of diplomats and politicians, and 'relations,' which refers to a much broader universe of contacts including unofficial and private activities. Only two of the chapters in this volume are primarily concerned with 'relations,' looking at Canadian missionaries and Chinese Canadians operating in private capacities. The remainder concentrate on the politicians and diplomats who engineered government policy.

The focus on policy, as compared to relations, is deliberate. In the era being examined, the Canadian agenda with respect to both Communist and Nationalist China focused on high politics. Governments were the main actors, with centre stage on the Canadian side reserved for cabinet and the Department of External Affairs (DEA). The level of direct societal contact with the PRC – principally in the forms of a *Globe and Mail* bureau in Peking opened in 1959, a trickle of Chinese emigrants after 1947, and a small number of private exchange programs – was extremely restricted. Grain exports after 1960 constituted the overwhelming dimension of substantive contact and even here government played a major role in initiating and sustaining the trading relationship. Similarly, there was very little commercial or social contact with the Republic of China on Taiwan until, paradoxically, after formal diplomatic relations were terminated in October 1970.

For diplomatic historians, the complicated and difficult policy problems of the era carry their own fascination. At the time they generated commentary and controversy far in excess of the actual level of substantive connections or of Canada's stake in East Asia. In part this was because China was an emotional and passionate issue to those individuals who had directly experienced its century of revolution. And in part it was because policy toward China touched a nerve on the sensitive issue of Canadian independence in foreign relations. To many Canadians, China policy symbolized and suffered from the undue dependence of Ottawa on Washington. Within the diplomatic service, the problem was posed somewhat differently. To the architects of the 'golden era of Canadian diplomacy' in the post-war years, China represented a painful and enduring reminder of the gap between aspirations and achievements. The objectives of internationalism, Canadian activism, and ending the isolation of a great power were frustrated by events abroad, bad timing, and the overriding importance of relations with the United States.

Unlike the strong national consensus which developed in the United States after the outbreak of the Korean War on the nature of Mao's China and the appropriate policy response to it, Canadian public opinion on China was consistently divided.[2] Few Canadians were deeply informed about China, but most held firm opinions which tended to divide along the lines of region, party affiliation, and education. Images and interpretations of Communist China that emerged in the press and Parliament were passionate and diverse, ranging from mildly favourable to strongly critical. On policy issues, there was general enthusiasm for trade relations but a very mixed response to the recognition of the PRC and its admission to the United Nations. Support for expanded relations with the PRC grew in the 1960s, to the point that by 1964 a little more than half of Canadians supported recognition of Peking and its admission to the United Nations.[3]

Canadian views of Communist China then and later have not had the mercurial quality that has characterized the Sino-American connection.[4] If Sino-American interaction has been a roller-coaster ride, Canada and the PRC have been on something closer to a merry-go-round. The highs have not been as high or the lows as low. This more stable attitude is likely a function of the diversity of Canadian conceptions of China and has been a major factor in explaining how since 1970 the Canadian and Communist Chinese governments have been conspicuously successful in managing what both sides have often identified, usually without cynicism, as a 'special relationship.' At the same time, it is unwise to minimize the controversy which China and China policy has engendered in the past. Viewed from the perspective of the emotional and angry response in Canada to the tragic events in Tiananmen Square in the summer of 1989, the potential for public rancour over relations with China is not of merely antiquarian interest.

It is beyond question that China received an inordinate amount of public attention. This was reflected in Parliament where between 1949 and 1974 China was mentioned more often than any other foreign country with the exception of the United States.[5] But how far did the Canadian public affect government policy in the 1950s and 1960s? As several of the essays indicate, a variety of interest groups and private citizens ventured into lobbying activities. These included church groups, Chinese Canadians, concerned academics, and business people. Two points deserve attention. First, the views they espoused ran in different directions. Second, major Canadian corporations did not have a large stake in the China trade and did not actively lobby in support of expanded political relations with either Peking or Taipei. As Lester Pearson acutely knew, there never emerged a compelling popular mandate to act in any particular direction. The main forces pressuring federal officials thus centred principally on intra-elite conflict and external considerations, not on an activist domestic constituency.

In assessing these external considerations, many have looked to Washington instead of across the Pacific to explain the distance between Canadian aspirations and achievements in Cold War China policy. Clearly, Washington was the key external player and was decisive in setting the agenda for the Asian policies of most Western governments. In addition to the skills of American diplomats and what John Holmes had adroitly called 'the fact of American policy,' perceptions of Washington's economic power conditioned the responses of all of these governments. The instruments and extent of American involvement in the economies of the allies varied considerably, but calculations of Washington's diplomatic and economic response were fundamental and abiding concerns. This sensitivity to Washington was amplified by the widespread acknowledgment of the passion and near unanimity of American hostility towards Communist China in the period between the Korean War and the mid-1960s. Even when Canadian officials disagreed with American attitudes and actions, they could not ignore them. On the other hand, as the essays make clear, the reasons for Canadian inaction were complex and cannot be attributed simply to American interference. For better or worse, Canadian China policy was indeed made in Canada.

In elite circles, China policy provoked debate and occasional rancour for more than two decades. DEA confronted the China problem from the position of a well-regarded, comparatively small elite operating out of the East Block on Parliament Hill. Canadian policy, of course, was made by elected politicians, not the department. But as several essays indicate, the relationship between the politicians and the civil servants was complex. Signals and directives from above shaped but did not completely dominate the policy advice that came from below. Within the department, policy advice came from officials who rarely had deep attachments to China or detailed conceptions of its internal dynamics. Expertise on China was not lacking, but the principle of rotation and the generalist ethic of the department worked against regional specialists dominating the policy formulation process.

The Essays

A major scholarly review of Canadian policy toward Eastern Asia has not been attempted since the study by H.F. Angus in 1953.[6] There have been several excellent book-length treatments of Canadian involvement in the conflicts in Korea and Indochina and of our bilateral economic relationship with Japan.[7] What has been missing is a general overview sensitive to strategic and political developments at the regional level. The essays in this volume go some distance in filling the gap by situating China in the broad outlines of Canada's post-war policy as it developed during and after the Second World War. China, of course, is only one part of Asia. But by the late 1940s, the fate of the Chinese revolution and international responses to the Communist regime were the main planks in the geostrategic thinking about Asia of much of the Western world, including Canada. The essays are all based on original interviews and documentary research, principally employing recently declassified DEA and Privy Council Office (PCO) records. The overall accomplishment is an unusually rich and detailed history of Canadian policy making over almost two decades from the perspective of a group of authors with visibly different disciplinary backgrounds and political sensitivities.

It is worth emphasizing that although the authors differ in their interpretations of key events and in their assessments of the wisdom of Canadian policy, they are all employing Canadian sources and materials. A fuller treatment of the period and the issues awaits the utilization of Chinese sources, from both Taipei and Peking. Until that time, the scholarly discussion of Sino-Canadian exchange will necessarily remain partial and out of balance.

The missionary enterprise provided Canada's first popular link to both mainland China and, slightly earlier, Taiwan, and is therefore the natural place to look for the roots of Canadian involvement. Peter Mitchell's chapter examines the missionary presence in mainland China and gives a broad overview of Canadian policy in East Asia up to the Communist victory. He contends that in the absence of significant trading and diplomatic activity, missions in the field and church organizations at home were the most sustained bridge between Canada and China for almost fifty years.

Mitchell examines an era in which private initiative flourished and in which Asia was not a major Canadian priority. At the same time, it was an era which witnessed the first glimmerings of a Canadian identity as a Pacific country as well as an Atlantic one. Three areas that Mitchell finds important are the missionaries' direct linkages with policy makers in Ottawa and overseas, several of whom were the sons of missionary parents;

their influence on public images and thinking about China; and the ways in which their activity foreshadowed later governmental policy, especially in the areas of developmental assistance and immigration. It is in the shaping of general perceptions rather than in direct influence on decision making that Mitchell locates the most important legacy of the missionaries in the policy realm.

The recognition issue was at the heart of Canada's China problem, and Stephen Beecroft examines the way in which the St Laurent government approached it. Continuing Mitchell's themes of Canadian insularity from Asian affairs and the identification of China as a low national priority, he traces the early debates in cabinet and DEA which were the first acts in a drama that ran for twenty-one years. Among the themes of the essay are the growing irrelevance of British influence on Canadian actions, if not attitudes, and the evolving views of St Laurent and Lester Pearson on the proper Canadian course of action and the importance of China in the post-war order. In this instance, as in others that followed, the secretary of state for external affairs was further out in front on the problem than the prime minister could support. The parallels between Pearson's frustration with St Laurent's procrastination in 1950 and 1955 and Martin's later frustration with Pearson in 1964 and 1965 testify to the importance of role variables in explaining policy preferences. A brief epilogue by Paul Evans describes the main lines of DEA's action on the recognition problem in the period between the fall of the St Laurent government and the Trudeau initiative of 1968.

Don Page gives a detailed account of Canadian thinking and action with respect to the representation of China at the United Nations. Like Beecroft, he relies principally on DEA and cabinet materials. The proper representation of China in international organizations, particularly the United Nations, was closely linked to the recognition problem, but by its nature demanded multilateral action and, as Page argues, represented an even greater threat to American interests and priorities. The efforts of Paul Martin, the secretary of state for external affairs, to solve the problem between 1963 and 1966 are a central focus. The representation issue was a high priority to Martin, his department's main cut at the China issue, and a source of friction with Pearson. Martin's slow progress on the problem and eventual abandonment of it underline both the domestic and international factors which produced the stalemate that would not be broken until 1971.

Norman St Amour uses both Canadian and American documentary material to examine the interaction between the Johnson administration and the Pearson government on China policy. Because of the Canadian focus at the time on the U.N. problem, the essay covers some of the same ground as Page but does so from a different perspective. The key confrontation in St Amour's essay is that between Paul Martin and Dean Rusk. St Amour emphasizes the conflicts and tensions within the U.S. government and the way these divisions were interpreted in Ottawa. The Pearson government's 'quiet diplomacy' towards Washington and its desire to influence events in Asia by influencing the United States was, St Amour suggests, coupled to an attempt by DEA officials to sustain and reinforce moderate opinion in the State Department and the White House. But he also makes clear that the ultimate objectives of at least some of the moderates in Washington were compatible, though not identical, with Canadian views. St Amour is more critical of Canadian policy than either Beecroft or Page, suggesting that fears of American retaliation were often exaggerated and were in fact more powerful in the minds of Canadian officials than in reality. Canadians were constrained as much by their own perceptions and domestic priorities as by external circumstances. He indicates, for example, that there is no hard evidence that the White House linked China problems to Canadian-American bilateral trade issues. Whether or not this linkage was or would have been made in Congress is less clear.

The third section of the book draws on the insight that policy making is a collective process but that individuals play an essential role. States do not act, individuals do. Lester Pearson emerges throughout as a major political player and the most articulate exponent of the main lines of Canadian policy. John English gracefully examines the origins of Pearson's thinking on China and the place he gave China in his conception of a post-war order. For Pearson, China was not an emotional or deeply personal subject, but an increasingly important country which needed attention, understanding, and, above all, careful treatment. Similarly, Pearson's China policy was not the product of a deep understanding of the specifics of the Chinese revolution or Asian affairs but, rather, of a calculation from the perspective of international relations on the future and significance of the region, Canadian opportunities for leadership, and his conception of stability, multilateralism, and moderation as the key to world peace. Pearson's close familiarity with American sensitivities also affected his judgment and was no doubt influenced by his time in Washington during the Second World War. English looks to the structure of Pearson's ideas on international politics, the vagaries of pragmatic political concerns, and volatile international conditions to explain Pearson's increasing procrastination on any major China initiative after 1954. In temperament, character, and calculation, Pearson was the 'Hamlet' of the China drama.

Brian Evans's portrait of Chester Ronning tells the story of a flamboyant individual who lived and breathed China through all of his life. Perhaps no

Canadian at the time was more closely identified with Canada-China relations. Ronning's sense of Chinese history and society was the overriding determinant of his policy prescriptions. The consistency and passion of his views were widely admired among his colleagues at DEA, even if they were rarely shared. They did, however, find consistent and vocal support in the Canadian left. The extent of this support and the fact that he was allowed to present his opinions in such forthright and visible fashion for more than two decades, much of this time as a civil servant, testify to the tolerance and diversity which characterized debate on the China question even at the height of the Cold War. In the late 1960s, after leaving DEA, he made his case in the United States, steadfast in his view that American policy was wrong and that it needed to be changed before the strategic situation in Asia could improve.

As Patrick Kyba persuasively demonstrates, Alvin Hamilton's involvement with China was cut of a different cloth. Hamilton was not concerned with the intricacies of diplomatic negotiations and strategy, but was an engineer of substantive trading relations in the tradition of Canadians intent on selling wheat to Asians. He was not of missionary parents and had neither prior exposure to China nor any deep feelings about the Chinese revolution. His concerns were first and foremost those of domestic political imperatives. The grain trade created the first significant link between the PRC and Canada and foreshadowed a major governmental role in the bilateral commercial relationship. Ironically, Ronning the Alberta socialist and Hamilton the Saskatchewan conservative found themselves in the late 1960s and early 1970s preaching a parallel message to Canadians and Americans about the virtues of expanded contact with the PRC.

Kyba's essay is also a useful look into China policy in the Diefenbaker years. The main pillar of the Conservative government's approach was to postpone serious discussion of PRC recognition and U.N. admission and instead to concentrate on developing trade relations. But even here there was controversy in Parliament and within the Conservative party. Kyba makes clear that the sales were possible only after sharp political in-fighting and extensive bureaucratic manoeuvring. In initiating the sales, and then later in protecting them at the time of the Sino-Indian border war in 1962, pragmatism and domestic priorities prevailed over ideological reflexes in a divided cabinet.

Bernie Frolic's focus is Pierre Trudeau and the chain of events which began in 1968 and eventually led to the normalization of relations between Canada and the PRC two years later. Frolic looks first at the origins of the Trudeau initiative as they grew out of Trudeau's own experience with China, his conception of Canadian objectives and priorities, as well as his political style. The coming of Trudeau, he notes, fortuitously coincided with a change in Chinese priorities, the loosening of American influence over its allies, changing attitudes and strategic assessments in the United States, and a noticeable shift in Canadian public opinion on China policy. The actual implementation of normalization was left to Mitchell Sharp and his officials at DEA. Behind the successful conclusion in Stockholm lay intense internal manoeuvring, hard work, and tough negotiations. The outcome was far from inevitable and en route involved several Canadian concessions. Frolic's essay benefits from extensive access to the documentary record and interviews with almost all of the Canadian officials involved.

If a single theme emerges in the chapters by Beecroft, Page, St Amour, and Frolic, it is that the Trudeau government differed little from its Liberal predecessors in wanting Canada to play a direct role in bringing the PRC into the mainstream of the international community. Where it differed was in having the will and good circumstances to do so.

Janet Lum looks at the recognition issue from the perspective of a significant but largely quiescent constituency. Her case study of the Chinese community in Toronto assesses the extent to which Chinese Canadians participated in the recognition debate and decision. At the outset, they appeared to give strong support to the Nationalist government in Taiwan and were largely hostile to the establishment of relations with the PRC. By the end of 1970, with recognition imminent, the community perceptibly shifted to acceptance of the new state of affairs. Fears soon subsided that local Chinese communities would be the focal point for conflict between supporters of the Nationalists and supporters of the Communists. Lum concludes with the provocative argument that the process of recognition of the PRC promoted a greater respect for China and indirectly improved the self-image of Chinese living in Canada.

Arthur Andrew played a major role in the negotiations with the Communist Chinese and in other aspects of China policy during his career in the Department of External Affairs. His essay examines the diplomatic complexities of severing the relationship with the Republic of China. The status of Taiwan had been a recurrent and fundamental dimension of Canadian thinking on the China problem. The Nationalist government and the anti-communist cause of 'Free China' had a small number of vocal supporters in Canada, but in government circles was less important than a commitment to the people of Taiwan. The fragile and temporary nature of the Canadian enthusiasm for the Nationalists was symbolized in the fact that unlike the United States, Australia, and France, Canada did not establish an embassy in Taipei after 1949 even though the Republic of

12 Reluctant Adversaries

China had established one in Ottawa. The termination of diplomatic relations was achieved comparatively gracefully as Andrew notes, but the divorce that followed was bitter.[8]

Beyond 1970

The opening to Peking ushered in a dramatically different era in bilateral relations. By the time of Trudeau's celebrated visit to the PRC in 1973, the 'China problem' had become the 'China opportunity.' The context shifted from the high politics of establishing a relationship to the less glamorous politics of its careful and patient management. Accordingly, the policy agenda became much more complex, the number of bureaucratic actors proliferated at both the federal and provincial levels, and the depth and breadth of contacts deepened considerably. China received extraordinary attention in the areas of cultural and academic exchange, immigration, trade promotion, and, later, developmental assistance. Many of the programs that were pioneered in China became models for relations with other Asian countries. Until the events of the summer of 1989, the pace and scope of the relationship moved in an ever upward direction and, to almost all observers, represented a major success for both sides. The chief casualty, at least in the short term, was Canada's relationship with Taiwan. Canada's 'one-China' policy was pursued with a vengeance and there developed no Canadian equivalent of the Taiwan Relations Act of April 1979 which the American Congress enacted to ensure ongoing unofficial contact with Taiwan after the Carter administration recognized Peking on 1 January 1979. However, bilateral economic contact between Canada and Taiwan flourished and, in time, a more pragmatic attitude evolved on how contact could be enhanced without jeopardizing Canadian links with the mainland.

It would be unwise to overlook the broader meaning of the Canadian opening to Peking which, in at least two ways, extended beyond the strictly bilateral context. First, contrary to the view of sceptics, the Canadian recognition of the PRC was a significant link in the complicated chain of events that facilitated the PRC's opening to the outside world. Trudeau's China initiative both benefited from and contributed to a vastly improved international context. Canadian actions in 1970 did not end the Cold War with the PRC, but they did move it to a lower level of hostility and set the stage for its eventual transcendence. The ensuing decade was extraordinary in reshaping the strategic environment in Asia and in bringing the PRC into the international community and the global economy.

Second, Canada's Pacific policy until the late 1960s had largely been born in the minds and carried in the hearts of officials in Ottawa. It was also largely reactive, a response to the geostrategic interaction of the great powers. The new connection to Peking both promoted and symbolized an expanded Canadian involvement in the Pacific which was built upon a clearer focus, considerable public enthusiasm, and far more points of contact. Canada's emerging identity as a Pacific nation has been the product of changing economic, social, and technological forces much larger than governments or state-to-state relations. By combining diplomatic aspiration and substantive societal contact, the new relationship with China became the foundation of a more mature and independent Canadian approach to Eastern Asia after 1970. With the basic diplomatic problem solved, Canada's Pacific era could begin.

Notes

1 R.F. Swanson, as quoted in Brian Evans's essay (ch. 6 in this volume). The second sceptic is Charles Burton Marshall, as quoted in Paul Evans and Daphne Gottlieb Taras, 'Canadian Public Opinion on Relations with China: An Analysis of the Existing Survey Research' (Toronto: Joint Centre on Modern East Asia, Working Paper No. 33, March 1985).
2 Among the Western allies, the Canadian pattern is more representative than the American. On Great Britain, see Robert Boardman, *Britain and the People's Republic of China, 1949–1974* (London: Macmillan Press 1976); on Australia, Edmund S. Fung, *From Fear to Friendship: Australian Policies towards the PRC* (St Lucia: University of Queensland Press 1985).
3 On the dimensions and development of Canadian public attitudes on China policy and the related images of China held by Canadians, see Evans and Taras, 'Canadian Public Opinion' and 'Looking (Far) East: Parliament and Canada-China Relations, 1949–1982,' in David Taras, ed., *Parliament and Canadian Foreign Policy* (Toronto: Canadian Institute of International Affairs 1988).
4 Two of the most thoughtful treatments of the historical pattern of American images of China are John K. Fairbank, *China Perceived: Images and Policies in Chinese-American Relations* (New York: Alfred A. Knopf 1975); and Harold R. Isaacs, *Scratches on Our Minds: American Views of China and India* (New York: John Day Co. 1958 and, with a new preface by the author, Armonk, NY: M.E. Sharpe 1980).
5 See Evans and Taras, 'Looking (Far) East,' 67–74.
6 The three main studies remain Arthur R.M. Lower, *Canada and the Far East – 1940* (New York: Institute of Pacific Relations 1941); Charles J. Woodsworth, *Canada and the Orient: A Study in International Relations* (Toronto: Macmillan 1941); and H.F. Angus, *Canada and the Far East: 1940–1953* (Toronto: University of Toronto Press 1953).

7 See particularly Denis Stairs, *The Diplomacy of Constraint: Canada, the Korean War, and the United States* (Toronto: University of Toronto Press 1974); Douglas A. Ross, *In the Interests of Peace: Canada and Vietnam, 1954-1973* (Toronto: University of Toronto Press 1984); James Eayrs, *In Defence of Canada*, vol. 5, *Indochina: The Roots of Complicity* (Toronto: University of Toronto Press 1983); Frank Langdon, *The Politics of Canadian-Japanese Economic Relations, 1952-1983* (Vancouver: University of British Columbia Press 1983).
8 See Paul Evans, 'Canada and Taiwan: A Forty-Year Survey,' in Frank Langdon, ed., *Canada and the Growing Presence of Asia* (Vancouver: Institute of International Relations, University of British Columbia, 1990).

SECTION I

Origins

CHAPTER ONE

Peter M. Mitchell

The Missionary Connection

From the late 1880s through much of the early twentieth century, the Canadian missionary community in China was Canada's most organized overseas presence with the exception of wartime military expeditions. In numbers involved, levels of contact, continual commitment, and scope of impact, this 'missionary enterprise' merits considerable attention in any study of Canada's relations with China.[1] Catholic and Protestant, mainline and pentecostal, fundamentalist and social reformist, their numbers signalled a distinctive place for China in the Canadian outlook for many decades.

This chapter is concerned not with theological issues or rates of conversion, but rather with how the missionary presence in China contributed to general patterns of contact between the two societies in the period prior to 1950. On what issues did the Canadian missionary community in China and its extensive support network at home seek to influence Canadian official attitudes and public opinion on Asian affairs? How did they exercise such influence? How successful were those efforts? What legacy did they leave when, in mid-century, political and commercial interests superseded their prominence in Sino-Canadian relations?

Although the story begins in the 1890s, the major focus here is the late 1930s and 1940s when war and civil war raised fundamental issues of the outside world's relationship to China. American policy heralded China as a future major actor on the world scene, just as the domestic forces of revolution were accelerating toward a 'new China' to which post-1950 policy and opinion makers would have to react. Simultaneously, the expansion of the Department of External Affairs (DEA) signalled Canada's maturing status and readiness for new activism in international circles. This inquiry thus focuses on how decades of Christian missions in China helped fashion the background for later Canadian opinion and policy.

The Early Years, 1880–1939

The major themes of Canadian foreign policy throughout the pre–Second World War era were peace, trade, and immigration. With respect to Asia and China, these concerns produced sporadic bursts of intense official and public interest. However, a quick glance at each of these themes indicates that such outbursts of interest in the Far East produced very few active policy initiatives.

Two incidents constituted Canada's active strategic involvement in the Pacific. First, between 1917 and 1921, a number of Canadian missionaries became British Army officers in the Chinese Labour Corps which represented China's only participation in the First World War. Canada also served as the major transit route to and from Europe for that group of over 100,000 labourers.[2] In the second case, flushed with Canada's wartime rise to new international status, Sir Robert Borden's Union government committed a small military contingent to the Allied Siberian Expedition of 1919. The first of these events merits no more than quixotic mention in a few Canadian histories, while the second received little more comment as it lasted only a few months before the unbloodied Canadian troops were abruptly withdrawn.

These two episodes only briefly interrupted the calm dominance of another perception of appropriate Canadian policy in Asia. In the immediate post-war period, Canada co-operated with other Dominions in pressuring Great Britain to abrogate the Anglo-Japanese Alliance. Consequently, the possible strategic obligations in the Pacific which that alliance entailed were replaced by the sweeping but non-committal rhetoric of the Washington Conference agreements of 1921–2. Thereafter, under the careful shepherding of O.D. Skelton and Loring Christie, the fledgling Department of External Affairs consistently prevented Canadian entanglement in periodic breaches of the peace anywhere outside its own borders. A brief flurry of activity came in the wake of the Cahan incident during the League of Nations debates over the Japanese invasion of Manchuria in the early 1930s. But the pro-Japanese echoes in Cahan's comments were quickly neutralized by more detached official pronouncements.[3] Officially, Canada had no national objectives in the Pacific area which required an identifiable political stand.

This official attitude undoubtedly mirrored the realities of Canada's international status as well as Canadian public opinion. While Canadians hoped for peace in the Pacific, few considered it an objective they could influence. Arthur Lower's 1940 study aptly summarized the effects of that attitude. Nine years after the Manchurian Incident and three years after the full-scale Japanese invasion of North and Central China, he noted, 'The Tokyo Legation has never yet dealt with a matter of "high policy" for the very good reason that none such has arisen . . .'[4] As Tokyo was Canada's only diplomatic representation in Asia at the time, that categorization held for Canadian official posture toward the broader issue of maintaining peace and security in the Asian region.

Trade was Canada's second major international concern and it prompted the first official representation in China. A commercial agent was appointed to Shanghai in 1906 and raised three years later to the status of trade commissioner. The CPR developed its renowned *Empress* fleet in the Pacific and some Canadian companies (particularly insurance firms) opened Asian branches. In 1929 another trade office opened in Hong Kong. Prospects for Asian trade in the late 1920s figured prominently in Mackenzie King's justification for establishing the Tokyo legation and in his personal instructions to Herbert Marler, the first Canadian minister to an Asian capital.[5] Ottawa periodically indulged itself in the myth of Asian trade potentials.[6] Yet Sino-Canadian commercial ties remained too marginal to prompt serious sustained consideration of closer official relations by either side.

Through the 1930s, Ottawa periodically contemplated either cross-appointment of the minister in Tokyo to China or separate diplomatic representation. Ottawa was acutely sensitive to China's growing nationalism over such issues. And some Canadian missionaries were urging representation in China. As late as 1939, however, King was still extremely tentative about adding diplomatic to commercial agents in China.[7]

If peace and trade produced little policy-related activity, oriental immigration was another matter altogether. Charles J. Woodsworth's classic study *Canada and the Orient* devoted one chapter each to political, trade, and missionary connections but gave over four chapters and five of seven appendices to the history of oriental immigration.[8] Virulent rhetoric and occasional explosions of physical violence surrounded this matter throughout the late nineteenth and early twentieth centuries. To many Canadians, immigration was primarily a domestic rather than a foreign policy question. The capitation tax system was designed to curb the influx of Chinese labourers in particular, but even progressive increases in the amounts ($50 in 1885, raised to $100 in 1900, and $500 in 1904) failed to mollify the opponents of oriental immigration. Diplomatic activity sought a negotiated solution similar to the so-called Gentlemen's Agreement governing Japanese immigration after 1907.[9] But the lack of diplomatic commitment to Asia prevented any effective brake on the swell of western Canadian hostility. This led to the unilateral passage of the Chinese Immigration Act of 1923, which effectively ended any new Chinese immigration into Canada.

While viewed by Canadians as domestic politics, the legislation (and similar restrictive domestic regulations) had dramatic effects on Chinese impressions of Canada. Throughout the late 1920s and 1930s, visitor after visitor from China commented to Ottawa on these negative policies as barriers to any substantial improvement in trade relations. An anonymous commentator in the influential *The Round Table* opined in 1933 that Canada escaped a Chinese economic boycott only because 'the Japanese [had] come to Canada's assistance by creating a diversion in Manchuria.'[10] Though he had been a leader in earlier British Columbia pressure for oriental exclusion, H.H. Stevens, the energetic minister of trade and commerce in R.B. Bennett's cabinet in the early 1930s, became convinced of the need for change, if only to compete with the ease of entry which the United States was according Chinese professional and commercial visitors. His efforts achieved some minor modifications in the procedures of the Department of Immigration, but these failed to lessen substantially Chinese concerns.[11] In 1936, Escott Reid, then national secretary for the Canadian Institute of International Affairs, urged N.W. Rowell to press the matter once again with Mackenzie King, but the issue remained unresolved before war in Europe and Asia put such matters temporarily on hold.[12]

Canada's low level of political and economic involvement in the Pacific magnified the missionaries' influence on official and public images of China and its Asian neighbours in Canada. The missionaries were Canada's only substantial community in Asia, supported by home constituencies in all regions, to which they regularly reported by circular and private letters. The network was highly structured among mainline Protestant sects, perhaps less so among the non-national pentecostal groups (though that may reflect archival deficiencies more than anything else). Catholics were equally anxious to recruit their parishioners' support for missions in China, though there is less documentary evidence of direct efforts to influence Ottawa's policies on China prior to the late 1940s.[13] Some mission societies reinforced the effect of missionary correspondence by arranging extensive public speaking tours during home leaves. Done mainly to strengthen monetary as well as spiritual support for missionary endeavours, such tours by these itinerating 'experts' on China often included newspaper interviews as well as pulpit and parish hall reports. In early twentieth-century Canada, church and church-related groups were a normal part of most Canadian families' weekly activities. For many Canadian youngsters, initiation in foreign knowledge was often through the reports of Canadian missionaries, incomplete or prejudiced as these might be. China's overwhelming predominance in Canadian mission efforts made it the focus of inordinate attention.

Missionary letters and addresses in the early twentieth century conveyed to their Canadian readers a split image of developments in China. They verified press and official views of constant domestic political turmoil. While deprecating China's political weakness, however, they also conveyed a sympathetic attitude which championed the Chinese people. Increasingly they expressed greater hope for China's future, especially if foreign friends stood by the people's struggle for a better life.

The upsurge of Chinese nationalism in the 1920s reinforced this dualism. The majority of Canadian opinion – missionary, official, and public – found it difficult to do more than suspend judgment before the bewildering violence of that anti-imperialist movement. Ottawa bureaucrats deflected suggestions of participation in foreign intervention and quietly expressed doubts about continued association with British consular authority under which Canadian missionaries technically operated in China. Privately, at least, Canadian officials became more critical of the legacy of Western treaty privileges in China and the inadequacies of British representation of Canadian interests there.[14]

At the same time, the missionaries were forced to confront the facts of their relationship to the unequal treaty system, a traumatic experience for many. The overtones of a Bolshevist element within the Chinese Nationalist movement made most missionaries back away from outright condemnation of the system which protected their work in China. However, a few in the West China mission of the newly formed United Church of Canada took the lead in stimulating the Canadian missionary establishment at home and abroad to go on official record as seeking a new relationship with China based on bilateralism, reciprocity, and equality of rights.[15] This did not immediately affect Canadian involvement in China, but it did gradually filter into public opinion at home, preparing the groundwork for later events.

One area demonstrates the tangible effect of missionaries and their secular allies on Canadian policy in the prewar years. Prior to 1949, the Christian missionary enterprise in China was deeply involved in education. Two prominent examples – West China Union University and Shantung Christian University – illustrate Canada's self-defined role. Both were 'Union Universities,' interdenominational and multinational corporate structures located in China, responsible to boards in New York and

London. Canada's position was expressed by Dr A.E. Armstrong of the United Church Board of Foreign Missions: 'The United Church of Canada, through its North Honan Mission, is proud to be the connecting link between the British Boards and the United States Boards in the happy fellowship of the Board of Governors of Shantung Christian University. Of the eleven Boards in that partnership, five are in England, five in the United States, and one in Canada. We rejoice in being the hyphen.'[16] China missionaries thus reflected the growing self-consciousness of a Canadian position between Europe and America. They also demonstrated the attendant problems of defining that position with any degree of confident commitment.

The presence of Chinese students in Western institutions of higher learning functioned as a focal point in international competition over the shaping of China's future as a modern society. Canadian efforts to join this competition were spearheaded by McGill University and the University of Toronto, two major suppliers of recruits for the Canadian missions in China. Spurred on by their alumni in the cloth and reinforced by private commercial interests, they did manage in mid-1917 to secure capitation tax exemptions for Chinese students attending Canadian institutions. Canada's competitive edge was soon lost, however, when Department of Immigration authorities in Ottawa declined to accept the popular work-study programs put in place by France and the United States immediately after the First World War.

These efforts continued in the 1920s. Education officials in Canada reached inter-university agreements on academic equivalences to ease the applications of Chinese students. Canada also attempted to emulate the Americans' diversion of Boxer Indemnity Funds, but British officials responsible for the Indemnity Fund were unwilling to support Chinese students studying in Canada. No other substantial public or private funds were found to underwrite a variety of suggested programs to foster Sino-Canadian relations.

Sporadic efforts by overseas missionaries and university and business communities failed to increase the very small numbers of Chinese students in Canadian institutions of higher learning. The vast majority of those few who came did so through the network of Canadian missionaries. Arthur Lower summarized the situation accurately, if bleakly:

> Too much could not be expected, for Canadian civilization is still not easily distinguishable from that of the United States or Great Britain. However, the efficiency, thoroughness and general stability of the Canadian [missionary] effort may be considered reflections of

recognized Canadian characteristics. Possibly the failure to arrange for an adequate proportion of Oriental students to attend Canadian universities is also a reflection of Canadian quality – a lack of imagination that might be expected in association with 'solidity.'[17]

In the search for national self-expression, the Canadian missionaries and their home allies had as much of a problem as officials in Ottawa in defining an identity based on the fundamental premise of being a hyphen.

In the Midst of War, 1939–1945

Canada's official reaction to intensified Sino-Japanese conflict after mid-1937 was less a conscious 'Pacific policy' than an effort to stay in the hyphenation between an embattled Britain and an isolationist America. The Pearl Harbor attack in December 1941 released Ottawa from the tense nightmare of a Pacific War without her southern neighbour fully involved. Canadian action between 1937 and Pearl Harbor has been recounted elsewhere: in brief, it carefully trod a half-step behind the escalating American hostility to Japan while concentrating on maximizing military commitment as Britain's ally in the European War.[18]

Canada's involvement in the subsequent Pacific War was minimal, but with it came a new political relationship with China. In February 1942 Liu Shi-shun presented his credentials as the first Chinese minister to Canada. Fourteen months later Major-General Victor W. Odlum of Vancouver followed suit in Chungking.

Considerable impetus for the establishment of diplomatic relations came from the United States. In contrast to Churchill's jaundiced view of China's potential, President Roosevelt promoted a rosy American picture of a Christianized, reformist leadership in a China destined for post-war greatness. While never convinced of the latter, Ottawa did wish to give Sino-Canadian relations a modicum of content beyond the mere exchange of diplomatic representatives. In February and March 1944 Liu and Odlum presented new credentials as ambassadors. Simultaneously, mutual aid agreements provided the Nationalist forces with Canadian munitions and supplies valued at $26.6 million, much of which remained stranded in Indian and Canadian warehouses. A month later a Sino-Canadian exchange of notes marked relinquishment of the old treaty rights of extraterritoriality. Although not engaged significantly in Far Eastern battlegrounds, Canada created a 'Pacific policy' by extending full diplomatic relations and material aid to a front-line wartime ally.

Public opinion was solidly behind China in its struggle with Japan. In June

1943 Mme Chiang Kai-shek addressed both Houses of the Canadian Parliament. While in Ottawa, she accepted cheques for $177,000 from the Chinese War Relief Fund, $1 million from the Canadian Red Cross, and $10,000 from the Junior Canadian Red Cross, indicative of the significant funds raised privately in Canada for Chinese war relief.[19] Sympathy for war-ravaged China grew quickly, and the ethnic ties of Canadian Chinese to the land of their ancestors now merited public approbation in official government ceremonies and laudatory press commentaries.

In this new era of direct bilateral relations and a sympathetic Canadian public, other areas of Sino-Canadian contact took on new life. Negotiators once again tackled the immigration issue. They failed, however, to find any common ground between Chinese nationalist resentment of particularized treatment and Canada's continued determination to limit Asian immigration. Immigration problems were postponed till peace-time, but travel restrictions on Chinese visitors in Canada were eased as the war multiplied officially sanctioned contacts with Canadian business and universities. Though never accepted by the Chinese, the draft treaty on immigration proposed by Canada in 1944 contained a provision for a student exchange program similar to that finally instituted in the early 1970s.[20] Less formal arrangements admitted substantial Chinese technicians for advanced training in Canadian factories and laboratories, and some Boxer Indemnity Fund scientists from China were side-tracked from beleaguered Britain to study in Canadian universities in 1944 and 1945.[21]

What of the missionaries' relationship to this expanded range of Canadian contacts with China in the 1930s and 1940s? Three related aspects warrant attention: the missionaries' information linkages which affected home reactions to escalating conflict in the Pacific; their relations with the new Canadian diplomatic presence in China; and their role in several experimental non-religious projects which functioned as early examples of aid and development programs. These helped mould a distinctive Canadian attitude towards a new China in the post-missionary age.

The relationship between opinion at home and the missionaries operating in China is complex. In the early 1930s, Canadian public opinion was muted, if not equivocal on Japanese expansionism. The caution of DEA was echoed by non-official commentators who similarly opined that 'in Far Eastern questions, we must be on the side of, if not the angels, at least the Americans.'[22] The business community and the public at large tended toward a positive view of Japanese 'law and order' replacing the 'latent anarchy' of previous Chinese administrations in occupied territories such as Taiwan and Manchuria, a view which some Canadian missionaries initially shared.[23]

A more critical tone gradually crept into the China missionaries' home-bound material, coinciding with a more apologetic voice in the correspondence of Japan-based missionaries. These positions converged as mounting tensions in the Pacific prompted Canadian churches to arrange debates between itinerating missionaries from the two countries.[24] Soon after full-scale hostilities broke out in mid-1937, the Canadian minister to Japan characterized Japanese imperialism as 'simply an attempt to put her neighbour country into decent shape.' The comment produced a storm of controversy at home.[25] Despite official denials of the minister's comments, a surge of public meetings, press notices, and petition campaigns swept across Canada, eventually producing a concentrated effort to organize a nation-wide boycott of Japanese imports and Canadian exports of key resource materials. Government files filled rapidly with letters, petitions, and motions, particularly from western Canada.

Canadian missionaries were forced out of inland stations in occupied North China and then, as the war zone spread, they and others faced repatriation home, transfers to other fields, or, if they remained, eventual internment. Their accounts of the war in China reinforced international press criticism of Japanese wartime conduct. In late 1940, Dr Robert McClure, the indefatigable missionary from North Honan, tried to reinvigorate the boycott movement. His vivid descriptions of extracting Canadian scrap metal from Chinese wounded civilians stirred up public and diplomatic concern over the export of strategic metals to Japan.[26] Well before Pearl Harbor, Canadian public opinion had decisively shifted in favour of China and against appeals for more patient assessment of the issues.[27]

But sympathy did not translate directly into concrete action. The early boycott movement lost considerable steam when it failed to secure endorsement at the Fifth General Council of the United Church of Canada in September 1938, although the deluge of correspondence tapered off only in mid-1939.[28] McClure's efforts attracted momentary attention, but they did not alter official policy. The boycott campaign failed to neutralize the powerful Canadian export community, whose influence was reflected in anti-boycott press across Canada.[29]

Missionary-influenced opinion thus failed to overcome the government's determination not to march ahead of other countries, especially the United States, in reacting to Japanese aggression in China. Exports of strategic materials were quietly restricted only as the European War placed increasing demands on Canadian production. In 1941, half a step behind similar moves in Britain and the United States, Canada finally froze Japanese credits and bank balances.

In China, the missionaries became closely connected with the new

Canadian legation and later embassy. Ambassador Odlum's wartime 'China' was Chungking-centred, with Chengtu, Kweiyang, and Kunming as its outposts. In the area was a concentration of Chinese refugees and the Canadian missionary community. Within the first few months, Odlum's staff had to deal with the missions' foreign exchange problems, their property rights following abrogation of the old treaties, and the first legal cases after abolition of extra-territoriality courts.[30] They were well equipped to do so as both the counsellor, George S. Patterson, and the third secretary, Ralph Collins, had personal backgrounds associated with missionaries. Odlum and his staff cultivated mission contacts. Leslie Kilborn was his aide and translator before the arrival of Patterson and Collins. Dr Gladys Cunningham lent her house and services as official hostess for his visits to Chengtu. Canadian mission homes welcomed the embassy officers on tour and, in return, several 'regulars' were encouraged to drop in at the embassy, especially when new quarters allowed overnight guests.

These linkages led naturally to a network of missionaries willing to correspond periodically on more than personal or mission business. The individuals involved and topics covered varied over the years of Odlum's ambassadorship. Bruce Copland frequently reported on conditions in the north, and Gerald Bell assessed Szechuan politics from the vantage point of Chengtu. A few, such as the Rev V.J.R. Mills, played multiple roles. Odlum suggested that Mills's Canton-area connections be used to communicate with Canadian POWs in Hong Kong, but this proved unworkable. Mills did provide contacts to improve post-war Canadian trade, and, following the example of several other Canadian missionaries, he acted as regional representative for the United Nations Relief and Reconstruction Agency (UNRRA), the Canadian Red Cross, and Chinese War Relief Fund agencies. Following the Japanese surrender in August 1945, missionaries proved useful in describing post-war conditions in previously occupied areas, such as Margaret Brown on liberated Shanghai and Dr Stewart Allen on North Honan.[31]

In such diverse ways the missionaries added breadth to the narrow base of official contact and information available to Canadian embassy personnel. Odlum himself was never stingy in directly crediting his missionary sources, often simply forwarding their communications with an accompanying gloss. On leaving China he remarked: 'Since the date of our first arrival, we have been tremendously interested in, and proud of, the Canadians in China. I have never failed to tell the Government at Ottawa that Canada's high standing in China is very largely due to the magnificent groundwork done by the band of Canadian missionaries who long preceded the arrival of Canada's diplomatic mission. The best we can claim for the

Embassy is that we have not upset the good work done by others.'[32]

Aid and development projects were also significant. Before the war, an assortment of mission-related experiments had centred on famine relief, medical services, and rural development.[33] During and after the war, several missionaries and missionary children worked directly with UNRRA and similar organizations. The range of work extended from distribution of relief supplies to an ambitious project to contain the Yellow River let loose in late 1937. Though sometimes disparaged by other missionaries, the dairy herd experiments of F. Dickinson of West China Union University received Mme Chiang Kai-shek's personal patronage.[34] Less idiosyncratic were various schemes for strengthening medical services, including McClure's association with the wartime Friends Ambulance Service and UNRRA-sponsored post-war rehabilitation of North Honan hospitals. Dr Gordon Agnew energetically recruited governmental, professional, and private support in Canada and the United States for West China Union University's dental program which trained both professional dentists and dental technicians. Don Faris produced plans for post-war Canadian development aid in agricultural extension, as did L.G. Kilborn for better Canadian publicity work in China.[35] Quixotic and imaginative, these non-governmental projects were the first Canadian initiatives in aid and development, although they collapsed in the dislocations of civil war and revolution of the late 1940s, leaving only intangible influences in goodwill and experience for later developmental assistance programs.

Gauging the missionary influence on Canadian China policy up to the war's end is difficult. Odlum's missionary network was both useful and problematic for DEA. On behalf of the department, Hugh Keenleyside commended Gerald Bell's analysis of Szechuan power struggles, but also warned:

> I think you are well advised in taking great care in obtaining even ordinary information from the Canadian missionaries not to entrust such enquiries or replies to the mails. As you know, foreign missionaries in China, as in Japan, have often been suspected and at times openly accused of acting as spies for their governments. We should not wish to compromise in any way the excellent reputation which the Canadian missionaries have established for themselves in West China. By exercising continuous discretion it should, however, be possible for you to obtain from time to time by word of mouth or by letters sent with some Canadian visiting Chungking further reports as interesting as we have found this one.[36]

Information itself did not generate active policy. Odlum queried whether DEA envisaged a positive policy in China or intended to 'sit on the side lines waiting and watching' British and American active engagement in China's modern development. Norman Robertson found it 'very difficult to furnish you with a useful reply,' but in the end expressed Ottawa's willingness to 'follow a positive policy (rather than following in the wake of other industrial and agricultural nations)' so long as China herself managed to create the unity and commitment to make it a true partnership.[37] Nevertheless, such elevation of China and the Canadian ambassador (and his missionary-based ideas) to the top levels of the policy process never occurred.[38]

This was in part due to the disparity between Odlum's self-image and the reality of his standing in Ottawa. The proof was Odlum's return to Canada in late 1944 when all Canada, and particularly Ottawa, was engrossed in the conscription issue. As Odlum later commented, 'no one could talk with me, or even think of me. I was just another headache, and was told to get out of the way; be sick, and to need a lot of rest.'[39]

Post-war and Beyond: The Question of Lasting Influences

The evidence is too inconclusive to prove direct missionary influence on Canada's China policy. The missionary establishments represented substantial links, but these were private and cultural, not matched by sufficient material or political investments to require committed policy positions by Ottawa. As W.L. Morton wrote in 1946, hitherto 'Canada cannot properly be said to have a positive Far Eastern Policy,' though he added that official and public opinion supported the evolving basis for such a policy in the near future.[40] The proclamation of the People's Republic of China in October 1949 and the outbreak of the Korean War nine months later radically changed the policy environment. It is important to consider the post-war years in that context, identifying the related elements which preconditioned the attitudes of the Canadian public and policy makers in a new and more threatening phase of the Chinese revolution.

Canada came out of the Second World War with a maturing view of its role in world affairs. This was especially true after Louis St Laurent became the first independent holder of the External Affairs portfolio in September 1946 and acquired the energetic Lester B. Pearson as his under-secretary. Pearson, along with Norman Robertson and Hume Wrong, formed the 'triumvirate most responsible for the shaping of peace, Canadian style, after 1945.'[41] They were assisted by an exceptional coterie of able young men as the department continued the dramatic expansion of the war period. Most of this new internationalism and the new personnel were absorbed in traditional continental and trans-Atlantic centres of interest or attached to multilateral organizations – NATO, the U.N., and the Commonwealth – which both DEA bureaucrats and the Canadian public saw as key arenas for Canada's new international role. In the later 1940s, the Atlantic-centred diplomacy of peace-time readjustment was critical to Canada's financial and political future.[42]

Viewed from Ottawa these were almost totally dominant prisms through which filtered the problems and potentials of post-war Asia and bilateral relations with China. The resulting compromise accepted Robertson's qualified openness to enhanced political and economic relations, combined with a limited role for Asia in defining where Canada's critical interests lay.[43] The tentative steps toward definable policies indicated initial glimmerings of public and official awareness of Canada as a Pacific nation.

Canadian relations with China in the immediate post-war period demonstrated the nature and limitations of Ottawa's interest. In early fall 1946 a commercial modus vivendi was signed in lieu of the evasive general treaty of friendship and commerce promised by Mackenzie King for six months after peace was achieved. When negotiations failed again, Canada unilaterally repealed the Chinese Immigration Act in May 1947. Such measures prompted initial optimism in Odlum's replacement, Ambassador T.C. Davis of Saskatchewan, who was a far more respected voice in DEA circles. Early in his tour of duty, Davis noted that Canada vied with France for ranking next only to the United States and Britain in the estimation of Chinese leaders.[44] Reinforcements strengthened Canadian embassy staff as well as the trade commissioner service in Nanking, and a consulate general replaced the pre-war trade commissioner's office in Shanghai.

Future commercial potentials were commonly cited rationales for strengthening relations and were also used to justify both official and officially sanctioned development aid. Canada extended an additional $60 million under the Export Credits Act, representing about 5 per cent of all credits granted by foreign governments to the Chinese. Economics also justified sales of surplus arms to the Nationalists, though Canadian official thinking had long since abandoned hope that they would emerge successful in the civil war with the Communists. These shipments continued into early 1948 despite DEA's growing unease over possible political ramifications in supplying an unpopular military regime.

Officially sanctioned non-governmental links also expanded. In late 1946, the Canadian government guaranteed a $12,750,000 loan by three Canadian banks to the Ming Sung Industrial Company's plans for modernized Yangtze transport using Canadian-built river vessels. Though modest in comparison with its commitments to British and European rehabilitation,

Canada's contribution of $20 million in cash plus industrial equipment, which amounted to 10 per cent of the total given to China, made Canada the third largest contributor to UNRRA's China program. Private Canadian donors added over $1 million through the Aid-to-China Fund. Plans were generated for training more Chinese scientific and technological workers in Canadian factories and research laboratories, as well as Chinese students in Canadian universities. Both sides expected that steady development in political and economic ties would complement the long-established cultural ties of missionary and immigrant communities.[45]

The missionary movement was also optimistic and active in 1945 and 1946. Church officials lobbied for, and then rejoiced at, the repeal of the Chinese Immigration Act. T.C. Davis sought their advice before his departure for China, and DEA consulted them while drafting a general treaty with China.[46] Chester Ronning carried the Chinese language and cultural skills, the humanitarian values, and the personal commitment of his China mission upbringing into a new career as diplomatic officer, first under Odlum, then Davis, and finally as chargé d'affaires. Catholic and Protestant missionaries returned to areas formerly evacuated, prepared their claims for damages under Japanese reparation programs, and promoted reconstruction and development projects under UNRRA and other auspices.

These promising signs could not obviate the other side of Norman Robertson's 1943 equation: a positive Canadian policy was dependent on China's ability to maintain unity and political stability. In Asia, Canada's primary diplomatic attention centred on stability. To post-war Ottawa this meant a satisfactory settlement with Japan and concentration on the Commonwealth and the United Nations. Canada could thus follow an 'independent policy' in Asia and elsewhere, without unduly antagonizing the United States. To those ends an expanded relationship with China was not of central importance.

The Department of External Affairs had not shared Odlum's rather rosy perspective on Chiang Kai-shek's regime, and did not harbour the image of post-war China as a major world power which enthralled important U.S. policy and opinion makers. As civil war intensified in China, T.C. Davis's reports from Nanking increasingly depicted a collapsing political order. Before departing China on leave in early 1949, he described the occupation of Nanking by the Communists who, he had already predicted, would soon gain control of all China.[47] Renewed civil war meant that active Canadian engagement lost whatever impetus two years of peace had generated. By the time of Davis's departure Canadian political and economic relations had returned to, in the words of one writer, a 'properly neutral stance, content to watch the transformation of China from the sidelines.'[48]

The end of the mission era was swift. In mid-May 1947, the North China mission of the United Church of Canada disbanded as Communist forces occupied North Honan. The next spring, as mission activities north of the Yangtze shrank to isolated enclaves, the last Canadian Anglicans left Kaifeng. Canadian Catholics of French and English background created their own records of travail and martyrdom as their former fields from Manchuria to Canton progressively came under Communist control. Numbers dwindled, though by early 1949 missionaries still constituted the largest segment of the 850 Canadians remaining on Chinese soil. The Korean War ended the various accommodations by which these last remnants of an impressive tradition had remained active in teaching, medical, or other service functions. Their exodus in 1950–1 left only a handful in official custody, objects for future diplomatic démarches as well as stimulants to periodic outbursts of hostile opinion in the press at home. Thus ended more than sixty years of Canadian missionary activity in China.

Specific legacies from the era of missionary-dominated relations merit assessment. First, many Canadians responded to revolutionary China with memories forged by decades of intensive missionary association with that country, creating emotional ties which underlay all future debates over Sino-Canadian relations. Second, one can raise the parallel question of the lasting influence of the missionary on Chinese images of Canada. Lastly, from that same experience came some of the key players in future debates on China policy, namely children of missionaries, the so-called Mish Kids. These combined to provide influences which, if difficult to measure quantitatively, nevertheless were very real in succeeding decades.

Canadian public opinion tended to be decidedly critical of the Kuomintang from the mid-1940s onwards, but remained ambivalent on the nature and promise of the Communist alternative. This reflected opinions within the missionary body itself. With mixed emotions perhaps many missionaries' private and circulating letters home catalogued the Kuomintang's failure to reverse the disastrous deterioration of the later war years. Both before and after leaving China, the missionaries held conflicting views on the likely consequences. Several hoped to work within areas controlled by the expanding Chinese Communist forces and sought to influence Canadian opinion and policies to facilitate such accommodation.[49] As the Communists consolidated their hold on territories in which Canadian missionaries had traditionally operated, other opinions worked in a contrary manner. The object of particular attention by Communist cadres and propaganda, Catholics generally responded with an emotional rejection of accommodation. Their tales of brutal repression in mission fields fed a militant anti-communist streak in Canadian sensitivities. Protestants were more sharply divided, especially within the United Church.[50] It is clear that returned missionaries were active on both sides of the debate in the late 1940s and those differences carried on into organized groups within and beyond church circles, seeking to influence public opinion and official policies on China during the 1950s and 1960s.

Did missionaries equally affect Chinese images of Canada and Canadians? Twentieth-century Chinese nationalists have often depicted the mission movement as a cultural wing of Western imperialism, an interpretation especially embedded in Communist historiography. Discriminatory Canadian immigration practices prior to 1947 also inflamed Chinese sensitivities. To many the system which replaced the repealed Chinese Immigration Act was only less obvious in its continued discriminatory intent. Did missionaries help mute such reactions?

At this stage, one can only point out the relevancy of certain aspects of the Canadian mission effort. A.R.M. Lower noted that on average, Canadian missionaries were more highly educated and trained than their American counterparts, adding that 'the temper of Canadian life has been less secular than that of American, and at the height of the missionary movement not only was it a national effort, from which few dissented, and to which not many were indifferent, but also some of the best brains of the country went into it.'[51] Another intangible is suggested by a comment by Bishop White of the Canadian Anglican mission in Honan to an Ontario Supreme Court judge in mid-1931: 'For some reason the Chinese do not associate the Canadians with the background which foreigners generally possess, notably the British, German, French, American and Russian. Those nations have all interfered and intervened in China, and have a background which is readily understood and known to the Chinese people. The Canadians, while British, are not in the minds of the people of that country directly associated with that background.'[52]

Many Chinese benefited from the training provided by Canadians in hospitals and universities in China, and the majority in later years were not practising Christians. This suggests an impact far beyond the simplistic dismissal often accorded mission influences under the logic of cultural imperialism. It also suggests that not all favourable Chinese images of Canadians derived from the legendary exploits of Norman Bethune.[53]

At home, mission-related organizations were in the forefront of efforts to mobilize Canadian opinion against the discriminatory Chinese Immigration Act from its inception until its abrogation. Hugh Keenleyside noted that Canadian politicians used such missionary-related activities to offset pressures for even more severe immigration regulations.[54] The missionaries were also prominent in early sinology, both in publications and in helping establish the first centres dedicated to East Asian research in Canada. The Royal Ontario Museum's celebrated Far Eastern section is only one of several prominent examples.

Missionary supporters sought to influence Canadian policy makers as well as public opinion and possessed their own avenues for private lobbying. As Alvyn Austin has noted, many prominent early twentieth-century leaders – Chester Massey and Sir Joseph Flavelle in private business, Hugh Keenleyside, Lester B. Pearson, and Hume Wrong in public service – had family associations with the missionary movement.[55] In one instance, a foreign mission secretary released confidential reports on the takeover in Honan by the Chinese Communist party not only to other selected missionaries but also to Arthur Menzies, China desk officer at DEA.[56]

Here arises the final unanswered question: what influence did the 'Mish Kids' have on Canadian images of China and policy towards it? Menzies was only one of several government officials with personal experience growing up in the mission compounds of China. The names of several others are well known – Chester Ronning (though not raised by Canadian parents), Ralph Collins, and John Small, to mention only those who, with Arthur Menzies, would at one time or another act as chief Canadian diplomatic representatives in China. That they rose to positions of influence is undeniable. It is immensely difficult, however, to make the linkages between individuals and policy. At least three need further thought and research: the relationship between missionary upbringing in China and other aspects of childhood experience; the connection between these experiences and the policy preferences espoused during later years of government service; and the connections between these preferences and the many other factors that affect policy outcomes.

The common denominator that runs through the careers of all these men cannot be found in their style or specific views but in their acute interest in China. The implications of this interest provide at least a partial explanation for why China became central to Canada's Pacific policy in the post-war years and why China seems to have assumed a significance among Canadians far in excess of the actual level of our contact with it.

Notes

1 The standard reference is Alvyn Austin's *Saving China: Canadian Missionaries in the Middle Kingdom, 1888–1959* (Toronto: University of Toronto Press 1986). The term 'enterprise' was developed in a book edited by John K. Fairbank, *The Missionary Enterprise in China and America* (Cambridge, Mass.: Harvard

34 Reluctant Adversaries

University Press 1974). The size of the Canadian missionary enterprise in China is difficult to estimate. It is possible to chart specific Protestant or Catholic missions, such as the 141 Canadian men and women appointed to the Presbyterian mission in North Honan between 1888 and 1925, or the 48 Canadian-born priests and 10 Grey Sisters who served in the Chekiang mission of the Scarboro Foreign Mission Society from 1902 to 1954. But aggregate national totals do not exist. Several mission societies, both Catholic and Protestant, rejected identifying national affiliations in their dedication to evangelical purposes. Surveys such as the standard work *The Christian Occupation of China: A General Survey*, ed. by Milton T. Stauffer (Shanghai: China Continuation Committee 1922), subsumed Canadians under British figures. A rough estimate would be 600 to 650 Canadian missionaries in China at the height of activity in the 1920s, approximately double the number in Japan and Korea or India, the other major Canadian mission fields. While small in comparison with Stauffer's rough total of 8,000 missionaries – 6,636 Protestant workers and 1,351 foreign Catholic priests and nuns – it ranked Canadians next to Americans and British, representing in terms of relative population and GNP a commitment at least equal to that of any other contributing country.

2 On the Chinese Labour Corps, see Peter M. Mitchell, 'Canada and the Chinese Labour Corps, 1917–1921: The Official Connection,' in Min-sun Chen and Lawrence N. Shyu, eds., *China Insight: Selected Papers from the Annual Conference of the Canadian Society for Asian Studies* (Ottawa: Carleton University Press 1985), 7–30, and Margo S. Gewurtz, 'For God and King: Canadian Missionaries and the Chinese Labour Corps in World War I,' in ibid., 31–55.

3 See Donald C. Story, 'Canada, the League of Nations and the Far East, 1931–3: The Cahan Incident,' *The International History Review* 3.2 (April 1981), 236–55. An excellent account of the Cahan incident and Canadian policy in the Pacific during the Mackenzie King years can be found in Gregory Johnson, 'North Pacific Triangle?: The Impact of the Far East on Canada and Its Relations with the United States and Great Britain, 1937–1948' (unpublished PhD Dissertation, York University, 1989).

4 Arthur R.M. Lower, *Canada and the Far East – 1940* (New York: Institute of Pacific Relations 1941), 14–15. Indicative of the need for a review of the whole historical record, Lower's book, along with *Canada and the Orient: A Study in International Relations* (Toronto: Macmillan 1941) by Charles J. Woodsworth, and *Canada and the Far East: 1940–1953* (Toronto: University of Toronto Press 1953) by H.F. Angus, remains the standard reference.

5 W.L.M. King Papers (PAC MG 26) J4 C2478, pp. C45508–13, C455023 (n.d., notes on speech for Commons, attached to N.M.R. to King, 7 May 1928); also Memo to File re interview with Marler, 5 Jan. 1929) (in ibid. C45551–8).

6 See James Morton, *In the Sea of Sterile Mountains* (Vancouver: J.J. Douglas, 1974), 222–3, and R.J. Gowen, 'Canada and the Myth of the Japan Market, 1896–1911,' *Pacific Historical Review* 39.1 (Feb. 1970), 63–83.
7 A.E. Armstrong to Mackenzie King, 18 Feb. 1937, and King to Armstrong, 19 Feb. 1937, in RG 25 G1, vol. 1585, file 142(c).
8 Woodsworth, *Canada and the Orient*.
9 The label 'Gentlemen's Agreement' was frequently questioned on the grounds that no documentary 'agreement' ever existed and some questioned whether such an arrangement justified the use of the honorific 'gentlemen' at all. Mackenzie King negotiated a draft Chinese emigration agreement while attending the International Conference on Opium in Shanghai in 1910, but the Manchu dynasty's fall doomed that effort. Successive Chinese consuls-general in Ottawa tried unsuccessfully to engage the Canadian authorities in similar negotiations. (See Robertson to Cory, 3 Jan. 1914, and Robertson to Roche, 13 Jan. 1914 in RG 76, vol. 121, file 23635, part I; also several related memos and communications around the same date in RG 25 G1, vol. 1142, file 308, and Robert Borden Papers, in PAC MG 26H, vol. 183A, pp. 100260–332, and vol. 183B, pp. 100642–8.) As late as 1922, a new consul-general tried once more to negotiate a solution to forestall the discriminatory legislation passed in the following year. (See Memo to File, 28 July 1922, King Papers C2694, pp. 61104–10.)
10 'Canada and the Far East,' *The Round Table* 23 (1932–3), 666. Other examples include John R. Imrie, 'China's attitude toward Canada's restrictions,' in R.B. Bennett Papers (PAC MG26K) M1072, pp. 241861–70, and Hussey to Bennett, 28 Feb. 1932 in M1328, pp. 405252–62. Imrie was leader of the first delegation sent by the Canadian Chamber of Commerce to China and Hong Kong in 1930, and Hussey was a Peking-based expert on international law who served as adviser to the Chinese delegation to the Leyton Commission of the League of Nations.
11 A number of letters and memos from Stevens on this issue, many of which were addressed to O.D. Skelton, may be found in RG 25 G1, vol. 1585, file 142(c).
12 Reid to Rowell, 7 Jan. 1936, in Rowell Papers (PAC MG 27-II) C934, p. 4491.
13 See Alain Larocque, 'Losing "Our" Chinese: The St. Enfance Movement,' University of Toronto–York University Joint Centre for Asia Pacific Studies, *Working Paper Series* No. 49, June 1987.
14 See Keenleyside to Marler, 13 May 1935 in RG 25 G1, vol. 1687, file 80H for a biting comment on British diplomats' mishandling of Canadian matters. See RG 24 C1, vol. 96, file 1857–10 for a sizeable number of enquiries regarding service in any expeditionary force, including two officers from the earlier Siberian episode.

15 For the united stand by Protestant Missionary Boards, see H.C. Priest to King, 20 Feb. 1926 in King Papers C2292, pp. 116418–19, and United Church of Canada Archives, Board of Foreign Missions (hereafter UCC/BFM) West China Correspondence, box 1, file 4. O.D. Skelton's memo, 'The situation in China,' 5 Feb. 1929, in King Papers J4 C2479, pp. 47114–28, points out that many old China hands were bitter about missionaries they held responsible for spreading unsettling ideas which inspired student agitation against Western privileges in China. For an excellent critical view of the slow Canadian response to the dynamic of Chinese nationalism, see John W. Foster, 'The Imperialism of Righteousness: Canadian Protestant Missionaries and the Chinese Revolution, 1925–1928' (unpublished PhD dissertation, University of Toronto, 1977).

16 *Twenty-five Years in Tsinan: Shantung Christian University* (n.p., 1943?), 5; see also Karen Minden, 'The Multiplication of Ourselves: Canadian Missionaries in West China,' in Ruth Hayhoe and Marianne Bastid, eds., *China's Education and the Industrialized World: Studies in Cultural Transfer* (Armonk, NY, and London: M.E. Sharpe 1987), 139–57.

17 Arthur R.M. Lower, *Canada and the Far East*, 48; see also Peter M. Mitchell, 'Oriental Students in Canadian Universities, 1890–1960,' unpublished paper at Symposium at Joint Centre on Modern East Asia, Croft Chapter House, April 1983.

18 See Gregory Johnson, 'North Pacific Triangle?' especially chs. 2 and 3.

19 'Canadian News Bulletin,' 1st ed. 7 Aug. 1943, in Odlum Papers (PAC MG 30 E300), box 39, file 'Canadian Bulletins re China, 1943–55.' Hugh Keenleyside noted the occasion as 'not, I thought, in the best of taste,' referring to Mme Chiang's wearing of jewellery perhaps equal in value to the amount donated, largely by schoolchildren; see his *Memoirs of Hugh L. Keenleyside*, vol. 2, *On the Bridge of Time* (Toronto: McClelland and Stewart 1982), 455–6. Relief funds for China raised in Canada, particularly among Chinese Canadians, amounted during the war years to $6.5 million, a considerable sum exceeding comparable private aid raised for France. (See *Canada in World Affairs: 1944–46*, ed. by F.H. Soward [Toronto: Oxford University Press 1950], 322.)

20 The original Canadian initiatives on this issue reach back to Keenleyside's 1933 version forwarded to Ottawa by Marler. The drafts of 1944 can be found in SSEA to Odlum, No. 123, 3 June 1944, in Odlum Papers, vol. 38, file 'Sino-Canadian Immigration Draft Treaty, 1944;' see also F.J. McEvoy, '"A Symbol of Racial Discrimination": The Chinese Immigration Act and Canada's Relations with China, 1942–1947,' *Canadian Ethnic Studies* 14.3 (1982), 24–42.

21 The materials on these trading and academic programs of the mid-1940s are

scattered in various sources, including RG 76, vol. 121, file 23635, part 7; RG 20 B1, vol. 205, file 28880, part 2; Odlum Papers, vol. 35; and DEA 72-VQ-40C and 7493-40.
22 'Canada and the Far East,' by 'T,' *Foreign Affairs* 13 (1934-5), 393.
23 See H.F. Angus, 'Canada and Naval Rivalry in the Pacific,' *Pacific Affairs* 8 (1935), 179-80; also Robert B. McClure, York University Oral History Interview (1970), 36-8.
24 Outerbridge to Arnup, 16 Nov. 1937, in UCC/BFM, Japan Correspondence, box 4, file 81; Outerbridge to Arnup, 18 May 1938, box 5, file 90. Howard Outerbridge, one of the most cerebral and articulate of Canadian missionaries in Japan, initially deplored these debates, but by early 1938 contemplated thus spending his furlough in order to counter the growing effect of the United Church's outspoken West China mission of which, ironically, his own son was a member.
25 Clipping from *Toronto Star*, 12 Aug. 1937, and Minister Bruce's statement to the press, 13 Aug. 1937, in King Papers J4 C4255, pp. C111107-8. Also Skelton to King, 28 Jan. 1938, in ibid., p. C111105. Also Lower, *Canada and the Far East*, 29-31, on the Opposition attempt to use this incident to attack Mackenzie King's government in Commons.
26 McClure's own account can be found in Munroe Scott, *McClure: The China Years* (Markham: Penguin 1979), 284-7. A different view is presented in J.L. Granatstein, *A Man of Influence: Norman A. Robertson and Canadian Statecraft, 1929-68* (Ottawa: Deneau 1981), 99-101.
27 See Arnup to Albright, 25 Nov. 1941, in UCC/BFM Japan Correspondence, box 15, file 101, and Arnup to G.E. Bott, 28 Nov. 1941, box 5, file 103.
28 Toronto *Globe and Mail*, 1 Oct. 1938, 1. This note shared front-page coverage with the picture of Neville Chamberlain arriving back from Munich, a sign of the contrary pressures directing most public attention elsewhere.
29 See Lower, *Canada and the Far East*, 23-41, for a still useful summary of the boycott's course in the popular press across Canada as reflecting the various interests connected to Asian trade.
30 On the origins of the exchange issue see Patterson to SSEA No. 2, 19 May 1943. On the court case involving Dr C.M. Hoffman, see Odlum to SSEA no. 40, 29 July 1943, both in Odlum Papers, vol. 34, file 'Dispatches and Memos.' Another case was a malpractice suit brought against Dr Stewart Allen. On Allen's case, see Odlum to SSEA No. 202, 14 June 1945; No. 245, 3 July 1945; No. 351, 27 Aug. 1945, in vol. 35.
31 On Copland, see several examples in Odlum Papers, vol. 3, file 'Copland'. For Bell's correspondence, see his file in vol. 1. On Mills, see Odlum to SSEA No. 57, 27 Jan. 1944, and No. 223, 1 May 1944, in Odlum Papers, vol. 38, file 'POWs in China and F.E., 1943-46.' Also Mills to Odlum, 10 Feb. 1946,

38   Reluctant Adversaries

and Odlum to Mills, 21 Feb. 1946, in vol. 9. For Brown's reports, see her file in vol. 1, and for Allen's on North Honan regions, see Allen to Odlum, 13 June 1946, in vol. 4.
32 Odlum to McClure, 20 Sept. 1946, in ibid., vol. 8.
33 See Margo S. Gewurtz, 'Famine Relief in China: North Henan in the 1920s,' University of Toronto–York University Joint Centre for Asia Pacific Studies, *Working Paper Series* No. 50 June 1987; Karen Minden, 'Canadian Development Assistance: The Medical Missionary Model in West China, 1910–1952,' ibid., No. 55 May 1989; Peter M. Mitchell, 'Canadian Missionaries and Chinese Rural Society: North Henan in the 1930s,' ibid., No. 56 1990.
34 Dr Daniel Dye (WCUU) to Odlum, 25 Aug. 1944, in Odlum Papers, vol. 4; also Dickinson to Odlum, 17 Sept. 1945, 4 Feb. 1946, 21 Feb. 1946, and 19 Apr. 1946, in vol. 3.
35 On McClure, the best source is Munroe Scott's biography, *McClure*. On Agnew's project, see his file in Odlum Papers, vol. 1, and also Department of External Affairs (DEA) file 8651-40. Faris's 'Suggestions for Reconstruction in China' was enclosed in Odlum to SSEA No. 28, 3 June 1943, and commented on in Odlum to SSEA No. 41, 30 July 1943, while Kilborn's ideas were attached to and developed in Odlum to SSEA No. 43, 31 July 1943. See Odlum Papers, vol. 34 file 'China Despatches and Memos, May–August 1943.'
36 Keenleyside to Odlum, 29 July 1944, in Odlum Papers, vol. 6.
37 Odlum to SSEA, 8 Sept. 1943, and Robertson to Odlum, 26 Sept. 1943, in DEA file 4851-40.
38 See Kim Richard Nossal, 'Strange Bedfellows: Canada and China in War and Revolution, 1942–1947' (Unpublished PhD dissertation, University of Toronto 1977); also his 'Chungking Prism: Cognitive Process and Intelligence Failure,' *International Journal* 32.3 (1977), 559–79, and 'Business as Usual: Canadian Relations with China in the 1940s,' in Kim Nossal, ed., *An Acceptance of Paradox: Essays in Honour of John W. Holmes* (Toronto: Canadian Institute of International Affairs 1982), 38–52.
39 Odlum to Cosgrove, 5 July 1945, in Odlum Papers, vol. 3.
40 W.L. Morton, 'Canada's Far Eastern Policies,' *Pacific Affairs* 19 (1946) 241–9. Robert A. Spencer similarly commented: 'Not until the Chinese revolution had dispossessed the wartime ally of its mainland possessions, and the emergence of the Asiatic dominions in the British Commonwealth [culminating in the Colombo Conference of January 1950], could Canada be said to have an Asiatic policy' (*Canada in World Affairs: 1946-1949* [Toronto: Oxford University Press 1959], 5).
41 John W. Holmes, *The Shaping of Peace: Canada and the Search for World Order, 1943-1957* vol. 1 (Toronto: University of Toronto Press 1979), 15.

42 See Holmes, *The Shaping of Peace*, and Robert Bothwell and John English, 'Canadian Trade Policy, 1943–1947,' in J.L. Granatstein, ed., *Canadian Foreign Policy: Historical Readings* (Toronto: Copp Clark Pitman 1986), 145–57.
43 Eric Downton (*Pacific Challenge: Canada's Future in the New Asia* [Toronto: Stoddart 1986]) coined the phrase 'Pacific Blind Spot' to describe 1941 Ottawa's lack of concern for the region's mounting tensions, a state of ignorance which, he asserts, still remains. For a more balanced view based on detailed research into the role of the Pacific question in Canada's efforts to steer an independent but collaborative path between American and British wartime diplomacy, see Gregory Johnson, 'North Pacific Triangle?'
44 Circular letter addressed T.C. Davis to W.L. Davis (Prince Arthur, Saskatchewan), 7 May 1947, in Odlum Papers, vol. 3.
45 On the short but critical post-1945 period, see Nossal's works cited above, and Donald H. Gardner, *Canadian Interests and Policies in the Far East since World War II* (11th I.P.R. Conference, Lucknow, October 1950; published Toronto: Canadian Institute of International Affairs 1950).
46 A copy of the circular letter to all MPs from the Committee for Repeal of the Chinese Immigration Act (which was dominated by mission bureaucrats) can be found in the King Papers, J2 vol. 430, file 1-20-14. Davis's briefing by mission board personnel is referred to in A.E. Armstrong to George K. King, 1 Feb. 1947, in UCC/BFM, Honan Correspondence, box 12, file 208. The solicitation of missionary advice on treaty preparation is contained in R.M. Macdonnell to A.E. Armstrong, 21 Dec. 1946, in DEA file 4851-40.
47 See Davis to Odlum, 13 April 1949, in Odlum Papers, vol. 3; Davis to SSEA No. 91: 'The takeover of Nanking,' 30 Apr. 1948, in Odlum Papers, vol. 36, file 'External Affairs – Canadian Documents on China – 1949.'
48 Nossal, 'Business as Usual,' p. 49.
49 Donald K. Faris was one example. While on furlough following his UNRRA assignment bringing the Yellow River back under control, Faris actively lobbied against shipment of arms to the government in Nanking. (See circular letter from Faris to all MPs, 30 Jan. 1948, in the St Laurent Papers [PACMG26L], vol. 18, file 100-1-17.)
50 In United Church circles, the major debate concerned ex-missionary James G. Endicott's efforts to elicit Canadian sympathies for the Chinese revolution, an effort which aroused more conservative mission bureaucrats, provided considerable news coverage of his eloquent public addresses, and exasperated Ottawa bureaucrats. (See the biography by his son, Stephen Endicott, *James G. Endicott: Rebel out of China* [Toronto: University of Toronto Press 1980], and the large number of references in various parts of the Odlum Papers, DEA files, and contemporary Canadian newspapers, and periodicals.)
51 Lower, *Canada and the Far East*, 49.

52 Noted in Justice F. Hodgins to Bennett, 4 Sept. 1931 (Bennett Papers M1218, pp. 14945–7).
53 On Bethune, see Roderick Stewart, *Norman Bethune* (Don Mills: Fitzhenry and Whiteside 1974) and *The Mind of Norman Bethune* (Toronto: Fitzhenry and Whiteside 1977), as well as the documentary film produced and written by John Kemeny and Donald Brittain, *Bethune* (National Film Board 1964).
54 Keenleyside, *Memoirs*, vol. 2, 269–70.
55 Austin, *Saving China*, 100–2, 262.
56 See George K. King to A.E. Armstrong, 6 Aug. 1947, and Armstrong to King, 18 Aug. 1947, in UCC/BFM, Honan Mission Correspondence, box 12, file 209. It was apparently Menzies who was responsible for soliciting the missionary establishment's views in treaty revision. See R.M. MacDonnell to A.E. Armstrong, 21 Dec. 1946; Menzies telegram to Canadian Minister (Wash), 10 Feb. 1947, and DEA to T.C. Davis No. 192, 13 June 1947, in DEA file 4851-40, vol. 1.

SECTION II

The Policy Problems

CHAPTER TWO

Stephen Beecroft

Canadian Policy towards China, 1949–1957: The Recognition Problem

On 16 November 1949, the Canadian cabinet decided in principle to accord recognition to the newly established Communist government of the People's Republic of China (PRC). It was to be twenty-one years, however, before this decision was finally implemented. My purpose is to examine the reasons for the discrepancy between objectives and actions during the St Laurent administration, 1949–57.

The recognition issue was at the heart of Canada's China problem, one of the most contentious and dangerous flashpoints of the Cold War period. It still represents the most controversial aspect of the historical record by raising questions about the extent of American influence on Canadian policy and the ability or willingness of Ottawa to follow an independent course in external relations.

Ultimately, three basic questions need to be answered. First, why did the Canadian government decide in favour of recognition and a constructive approach to the China problem in 1949? Second, why, despite the consistent efforts of secretary of state for External Affairs Pearson and the Department of External Affairs (DEA) did they not act on this decision either prior to the Korean War or after it? Finally, what can be learned about the mechanics of foreign policy formulation in Canada from an analysis of this matter?

My approach to this subject is clearly from the perspective of DEA. This is appropriate given that the department and its minister had paramount responsibility for the management of Canada's external relations and were the consistent initiators of policy ideas regarding the China issue. The influence of DEA in setting out foreign policy alternatives was less diluted in the 1950s than later. A departmental perspective, however, is not the only possible basis for analysis. The attitudes of other ministers and government departments were also crucial and their influence at the cabinet level is considered in this work.

An analysis of Ottawa's responses to developments in China must bear in mind the way in which these fitted into and were influenced by the wider spectrum of Canada's foreign relations. For China policy did not evolve in a vacuum. The St Laurent government reacted not only to external events but to the responses of its major partners, in particular its North Atlantic Triangle associates, the United States and the United Kingdom. The seeds of division over China between these two allies were evident as early as the autumn of 1948 and persisted throughout subsequent decades, thus complicating the political environment in which all Canadian decisions were made. Since most of the Asian Commonwealth and many European states disagreed with the American position as well, Canada's position in the middle became more and more uncomfortable. The desire to implement the policy External Affairs officials believed to be correct and to maintain the support of Asian democracies for Western causes in the United Nations and elsewhere came into conflict with the government's distaste for damaging NATO unity (even though the United Kingdom had recognized Peking in 1949) or undermining the power that was ultimately responsible for maintaining Western security in the Pacific. The tendency toward inaction was increased by such competing foreign policy objectives.

Above all, however, Ottawa's responses to developments in China in 1949 and thereafter were conditioned by one basic factor: the limited nature of Canadian interests in that country and the Far East as a whole. Canadian trade with China was minimal and showed little prospect of increasing markedly in the near future.[1] In financial terms, the government's commitments included a $60 million credit to the Nationalist government and a guaranteed loan of $12.75 million by Canadian banks to the Ming Sung Industrial Company. Concern about repayment of these loans initially cautioned against a precipitate break with Chiang Kai-shek's regime. The amounts involved, however, were insignificant and the long-term influence on policy was minimal.

On the strategic level, the victory of Communist forces in China was not expected to present an immediate threat to Canadian security. Some felt the victory might have dire repercussions for Southeast Asia, but this was outside Ottawa's range of responsibilities. Canada had never had an abiding strategic involvement with the Asian continent. The humiliating capture of the Canadian garrison in Hong Kong in 1942 eradicated any Canadian taste for future participation in the strategic affairs of the region.

Throughout 1949 and the subsequent decade, the Liberal government resolutely maintained its opposition to Canadian participation in any form of Pacific defence pact. With its gaze and limited resources focused entirely on Europe and North America, Ottawa was content to rely on American forces to defend Canada's western frontiers.

In part, this represented a logical division of labour between Western countries of unequal capabilities. But it was also a reflection of Canadian insularity. Despite the fact that Canada was a Pacific power, ministers and officials in Ottawa during the forties and fifties considered the Asia Pacific region to be peripheral. The nation's entire history, reinforced by continuing economic, cultural, and strategic ties, predicated a North Atlantic preoccupation which left little room for the Far East. In the mental maps of Canadian policy makers based in central Canada, Europe hovered affectionately just off the coast of Newfoundland while China remained a distant and alien shore almost beyond the realm of comprehension. Most of the leading officials at DEA had never set foot in the Far East and had little knowledge of, or interest in, the region.[2] The situation within the cabinet and other branches of the civil service was even more extreme. It is not surprising, therefore, that the China issue was generally given a low priority in Ottawa during the period in question. With few direct national interests at stake, there was little imperative to act. Instead, the government displayed a consistent tendency to put off until tomorrow what did not have to be done today.

The Position of the Department of External Affairs

The policy preferences of DEA officials were evident from an early stage and were shaped clearly by their images of the situation in China. In their view, the Communists were not winning the civil war so much as the Nationalists were losing it through their own incompetence and internal failings; this despite having had all the material advantages at the outset of the struggle.

There had never been any real affection for Chiang's regime among the denizens of the East Block. Such sympathy as had existed for its struggles during the Second World War was quickly eroded after the end of that conflict by the Nationalists' refusal to co-operate fully with Marshall's efforts to achieve a peaceful solution to China's internal problems. The Nationalists' brutal suppression of the popular rebellion in Taiwan in early 1947 also caused widespread abhorrence in Canada and throughout the world. However, it was not one or two events which undermined confidence and support for Chiang's government in Ottawa and other capitals, but rather the very nature of the regime itself. Over the previous years, a steady stream of damning reports had emanated from Western diplomats, missionaries, and journalists in China and it was these reports which shaped Canadian attitudes, both official and public, over the long term. The image built up was decidedly negative. Indeed, virtually no one with first-hand experience of China seemed to have anything but contempt for the Nationalist regime, a salutary comment which did not go unnoticed in Ottawa.

The one notable Canadian exception was Major General Victor Odlum, Canada's first ambassador to China, 1943–6. An ardent Cold War warrior and a great admirer of Chiang Kai-shek, Odlum was inclined to overlook the Nationalists' many faults and excesses for the sake of strategic goals. Convinced that the Chinese Communists were merely the 'Asiatic striking force' of the Kremlin, he insisted that Canada should support the Nationalists as the only pro-Western alternative in China.[3] He continued his pro-Chiang campaign even after leaving Nanking, frequently opposing the recommendations of Ambassador Davis and Chester Ronning.[4] However, the general was so completely out of step with his colleagues both in China and in Ottawa, and was himself such a focus of ridicule, that he was entirely without influence in DEA.[5] It is possible that his opinions carried greater weight with certain politicians already inclined toward a similar worldview, but his impact on Canadian policy in 1948–9 was negligible.

More potent in shaping Canadian images of China were the various missionary societies active in that country.[6] They expended considerable money and effort publicizing the abysmal human rights record of Chiang's government and the deplorable conditions of life which continued to exist unabated under its rule. In doing so, they played an important role in preparing Canadian public opinion for an eventual change in China policy. Their reports also had some influence on External Affairs officials, a significant number of whom, as we have seen, were of missionary stock themselves.

Far more important in shaping the attitudes of officials in Ottawa, however, were the regular dispatches of their own and other diplomatic representatives in China. Throughout the latter stages of the civil war these painted a consistently black picture of the Nationalist regime. Ambassador T.C. Davis and his staff were appalled by the corruption, brutality, and repression which they witnessed in China and reported their own views to Ottawa in the strongest possible terms.[7] As the civil war progressed toward its climax, their abhorrence of Nationalist methods was augmented by scorn for their incompetence. The views of Ambassador Davis were typical: 'While I am at it let me say, that when the history of this period is written ... the man who will be given the greatest credit for pulling this whole nation down about him and who has more that any other person given China over to Communism, will be the Generalissimo. Never has a man made a sorrier mess of things than he.'[8]

This image of the Nationalists, shared by most diplomatic representatives in China and a large proportion of their colleagues at home, helps explain the reactions of Western governments to the crisis in China in late 1948 and 1949. For the pervasive distaste for Chiang's government both limited their policy options and coloured their attitude toward Mao's Communists. Had Chiang's regime been viewed with greater sympathy, Britain, Canada, and other countries would not have found it so easy – intellectually, morally, or politically – to advocate abandoning the Nationalists and seeking an accommodation with the new rulers of China, particularly given events in Europe at the time. An intervention in the government's favour, at least by the United States, might have been a possibility. Indeed post-war American policy toward China might have been entirely different. As it was, however, there was little remorse about the Nationalist downfall. A Communist victory had long been expected. When it arrived, it was viewed with relative equanimity. With no emotional baggage to be carried forward and few strategic or economic interests to cloud their vision, DEA officials were able to base their policy prescriptions on a pragmatic acceptance of the facts of the situation in China. Since the Nationalist cause was both hopeless and discredited, there was no point in continuing to support Chiang's government in any way. Like it or not, the Chinese Communist party was going to rule China. It thus behooved Canadian leaders to accept reality and attempt to find some constructive way of living with it. Only in this way could Western powers hope to maintain their interests and influence on the mainland. There was also speculation that a positive approach might have long-term strategic benefits.[9]

Canadian and other representatives in China had long been suggesting that Mao Tse-tung and his supporters might prove to be independent of the Soviet Union if not forced into Moscow's arms by hostile Western policies.[10] There was no questioning the fact that the Chinese Communists were Marxist-Leninists who, initially at least, would tend to align with Moscow in international affairs. There were, however, thought to be numerous sources of potential friction between the two Communist powers. Doctrinal differences and contending interests in Manchuria, Sinkiang, and Inner Mongolia all seemed likely to undermine long-term Sino-Soviet harmony. T.C. Davis argued that Western powers should attempt to encourage and exploit this possibility: 'I am positive that when the smoke clears away here that Russia is not going to be able to run this country and that Tito will have nothing on the leaders of China. As against that day, much more can be done with candy than with clubs and we should accept the inevitable and let nature take its course.'[11]

Throughout 1949, Davis and Chester Ronning, the counsellor of the embassy, consistently recommended that Canada should be prepared to trade with the new regime and to recognize it whenever a central government was formed.[12] The influence of their views in Ottawa was considerable, enhanced in part by the conspicuous unanimity of most of the diplomatic community in Nanking.

The virulence of the anti-Western propaganda emanating from Peking caused some questioning of the Titoism thesis. But to Arthur Menzies and his colleagues in the American and Far Eastern Division, if there was any prospect, however slight, of keeping China out of the Soviet orbit, then it was worth encouraging.[13] A Joint Intelligence Committee study dated 21 February 1949 acknowledged that Communist rule in China would have dangerous repercussions in Southeast Asia.[14] But as a report by British military and diplomatic representatives in the region suggested, these would exist whether or not recognition were accorded to Mao's government and might in fact be lessened if the latter were treated diplomatically.[15] At any rate, there seemed to be no other workable policy option. With Chiang Kai-shek's armies rapidly being pushed off the mainland, Western powers had either to reach a modus vivendi with the Communists or pull out of China completely and resign themselves to an indefinite period of Sino-Western hostility, with all its attendant dangers. To DEA officials this was no choice at all.

Policy makers in Ottawa had already displayed their resolve to accept the fait accompli in China by leaving Ambassador Davis in Nanking when the Nationalist government retreated to the south. Subsequently, they followed the British lead in attempting to establish de facto consular relations with the new authorities. These efforts failed and in May the Western powers tacitly agreed to defer any further moves toward the establishment of relations until after the formation of a national government. There was, however, never any intention of pursuing an extended policy of non-recognition. In a memorandum of 3 June 1949, the American and Far Eastern Division insisted that it would be impractical from the point of view of protecting Canadian interests to avoid dealing with the effective rulers of the bulk of the country.[16]

During the summer of 1949, officials were preoccupied with following the disturbing and intensifying divergence between Britain and the United States over all aspects of China policy. Nonetheless, when the recognition question was formally raised by the establishment of the People's Republic of China in October, there was little doubt as to the course the department would recommend. In memoranda of 4 and 15 November, it argued that for legal and practical reasons Mao's government should be recognized.[17] The Communists had effective control of a definable territory with a reasonable prospect of permanence. They also appeared to govern with the acquiescence, if not the overt support, of the bulk of the population. The standard requirements in international law for de jure recognition were therefore satisfied, and in the department's view actions should be taken accordingly. Recognition was not in its view a sign of approval but merely an acknowledgment of facts. Or as Sir Winston Churchill aptly put it, the purpose of recognition was 'not to confer a compliment but to secure a convenience'.[18] Ultimately, of course, the decision of whether or not to recognize China was a political, not a legal matter. There, too, the balance of argument seemed to favour positive action. By establishing constructive diplomatic and economic relations with Peking, it was hoped that Canada and other Western powers could promote democratic ideas in China and perhaps strengthen the hand of more moderate elements in the government. It might also put them in a position to exploit any future Sino-Soviet conflicts. The issue was by no means clear cut, but DEA concluded that 'the political arguments in favour of recognition, without too great delay, outweigh those against.'[19] On 16 November the question went before cabinet where the decision in principle was made to accord recognition to the PRC.[20]

Missed Chances

The actual timing of recognition was left open for later discussion. Some delay was necessary to avoid raising the potentially divisive issue of Chinese representation in the United Nations while the General Assembly was still in session. Ottawa was also anxious to consult and co-ordinate with as many other powers as possible, and to this end decided to defer any decision until after the Commonwealth foreign ministers' meeting in Colombo, Ceylon, in January 1950. When Britain and the Asian Commonwealth countries decided to recognize Peking in advance of the conference, the Canadian government held to its course. It had few interests of substance in Asia and thus little reason to be in the first group of nations to accord recognition.[21] Moreover, the delay would leave others to test reactions in Peking and Washington.

Both Pearson and his department expected recognition to be accorded at some point during the spring of 1950. In Colombo, the minister was profoundly influenced by his conversations with the British foreign secretary, Ernest Bevin, and Pandit Nehru of India.[22] On 24 January Pearson sent a telegram to Prime Minister St Laurent emphasizing his conviction that recognition should be accorded as soon as possible. 'If we are to get any advantages out of recognition, I think we should avoid being the last to do so. My present inclination, therefore, is to recommend on my return to Ottawa that we should, without further delay, recognize the new Government.'[23] In view of the minister's enthusiasm, the department surreptitiously took an option on a building in Peking in preparation for the transfer of the embassy from Nanking.[24] Bruce Rankin, a foreign service officer recently back from Shanghai, was informed that he would be returning to his post once recognition was accorded, and throughout the spring was kept living out of a suitcase in Ottawa in preparation for this eventuality.[25] In late February 1950 several Commonwealth governments were informed that recognition would be accorded toward the end of March.[26]

Despite these developments, Pearson was failing in his efforts to convince cabinet of the desirability of early recognition. According to official records, opposition arose on two fronts. The minister of finance, D.C. Abbott, insisted that action should not be taken until arrangements were made to minimize Canadian financial losses resulting from loans to the Nationalist government. He was fearful that the Communists would refuse to accept any responsibility, that recognition would lead the Nationalists to default completely, and that the Canadian treasury would consequently lose its investment.[27] The prime minister expressed concern about Canada being the first country to break Western Hemisphere solidarity regarding China, a rather flaccid cover for his fear of annoying the Americans.[28] As a result of this opposition, at its meetings of 23 February and 10 March, cabinet decided to put off a final decision on recognition. The issue was not raised again for nearly two months.

External factors also militated against early action. The Soviet boycott of the United Nations over the Chinese representation question made any concession by Canada on this issue of recognition untimely. Of even more concern was the position of the Far Eastern Commission which had been established to oversee the occupation of Japan at the end of the Second World War. A Canadian initiative during the spring of 1950 would have altered the balance between recognizing and non-recognizing powers and thus possibly have precipitated a change in Chinese representation in that body. To the East Block the prospect of being responsible for seating Chinese Communist officials in Washington under the nose of Congress was not appealing. It was decided, therefore, to follow the advice of the Canadian ambassador in the United States and delay recognition for a time.[29]

Equally important in preventing Canadian action in the spring of 1950 were the difficulties experienced by Britain, India, and other governments which had already extended recognition unilaterally. Their attempts to establish diplomatic relations with Mao's government had met with a humiliating series of procedural delays on the part of the Chinese. Many felt that until these problems were resolved it would be imprudent for Canada to move. In mid-April, DEA came up with a strategy for circumventing the problem by seeking informal negotiations on the establishment of diplomatic relations prior to recognition. This would enable the department to announce recognition and the establishment of relations simultaneously so as to avoid the predicament faced by other governments. If the government in Peking would agree to this procedure and a satisfactory arrangement was reached, Canada, the department argued, should be prepared not only to accord recognition and withdraw the same from the Nationalists, but also to support the seating of Chinese Communist representatives in international organizations, something which Britain had not done.[30]

On 4 May the idea was placed before the cabinet and approval was given to go ahead with the first phase of the initiative. Ronning, now chargé d'affaires, was instructed informally to sound out the Communist authorities in Nanking to determine if they were amenable to such an approach. His initial enquiries on 15 and 16 May elicited a favourable response. Several days later a reply was received stating that the Chinese foreign minister would welcome him to Peking for preliminary negotiations if Canada would formally indicate its desire to recognize the central People's government. Ronning felt that an oral statement from him would satisfy this requirement and he implored Ottawa for authorization to issue such a statement and proceed on to negotiations.[31] These would, he recognized, have to be purely procedural. The Chinese had made it clear that they would not agree to discuss substantive matters, such as the position of Canadian loans to China, at the preliminary stage. Despite the caveat, DEA was generally encouraged by Peking's response, and in a memorandum of 29 May urged the minister to push ahead with the initiative.[32] If successful, Canada would not only achieve a considerable diplomatic coup, but might also help break the deadlock which had developed in the United Nations over the question of Chinese representation. Action would have to be taken soon, though, if it were to have any impact before the General Assembly session in September.

The minister agreed but, surprisingly, the matter was not referred to cabinet for several weeks. Pearson had been absent from Ottawa during most of May and this in good part explains the slow pace of the initiative that month. The causes of delay in early June are more difficult to determine, though the backlog on the cabinet agenda played some part.

Whatever the reason, it is clear that Ottawa's vacillation was a source of annoyance and exasperation both to Canadian officials in China and to the Peking government. On 16 June Ronning reported that he was being embarrassed by Canadian dilatoriness, particularly as he had initiated the discussions.[33] With obvious frustration he insisted that the time had come for Canada either to proceed to the establishment of diplomatic relations or to withdraw completely from China as the Americans had done. The need for action was reinforced in Ronning's mind when Communist police invaded the embassy in June and began harassing Ronning and his staff.

Still, Ottawa did not move. On 14 and 21 June Pearson sought approval from cabinet to proceed to negotiations, but on both occasions the matter was deferred for later discussions. Undaunted, DEA drafted two telegrams of instruction for Ronning in case a favourable decision should be forthcoming. These authorized him to deliver a confidential oral message to the authorities in Nanking stating that the Canadian government was prepared to announce recognition of the Central People's government 'if and when a satisfactory agreement has been reached on the establishment of diplomatic relations.'[34] Ronning was not to proceed to Peking to negotiate such agreement, however, until a favourable reply had been received from the Chinese foreign ministry. Commonwealth governments, as well as those of the United States, France, Belgium, Italy, and the Netherlands, would be informed in advance of Canadian plans. The draft telegrams were dated Friday, 23 June. They were seen by the minister but not sent. Two days later the Korean War broke out, and the situation was changed irrevocably.

It is a matter for speculation whether Canada would have accorded recognition during the latter half of 1950 even if events in Korea had not intervened. While Pearson and DEA undoubtedly would have pushed the matter, cabinet might well have continued to procrastinate. At its meeting of 21 June, James Gardiner, the minister of agriculture and one of the senior members, argued strenuously that recognition would create political difficulties for the government, both in parliament and at the constituency level. The opposition Tories could be counted upon to exploit Canadian action for partisan purposes. So too could Maurice Duplessis, the premier of Quebec, who for years had been castigating Ottawa for being lax in dealing with the communist threat to the Christian world. Gardiner therefore suggested that recognition be delayed until it was virtually inevitable.[35]

This sort of political logic commended itself to ministers from Quebec who, though junior, nonetheless held some cumulative influence. Paul Martin, for one, has recalled that he was opposed to recognition of the PRC at the time because of this factor.[36] D.C. Abbott retained his reticence for the same reasons he had expressed in February.

Officials at the Department of External Affairs were convinced that C.D. Howe, the mercurial and influential minister of trade and commerce, also played a significant role in blocking their efforts.[37] Though his opinions are not recorded in the cabinet minutes, Howe's main interest was trade and economic development and he was no doubt fearful that recognition would sour relations with the United States and thus rebound against Canadian interests.

When the decision in principle to accord recognition had been taken by cabinet in November 1949, it was widely expected that Washington would not disapprove too ardently of the Canadian action and might even follow suit at some later point. By the spring of 1950, however, American attitudes had hardened considerably. The State Department appeared to accept that Canada was going to recognize and made no attempt to influence Ottawa's actions. However, with the rise of McCarthyism in the United States and the increasing stridency and influence of the China lobby in Washington, it became clear, as Hume Wrong warned, that Canada would have to expect an adverse reaction from both Congress and the American press were it to accord recognition.[38] Given the sensitivity and vast scope of the Canadian-American relationship and the powerful impact Congress could have upon it, this was a potent consideration, particularly to ministers whose departmental focus was more limited than that of Pearson. Whether Canadian recognition during the spring of 1950 would in fact have had any negative effect on relations with the United States is questionable. But given the limited nature of Canadian interests in China, cabinet preferred not to risk antagonizing the United States at that time, even if the risk was small.

Certainly the prime minister was guided by such considerations. Though he later became a firm advocate of recognition, at the meeting on 21 June, and earlier in March, he cautioned against moving too far in advance of Washington.[39] St Laurent was no doubt influenced as well by the division in cabinet over the issue. Though Pearson was supported by Brooke Claxton, the minister of defence, the duo was no match for the heavyweights arrayed against it.[40] With several of his most powerful colleagues opposed, the prime minister felt that delay was the wisest policy. At any rate, there seemed little reason to rush into recognition. They could not possibly know that the Korean War was coming and so decided to adhere to a wait-and-see approach. As a result, Canada missed the one real opportunity to accord recognition free from deleterious consequences.

The Korean Watershed

With the outbreak of the Korean conflict and the subsequent intervention of Chinese forces, the entire China problem became immensely more complicated. The war not only necessitated that recognition be delayed for its duration, but it also made such an action more difficult to justify thereafter. The PRC was declared an aggressor by the United Nations General Assembly in February 1951, a stigma which placed major obstacles in the path of recognition for some time. At home the war aroused intense emotions which the St Laurent government could not easily ignore. In the United States the accession to the White House of a Republican administration virulent in its hostility to Peking ensured that recognition by Canada or other allies would provoke a negative response from Washington far in excess of anything contemplated in 1950.

There was also the Taiwan question to consider. Prior to the Korean conflict, most governments, including the Truman administration, had expected the island to fall eventually into the hands of the Communists, through either subversion or direct attack.[41] But the American commitment to the defence of the island during and after the Korean War guaranteed the continued existence of two competing and antagonistic Chinese governments, with all the dangerous consequences which that involved. The Taiwan problem became the central focus of Sino-American hostility, precluding any general Far Eastern settlement. In 1950, DEA had hoped to follow the British and Indian example by according recognition to the Communist government without commenting on the status of Taiwan. After Korea, the PRC was less willing to accept this. Concern arose that a gesture by Ottawa might be rebuffed if not accompanied by an acknowledgment of Peking's claims to the island, a condition which would be unacceptable to most Canadians. Though the Nationalist regime was viewed with little favour, there was much sympathy for the Taiwanese people who, it was felt, should have the right of self-determination. The Canadian government held consistently to the view that the eventual disposition of the island should be decided by an international conference, taking into consideration the wishes of the people. A 'two-Chinas' solution seemed the most logical way of dealing with the situation, but this was unacceptable to both the Nationalists and the Communists. Throughout the 1950s and 1960s the Taiwan problem remained a major barrier both to recognition and to the admission of PRC representatives to the United Nations.

The legal, political, and strategic environment surrounding the recognition question after the Korean War was, therefore, vastly different from what it had been in the spring of 1950. Yet three years of bloody conflict had not altered Pearson's and DEA's preference for the pragmatic, conciliatory China policy which they had espoused since 1949. If anything, it convinced them and the prime minister that recognition and the establishment of diplomatic relations were essential to the maintenance of world peace. Unlike their American counterparts, for whom events in Korea provided demonstrable proof that the Peking regime was a reprobate government unworthy of international recognition, Canadian officials drew different conclusions. The war made them more concerned than ever to bring the Chinese government into the world community, to bind it by international organizations such that disputes could be settled amicably. They shared American fears that recognition and U.N. membership could increase the potential for trouble-making of a regime which had already demonstrated its aggressive nature. But in their view, this risk had to be balanced against the proven dangers of isolation.[42] The desire to facilitate a normalization of relations between mainland China and the West was based largely on the fear that continued tension might result in another confrontation which could prove impossible to contain. By bringing Peking into the world community, it was hoped that conflicts could be resolved through negotiation, and future wars prevented. In Asia DEA's objective was the establishment of a lasting peace which, in turn, would ensure that scarce Western resources, so badly needed in the North Atlantic area, would not again be siphoned off into this peripheral region. For this to be achieved, some sort of modus vivendi would have to be reached with the PRC: 'Until Communist China is generally recognized we can see no end to the tension in the Far East.'[43]

In a memorandum of 15 May 1953, DEA emphasized that recognition and the eventual seating of Chinese Communist representatives in international organizations would be the goals of Canadian policy in the post-war years. Washington was not likely to be favourably impressed by Canadian action, while the Nationalists were liable to use it as an excuse to default on their loans (though the chance of recovering these was seen to be virtually nil). To DEA, however, the issue of peace or war took priority over all others and it made its recommendation accordingly: 'On balance we suggest that in the event of an armistice, the arguments in favour of recognition are overwhelming – recognition being understood to entail derecognition of the Nationalist government and our support of Communist China for membership in the United Nations.'[44]

Seeking the Right Moment

No one doubted that a substantial delay would be necessary, even after the armistice, in order to allow emotions influenced by the war to cool. To act hastily would be unseemly and could risk antagonizing public opinion in both Canada and the United States. Hasty action might also be misconstrued as a reward for ending aggression. It was therefore decided that no

56 Reluctant Adversaries

move would be made at least until after the political conference on Korea and Indochina, expected in the spring of 1954. Pearson and St Laurent meanwhile sought gradually but deliberately to prepare the ground for Canadian action through a series of public speeches.[45] Their constant refrain was that, although the time was not yet ripe for recognition, Canada would have to reconsider the question if an honourable settlement was reached in Korea, and if Peking refrained from further aggression. In the meantime options were to be kept open and a rigid commitment against recognition of the Communist government avoided.

In March 1954, while on a Far Eastern tour, St Laurent made an unfortunate faux pas, stating in a press conference that Canada would eventually have to recognize the government that the Chinese people wanted.[46] This created a storm of controversy at home. The opposition Tories, led by Drew and Diefenbaker, attacked the government for creeping appeasement.[47] The prime minister's office was flooded with letters and petitions, many of them orchestrated by the Roman Catholic church in Quebec, expressing abhorrence at the prospects of any rapprochement with the Communists in Peking.[48] A large volume of correspondence was also received from individuals and organizations supporting St Laurent's views, but its impact appears to have been overshadowed by the stridency of those opposed.[49]

The effect of this furore was to reaffirm the need for delay in moving toward recognition and to strengthen the hands of those in cabinet who opposed it for domestic political reasons. Not surprisingly, it also seems to have made the prime minister more wary of approaching the issue in the years that followed. Though he held consistently to the view that the fact of Communist power in China would eventually have to be recognized, he became even less disposed to take political risks to achieve this end. In a lengthy speech on 25 March he apologized to the House of Commons for his poor choice of words and gave assurance that recognition was not being contemplated at that time. However, he also reiterated his belief that the government should 'keep an open mind as to when, if ever, conditions may be such that it will be in the interests of peace and stability in the world to recognize diplomatically whatever government happens to be in control of China.'[50]

After the Geneva conference in April the prospects for movement seemed greatly enhanced. A settlement of sorts was reached in Indochina and, in private discussions, Chou En-lai and his subordinates adopted a surprisingly conciliatory posture. An Anglo-Chinese rapprochement was facilitated including, at last, the exchange of diplomatic representatives and a visit by a Chinese trade delegation to Britain. Talks between Ronning and mainland Chinese officials were cordial and resulted in the release of several Roman Catholic missionaries as well as Squadron Leader A.R. Mackenzie, the only Canadian prisoner-of-war in China.[51] Although the Korean conflict remained unresolved, there was a clear trend toward improved Sino-Western relations which DEA officials found most encouraging.

Another positive development arose out of private discussions at Geneva between Pearson, Richard Casey of Australia, and Paul-Henri Spaak of Belgium.[52] The three foreign ministers were like-minded in their belief that recognition of the PRC was both sensible and necessary to reduce Far Eastern tensions. However, given the common importance of their relations with the United States, it was realized that action would have to be timed in such a way as to minimize Washington's anger and ease the path to Sino-American détente. The three agreed to consult regularly and seek an opportunity to move together on this basis. The agreement existed only between the foreign ministers and there was no guarantee that their respective governments would support them. Upon returning to Australia, Casey was in fact repudiated by his prime minister, Robert Menzies. Nevertheless, for several years, Ottawa, Brussels, Canberra, and later Wellington kept in close contact on the recognition question.

To Pearson and his officials, the results at Geneva raised considerable hope for the future. A gradual normalization of Sino-Western relations at last seemed possible. But no sooner had this window of opportunity been partially opened than it was slammed shut by Chinese actions in the Taiwan Straits. On 3 September 1954 Communist forces on the mainland began shelling the Nationalist-held coastal island of Quemoy. Over the following nine months the attacks were continued and extended to other islands, raising the spectre of American intervention in support of the Nationalists, and of a consequent Sino-American confrontation. The effect of the crisis on Canadian attitudes toward the recognition of the PRC was similar to that of the Korean War. On the one hand, Peking's aggressive behaviour made it more difficult for Ottawa to justify direct contact with the PRC; on the other, it re-emphasized the dangers of allowing China to remain isolated and hostile to the West. Pearson and DEA were strongly influenced by the latter consideration but accepted that nothing could be done while fighting continued in the Taiwan Straits.[53]

When the Taiwan Straits crisis dissipated in the spring of 1955, another opportunity to move toward recognition arose. During the summer, there occurred a significant reduction in tension, not only in Asia, but between the Communist bloc and the West generally. In July, the heads of state of the 'big four' powers met in Geneva for talks which took on a surprisingly positive air. The highly touted 'spirit of Geneva' emanating from the conference seemed to offer the prospect of peaceful coexistence between East and West. Hostile rhetoric on both sides cooled. Further meetings between NATO and Warsaw Pact leaders were arranged.

There were encouraging developments in the Far East as well. Peking's statements and actions became less aggressive; Chou En-lai even raised the possibility of a peaceful settlement of the Taiwan and offshore islands disputes. In August, Chinese and American officials began meeting in Geneva to discuss their differences. Canadian observers felt that there were indications from Washington that American policy was beginning to moderate. Opinion in the State Department was moving toward acceptance of 'two Chinas.'[54] The words of certain influential Americans such as Walter George, the Democratic chairman of the Senate Foreign Relations Committee, suggested that a Canadian lead might be welcomed in many quarters of the United States.[55] Officials in Ottawa seriously contemplated the possibility of a Sino-American rapprochement to be followed by U.S. recognition of the PRC.[56] Concern was expressed by DEA that Canada might be beaten to the punch and thus made to appear a lackey, obediently following behind the American lead. This prospect was galling to DEA officials who had pushed for recognition for so many years.[57]

> It has all too frequently been alleged that we have in our policy on recognition humbly followed the U.S. and not taken a position of our own. We have constantly denied this charge and have pointed to the clear differences in many ways between our policy toward China and that of the U.S. However, if we delay recognition until a short time after the U.S. or even till the same time we should confirm in the minds of most people that the charge had been correct.[58]

Moreover, it was realized that if any practical advantage was to be gained in Peking through the establishment of diplomatic relations, Ottawa would have to move in advance of the United States.

A thorough memorandum was completed by the Far Eastern Division on 8 August 1955 setting out in detail the arguments for and against action.[59] In addition to the usual points, it was suggested that recognition would enable Canada to play a more effective role in helping to resolve Far Eastern problems. A Canadian initiative might also be followed by other powers, thus further improving Sino-Western relations and easing the path to American recognition. DEA, therefore, concluded that the moment was propitious to once more consider moving on the recognition issues.[60] The memorandum was approved by both Pearson and St Laurent and authorization was given to begin discussions with other interested powers.[61] In a speech to the Women's Canadian Club of Vancouver on 25 August Pearson flew a trial balloon to test reactions at home and abroad to the prospect of Canadian recognition. Though the government had no intention of rushing into action, he suggested that 'the time is coming, and soon, when we should have another and searching look at the problem.'[62]

The Canadian press responded favourably to the suggestion, most newspapers welcoming the Pearson démarche.[63] From other countries too there was considerable support. The Australian and Belgian foreign ministers expressed interest and made it clear they would welcome a Canadian lead. Even in the United States the reaction was mild. The American ambassador in Ottawa expressed his government's 'concern' regarding the possibility of early Canadian action but did not pursue the matter vigorously.[64] The international and domestic political environment in 1955 clearly offered the best opportunity to move since the spring of 1950. Yet the moment was allowed to slip away. The problem was not with the merits of the case, but rather the timing, and here DEA acted with undue caution. A memo signed by Jules Leger, the under-secretary, stated that 'it would seem the wisest policy to sit back for several months at least, encourage public debate and watch developments in Geneva, Washington, Peking and perhaps Phong Saly.'[65] As always, there were legitimate reasons for delay, and in the absence of any political imperative to act, these were allowed to determine policy. The department was concerned about moving before or during the tenth session of the General Assembly lest it cause an acrimonious debate on the Chinese representation question and so set back recent improvements in Sino-Western relations. Canada was about to introduce its 'new members' initiative in the assembly and wished to avoid anything which might jeopardize this. Moreover, Pearson was set to leave on a trip to the Soviet Union and India in late September and there was insufficient time to prepare action before his departure. To move soon after his return in November would give the wrong impression about the influences under which he had acted.

By this time, it had also become clear that Ottawa's initial hopes regarding the moderation of U.S. China policy were overly optimistic. At the Geneva bilateral talks and in their dealings with the allies throughout the autumn, Washington maintained a consistently tough line. In these circumstances, officials in Ottawa were concerned that Canadian action would not only provoke a harsh response from Washington, but might also force the China issue to the forefront of the approaching presidential election campaign.[66] If it did, both candidates would no doubt publicly commit themselves to maintaining a hard line, thus eradicating all hope of an improvement in Sino-American relations for another four years. To

Canadian officials, the central prerequisite for any improvement of the situation in the Far East was the moderation of U.S. China policy. If Canadian recognition were to reverse or hinder this process, it would be counter-productive.[67] It was, therefore, decided to defer action yet again.

Speaking in Parliament on 31 January 1956 Pearson announced that, after conducting the promised re-examination of China policy, the government had decided to adhere to its cautious wait-and-see approach: 'we feel that the careful policy we have been following, and are still following, has been the right one; rejecting on the one hand immediate, diplomatic recognition but rejecting on the other hand the view that a communist regime in Peking can never be recognized as the government of China.'[68] Canadian representatives abroad were informed that no action was likely until the end of the year at the earliest.[69] Not surprisingly, DEA became less active in promoting new initiatives in China policy. Holmes, Menzies, and the Far Eastern and American Division continued to suggest incremental steps toward recognition and movement on the U.N. issue, but their appeals fell on deaf ears. One official wrote: 'I think it is not to be expected that Canada will be found in the van of a movement for recognition or for seating Communist China in the United Nations. I think that we must be prepared to follow a less heroic course, to be among the late-comers in recognition, to be an abstainer or an opposer on a vote changing representation.'[70] Ottawa's course was set. Until American policy showed signs of moderating, the China issue was effectively shelved.

The combination of favourable international and domestic circumstances which had made the summer of 1955 so promising was not to return during the remaining life of the St Laurent government. During 1956 the American election and, later, events in Suez and Hungary forced the China question into the background. In the first half of 1957 the Liberal government was too preoccupied with its own re-election to take any action liable to alienate even a small proportion of voters. In June the Progressive Conservatives, led by John Diefenbaker, took office and any realistic possibility of immediate movement on the recognition issue disappeared. Though the new secretary of state for external affairs, Sidney Smith, was eager to move toward recognition, he did not have the support of the prime minister, who maintained a tight hold on policy. Trade with China would be opened up again under the Conservatives. But as Basil Robinson, one of Diefenbaker's closest foreign policy advisers, has recalled, the new prime minister was philosophically disposed against recognition and never seriously considered moving in that direction.[71] The cycle of procrastination was to continue for another eleven years.

Bureaucratic Dynamics within DEA

Canadian policy toward China during the St Laurent years was a chronicle of unfulfilled wishes. For Pearson and his advisers it was a source of great frustration. Their policy preferences, based on pragmatic acceptance of the situation in China and the need to find some constructive way of living with it, had developed early and were held consistently throughout the period in question. Prior to the Korean conflict there was virtual unanimity within the department regarding the need not only for recognition but for action as soon as prudently possible. After the war, differences did develop among External Affairs officials, but these were concerned primarily with tactics and timing rather than the substance of policy. There are no principled arguments against recognition or a positive, if guarded, approach toward relations with the PRC in the department's files. The issue in question to Canadian diplomats after the Korean War was not the appropriateness of their preferred policy, but rather the extent and speed with which Canada should push forward with it in the light of Chinese Communist actions and the intense hostility of the new American administration toward the Peking regime. On this matter a considerable variety of views were expressed.

It would be over-simplifying reality to attempt to explain these divisions on the basis of the three schools of thought which Doug Ross had discovered in DEA opinion toward Indochina. His policy tendencies – 'left liberal, liberal moderate, and conservative' – were based on the general political dispositions of the adherents.[72] In the case of China policy, however, the differing viewpoints were based squarely on dissimilar functional and regional responsibilities.

Members of the Far Eastern Division generally called for a more progressive, if still balanced, approach to the China question because they were engaged continually in studying this matter and felt more strongly than most the illogicality and danger of the existing situation. Similarly, those concerned primarily with Commonwealth affairs were continually faced with the very strong views of the Indians and other Asian members on this subject and became worried about the effect that Ottawa's dilatoriness was having on their relations with these countries. However, personnel in the American and Economic Divisions and in the embassy in Washington tended to drag their feet on the China issue because they were exposed daily to the vast scope and overwhelming importance of the Canadian-American relationship and were loath to see any action taken which might threaten this. The United Nations Division and the delegation in New York likewise generally opposed taking chances on the China question because they more than others were aware of the specific extent to which Canada needed American co-operation at the U.N. if it was to achieve some of its other more important goals there, for instance the 1955 'new members' initiative.

Jules Leger, under-secretary of state for external affairs, seems initially to fit neatly into the conservative mould as defined by Ross, particularly in his strong emphasis on allied unity and his more evident anti-communism. But his opinions regarding the implementation of China policy were as much a consequence of his position as senior official responsible for the work of the entire department. His order of priorities was clear and China, with its limited relevance to immediate national interests, was given a low position.

Even Chester Ronning and Escott Reid, whose views regarding China conform so closely to Ross's left-liberal categorization, appear to have been influenced by other factors beyond their general left-wing approach to international affairs. Their advocacy was also the result of specific personal experiences or interests which led to a preoccupation with the China issue. In the case of Ronning, his deep sympathy with the Chinese people and their revolution stemmed from his long experience of the country and its problems. Reid, however, was influenced by his constant exposure to the views of Nehru, whom he deeply respected, and by his intense desire to promote the Canadian-Indian 'special relationship,' which he saw threatened by Ottawa's failure to act on the recognition and U.N. issues.

Regional and functional preoccupations seem therefore to have played a significant role in influencing individual attitudes toward the implementation side of China policy. The differences of opinion discussed above should not, however, be exaggerated. The most remarkable aspect of the departmental record was the degree of unanimity expressed, not only regarding the most logical policy to be followed in dealing with revolutionary China, but also on the reasons why implementation should be delayed. The basic restrictions imposed by Canada's limited capabilities and the priority of other foreign policy objectives were accepted by all but a very few officers. Divisions within DEA no doubt reinforced the tendency toward delay and complacency after 1955. However, Canadian inaction was based on far more substantive reasons than merely bureaucratic dynamics. The inability of DEA to translate its policy preferences into government action was due to a host of internal and external restraints beyond its control.

Sources of Canadian Inaction

When assessing the reasons for the St Laurent government's failure to accord recognition during the 1950s, one must be aware that the Canadian experience was by no means unique. Australia, New Zealand, Belgium,

France, and many other countries followed a similar path for much the same reasons. Like Canada, they lacked sufficient interests in China to warrant risking a major strain in their relations with the United States, which recognition might produce. For their part, St Laurent, Pearson, and DEA were firmly convinced of the need to normalize relations with Peking but were not willing to take the necessary actions if these were likely to prejudice other, more vital domestic and foreign policy goals.

In the spring of 1950 the probable costs of recognition seemed slight, yet still too high for a cabinet which can only be described as excessively cautious. After the Korean War the expectation of cabinet opposition remained, and this in itself encouraged caution within DEA. To Pearson and his senior advisers there seemed little point in pushing the issue unless there was some hope of success. The tendency was, therefore, to delay, waiting for optimal domestic and international conditions before moving ahead. Since these never occurred, recognition initiatives, such as that in August 1955, tended to die within the department without ever reaching cabinet.

Ottawa's inaction was partly a reflection of the ambivalence of Canadian opinion regarding the matter. Throughout the 1950s newspaper articles, opinion polls, and the considerable flow of letters entering the offices of the prime minister and the secretary of state for external affairs indicate that those Canadians who thought about the China problem were deeply divided in their attitude toward it. So too was Parliament. And while this in itself did not present an obstacle to recognition, neither did it encourage the government to move. Had there been a consensus in favour of recognition, DEA might have had a substantive political reason to justify a new policy action both to cabinet and to the Americans. Under these circumstances, however, it was easier and politically safer for the government to do nothing. Recognition might win the support of certain individuals and groups in the country, but it would also alienate a considerable number of voters, particularly in the Liberal stronghold of Quebec. These were risks that cabinet was unwilling to accept.

Externally, the actions of the Chinese Communists were seen by Canadian policy makers as decisive in preventing Canadian recognition. Every time momentum seemed to be building toward a normalization of Sino-Western relations, it was reversed by a new crisis. The slow process of reconciliation would then have to begin again. In addition to causing delay, the regular recurrence of what mainstream opinion in the department interpreted as aggressive behaviour by Peking – in Korea, the offshore islands, Tibet, later on the Sino-Indian border and in support for Communist parties in Southeast Asia – made it increasingly difficult to justify action. It also served continually to enflame American opinion, thus raising the potential costs of Canadian recognition. Although not a member of the Southeast Asia Treaty Organization, Canada deemed it prudent to take account of the views of its members that Communist China threatened to push over the line of dominoes.

Given the economic and political importance of Canadian-American relations and the pivotal role played by the United States in the defence of Western interests in the Far East, policy makers in Ottawa could not help but be influenced by the policies of Washington, however irrational they felt them to be. It would be incorrect, though, to assume that Canadian inaction on the recognition question was merely a submission to American pressure. To be sure, Washington sought continually to keep its allies in line, both by generalized threats to withdraw from the United Nations should Chinese Communist representatives be admitted, and by repeatedly warning other governments of the effect recognition of the PRC would have both in Southeast Asia and on American opinion. There is no evidence, however, that intimidation or blackmail was used. This was unnecessary. Officials and ministers in Ottawa were only too aware of the vital importance to Canada of maintaining harmonious relations with the United States and within NATO and had little desire to put them at risk for the sake of pursuing a matter of principle.

Canada's main concern in the Far East during the 1950s was to prevent conflicts in that region from escalating into a major East-West confrontation. When this danger arose, as in Korea and the offshore islands, Ottawa was prepared to break with the United States and endeavour to restrain them from rash actions. The recognition issue was not, however, considered of sufficient importance to warrant such a forthright step.

Washington had committed itself to keeping Peking diplomatically isolated and militarily contained. Were Canada and other states to break with the United States on these two basic premises, it would undermine the prestige of their great ally, an intangible yet vital element of their own security. It might also have serious repercussions for the Canadian economy. The fear was not so much that Canadian recognition would lead to direct retaliation by Congress, but rather that it would erode the store of goodwill in Washington upon which the smooth operation of Canadian-American relations depended. This might be reflected in import quotas, trucking legislation, co-operation on the St Lawrence Seaway, or any of a vast range of bilateral concerns. An independent stand on this, perhaps the most emotive of issues to the Eisenhower administration, might also make it more difficult to attain American co-operation in other sectors of foreign policy.

In the complex post-war agenda, China policy did not rank as a high priority in either cabinet or DEA. The benefits expected to be gained from recognition were too esoteric, long range, and indefinite to justify the potential costs this might have for Canadian-American relations, costs which would be immediate and tangible. The government's inaction was, therefore, based on a clear realization of where the national interest lay at the time.

The appropriateness of this cost-benefit approach to foreign policy decision-making is unquestionable. However, it is open to speculation whether, during the 1950s, Ottawa exaggerated the cost side of the equation and in so doing unnecessarily curtailed its own freedom of movement. There is no doubt that Canadian recognition would have caused annoyance and anger in Washington. But, if well timed, as in 1955, it probably would not have resulted in any serious or lasting damage to the Canadian-American relationship. Britain repeatedly broke with the United States over China policy throughout the 1950s without dire repercussions on bilateral co-operation. It was, however, a major power and had extensive commercial and colonial interests in China and Asia to justify such an independent policy. Herein lay the key.

In the last analysis, the inaction of the St Laurent government on the recognition issue was a reflection not of its subservience to Washington, but rather of Canada's limited stake in the Far East. In the absence of any major interests in China, there was little imperative to move.

EPILOGUE: CANADIAN RECOGNITION INITIATIVES, 1958–1968
(by Paul M. Evans)

Between the defeat of the St Laurent government in 1957 and the Trudeau initiative of 1968, the recognition problem was under continuous but generally low-level consideration by DEA. The department file on the subject fills several volumes containing scores of reports, memoranda, clippings, and cables. Two of the more important reviews which reached the level of the prime minister were undertaken in 1958 and 1963, both in the early years of new governments. Neither produced any decisive change of policy, but they did reveal changing patterns of thinking in the department and the political leadership.

1958

In opposition, firmly anti-communist in ideology and strongly committed to the people and government of the Republic of China on Taiwan, John

Diefenbaker had strenuously opposed any attempts to expand diplomatic contacts with the PRC bilaterally or through the United Nations. In his first statement on the subject as prime minister he made two main points. First, his government would support expanded trade with the PRC. Second, it would not recognize Peking 'until such time as ... the Communist Government of China expiates its wrongdoing under international law.' Recognition, he continued, 'would be interpreted as recognition of Communism as such' and would harm Asian countries standing 'firmly against the on-rush of Communism.'[73]

The Diefenbaker government undertook only one major reassessment of the issue. Shortly after being appointed secretary of state for external affairs (SSEA), Sydney Smith surprised his department and government by indicating to a group of journalists that he intended to recognize the PRC as soon as possible. He quickly qualified his statement and launched an internal review. Its findings were communicated to the prime minister in a memorandum dated 16 June 1958.[74]

The memorandum identified several principal arguments which supported Canadian action. One set of arguments listed several potential benefits to direct Canadian interests, among them the establishment of a listening post on the mainland, enhanced prospects for trade promotion, settlement of outstanding bilateral issues including the Ming Sung loan issue which had so agitated D.C. Abbott ten years earlier, and the sending of a signal to the international and, presumably, domestic community that Canada could operate independently of the United States on major world issues. This last point received considerable attention, responding to frequently voiced opinion that the Conservative government, like its Liberal predecessor, was allowing Canadian policy to be made in Washington. The legal case covered familiar ground but also made the point that it would be valuable to dispel suggestions that the government was using a double standard which applied more strenuous criteria for recognition in Asia than elsewhere. There were as well recurrent echoes of earlier Canadian aspirations to use recognition as a vehicle for ending the diplomatic isolation of mainland China, committing it to international agreements, including it in international organizations (among them the U.N.), and reducing the PRC's reliance on the Soviet Union.

The memorandum also examined liabilities of moving on the recognition issue. They included a potential and probably significant souring of relations with the United States; extra complications at the U.N. if the United States suffered a major defeat on the question of Chinese representation; ongoing conflict over the future of Taiwan; the danger that 'derecognizing' the Republic of China would de-stabilize countries with a large overseas

Chinese population in non-communist Asia (especially in Indonesia and Malaysia); worries that the PRC might actually rebuff Canadian overtures; worries that if recognition of the PRC did proceed, the Chinese might use their presence in Canada for purposes of subversion and intimidation of the local Chinese communities; and, finally, a concern that recognition might reinforce the PRC's intransigence in refusing to agree to the final terms of a peaceful solution to the Korean problem.

The conclusion was indecisive, it being noted in the memorandum that 'there is no clear cut balance of argument discernible in this issue.' Smith nevertheless outlined a long-term plan of 'incremental action.' This staged approach would involve gradual expansion of unofficial contacts, particularly in the field of trade. It would also involve 'careful diplomatic preparation' entailing informal discussions with the Chinese to sound out their views and constant contact with the Americans and other interested parties.

The memorandum was sufficiently general and equivocal to render it inoperable as a foundation for action. Smith's death in March 1959 effectively ended any cabinet-level interest in forcing a re-examination of the recognition issue. Perhaps its only lasting significance for policy was the plan to employ gradual measures to expand non-governmental relations, thereby preparing the political ground for the most important Conservative initiative in relations with the PRC, the grain sales in 1960.

The memorandum pointed to a slightly altered pattern of thinking in the department. It indicated that recognition was at least temporarily linked to Communist Chinese behaviour and no longer offered as a matter of simple diplomatic expediency. Further, the domestic considerations included a concern about a likely negative response to recognition by the Chinese community in Canada as well as a worry that an exchange of diplomats with the PRC would result in subversion and harassment by PRC personnel posted in Canada.

1963

The election of a Liberal minority in April 1963 renewed the prospect that a major reorientation in China policy would be forthcoming. International conditions appeared favourable in light of the Sino-Soviet split, the quick termination of the Sino-Indian border war, and the institution of a period of comparative calm on China's frontiers. In August Norman Robertson, then serving as under-secretary of state for external affairs, prepared a report which summarized an internal departmental review.[75] The case against recognition included most of the arguments that had been presented in the review five years earlier, though there was considerably less emphasis on potential internal security problems and more emphasis on the difficulties of dealing with the future status and security of Taiwan. Significantly, the maintenance of Canadian bilateral relations with Taiwan did not even receive mention in their memorandum.

In favour of recognition, Robertson noted that the climate of opinion in the United States, especially among intellectuals and the business community, was gradually shifting away from the policy of military containment and diplomatic isolation of the PRC. He agreed that there might be enhanced prospects for bilateral trade but emphasized the broader view that if Canada wanted to become a major Pacific trading power, a first and necessary step would be expanded contact with the PRC. Canadian public opinion, he noted, was also shifting in favour of recognition of Peking, most dramatically in Quebec.

A few weeks earlier Paul Martin, the secretary of state for External Affairs, had given a major speech which questioned the wisdom of isolating and containing the PRC rather than 'broadening contacts at a variety of levels in an endeavour to penetrate the curtain of ignorance and blunt the edge of ideological differences.' The speech did not advocate an immediate initiative but did promote a 'progressive attitude.'[76] Mindful of these views and of Martin's rising interest in finding a solution to the U.N. representation problem, Robertson outlined a three-point strategy to link the recognition and representation issues. He advocated admitting the PRC to the United Nations, initiating informal contact with the PRC through an emissary like Chester Ronning, and keeping Washington closely informed of developments so as to dampen any retaliatory action.

The proposal did not produce a quick response though it appears to have had considerable support within the department. The prime minister was sympathetic to the main lines of the argument, if not to the specific prescriptions. A year later Pearson reiterated his familiar view that the strongest argument in support of a Canadian initiative would be to end the isolation of China which 'encourages recurring crises.'[77]

Increased American involvement in Vietnam and the concomitant hostility towards the PRC shattered any hope that the long-awaited improvement of Sino-American relations would soon occur. For the remainder of the period of Pearson's tenure as prime minister, Vietnam played the same role in forestalling a Canadian initiative that Korea and the offshore islands crises had at an earlier time. As John Holmes stated in 1965: 'To risk American irritation is one thing; to take what Americans would inevitably look upon as a friendly gesture toward those who are abetting the killing of American soldiers requires a degree of boldness and confidence which has not characterized Canadian policy toward China.'[78]

In light of American views after the Gulf of Tonkin Resolution in August 1964, the ensuing escalation of American military involvement in Vietnam, and the approach of a presidential election, a DEA meeting in September 1964 came to the conclusion that recognition would not serve any immediate Canadian national interests.[79] It is thus not surprising that most of the activity during the Pearson years shifted from Pearson to Martin, and from the recognition issue to the U.N. representation problem.

Notes

1 Canadian exports to China actually decreased from approximately $43 million in 1946 to only $13 million in 1949 (Dominion Bureau of Statistics, *Trade of Canada*, 1948 and 1949, vol. 2, *Exports*, 5).
2 In 1949 this included Norman Robertson, John Holmes, Jules Leger, Hume Wrong, A.D.P. Heeney, Escott Reid, and many others. Pearson's first exposure to the Asian continent did not come until January 1950 with the Commonwealth foreign ministers meeting in Colombo, Ceylon.
3 DEA 50055-40, vol. 4, despatch 53, Odlum (Ankara) to SSEA, 1 Apr. 1948. Also Odlum (Chungking) to SSEA, 4 Sept. 1946. A full analysis of Odlum's images of China and the way these affected his reporting is to be found in Kim Richard Nossal, 'Strange Bedfellows: Canada and China in War and Revolution, 1942–47' (Unpublished PhD thesis, University of Toronto 1977). See also his 'Chungking Prism: Cognitive Process and Intelligence Failure,' *International Journal*, 32.3 (1977), 559–76. For an impression of Odlum by one of his contemporaries see John Holmes, *The Shaping of Peace: Canada and the Search for World Order 1943–1957*, vol. 2 (Toronto: University of Toronto Press 1982), 134–5.
4 Nossal, *op. cit.*, 'Strange Bedfellows.'
5 Interviews with Campbell, Maybee, Holmes, Menzies, Reid, and Rogers.
6 See Mitchell, ch. 1 in this volume; older works include Charles J. Woodsworth, *Canada and the Orient: A Study in International Relations* (Toronto: Macmillan 1941), ch. 8, and Arthur R.M. Lower, *Canada and the Far East – 1940* (New York: Institute of International Relations 1941), ch. 4.
7 See, for example, DEA 50055-40, vol. 5, dispatches 305 and 72, Davis to SSEA, 16 June 1947 and 3 Feb. 1948; also 50056-40, vol. 2, telegram 214, Davis to SSEA, 2 Nov. 1948, and interviews with Maybee, Ballachey, and Rankin.
8 DEA 50055-40, vol. 7, despatch 81, Davis to SSEA, 12 Apr. 1949; also DEA 4458-V-40, vol. 2, despatch 91, Davis to Pearson, 30 Apr. 1949.
9 This assessment of Canadian policy preferences in 1949 is derived both from the documentary record and from interviews with several of the Canadian officials involved in China policy at the time, among them Arthur Menzies,

70 Reluctant Adversaries

Bruce Rankin, Escott Reid, Jack Maybee, and Frank Ballachey. (See DEA 50055-40, vol. 4, secret letter, Davis to Pearson, 5 Dec. 1948, and DEA 50055-B-40, vol. 1, minute by Menzies, 23 Apr. 1949.)

10 DEA 50055-40, vol. 4, Davis to David Johnson, 19 Jan. 1948, enclosing the opinion of Chester Ronning; also DEA 4457-40, part 2, Davis to SSEA, 21 Feb. 1949.
11 DEA 4457-40, part 2, Davis to SSEA, 21 Feb. 1949.
12 DEA 50056-40, vol. 2, telegram 214, Davis to SSEA, 2 Nov. 1948; also 50055-40, vol. 4, secret letter, Davis to Pearson, 5 Dec. 1948, and 50055-B-40, vol. 1, telegram 108, Davis to SSEA, 9 May 1949.
13 DEA 50055-B-40, vol. 1, minutes by Arthur Menzies, 23 April 1949, also 4 Nov. 1949.
14 Public Archives, RG25 A12, vol. 2078, dispatch 531, Mayrand to High Commissioner London, 1 March 1949 containing Joint Intelligence Committee report, 21 Feb. 1949.
15 PRO, FO, 371/1023, file 75619, telegram 919, Singapore to FO, 4 Nov. 1949. Circulated to Ottawa; see DEA 50055-B-40, vol. 2.
16 DEA 50055-B-40, vol. 1, exploratory memo by American and Far Eastern Division, 'Relations with the Chinese Communists,' 3 June 1949.
17 Ibid., vol. 2, memo, 'Policy towards Communist China,' 3 June 1949.
18 Hansard, British House of Commons, *Debates*, 17 Nov. 1949, column 2225.
19 Ibid., 'China situation – recent developments,' 15 Nov. 1949.
20 PAC, *Cabinet Conclusions*, vol. 18, meeting of 16 Nov. 1949.
21 DEA 5055-B-40, vol. 2, SSEA to the Canadian High Commission, London, 9 Nov. 1949.
22 See Pearson Papers, vol. 8, Pearson to Heeney, 17 Jan. 1950.
23 Ibid., vol. 4, telegram 22, Pearson to St Laurent, 24 Jan. 1950.
24 DEA 11152-E-40, vol. 1, 'Peking Premises,' H.F. Clark (officer in charge, supplies and properties) to Mr Harry Hussey, 22 May 1950. An option on a different house in Peking was taken by Ronning in Dec. 1949 and held until the following May.
25 Interview with Bruce Rankin, 19 Dec. 1983.
26 DEA 50055-B- 40, vol. 4, Pearson to Spender (foreign minister of Australia) enclosed in a letter to the Australian High Commission in Ottawa, 24 Feb. 1950. Similar messages were sent to Wellington, Pretoria, and London.
27 PAC, *Cabinet Conclusions*, vol. 18, meeting of 23 Feb. 1950.
28 Ibid., vol. 19, meeting of 10 Mar. 1950.
29 DEA 50055-B-40, vol. 4, Wrong to acting SSEA, 4 Feb. 1950.
30 DEA 550055-B-40, vol. 5, telegram 42, SSEA to Ronning, 28 April 1950.
31 Ibid., vol. 5, telegram 43, Ronning to SSEA, 22 May 1950.
32 Ibid., vol. 5, Memo to Minister, 'China – Relations with the Peking Government,' 29 May 1950.

33 Ibid., vol. 6, telegram 51, Ronning to SSEA, 13 June 1950; also telegram 54, Ronning to SSEA, 16 June 1950.
34 Ibid., vol. 6, two draft telegrams, SSEA to Ronning, enclosed in Memo for the Minister by Heeney, 23 June 1950.
35 Ibid., vol. 20, meeting of 21 June 1950.
36 Interview with Paul Martin at the Montebello Conference on Canada-China relations, May 1985.
37 Interviews with John Holmes, Peter Campbell, Arthur Menzies, Escott Reid, R.L. Rogers, and Jack Maybee.
38 DEA 50055-B-40, vol. 4, conference dispatch 374, Wrong to acting SSEA, 4 Feb. 1950.
39 PAC, *Cabinet Conclusions*, vol. 20, meeting of 21 June 1950.
40 Ibid., meeting of 4 May 1950.
41 See, for instance, DEA 50055-B-40, vol. 5, Memo for the Minister, 'China – Relations with the Peking Government,' 29 May 1953.
42 DEA 5005555-B-40, vol. 6, Memo for the Minister by the Far Eastern Division, 'Far Eastern Problems,' 15 May 1953.
43 Ibid.
44 Ibid.
45 See, for instance, Pearson's speech to the Canadian Club of Vancouver, 27 May 1953 (in *Statements and Speeches*), 1953, No. 50 and his article in the December 1953 issue of *World*, see also the report of Prime Minister St Laurent's press conference on 12 June 1953 in the *Ottawa Citizen*, 13 June 1953.
46 This statesment was made off the cuff in response to a press question so there was no official record of what was said; St Laurent did not think he had used the word 'wanted' but in his apology to Parliament he took full responsibility for any misinterpretation of his statement by the press. (*Debates*, 25 Mar. 1954, 3332–5; also St Laurent Papers, PA, MG26L, vol. 220, file U-25-8.)
47 Canada, House of Commons, *Debates*, 25 and 26 Mar. 1954, 3335–6, 3373.
48 PAC, St Laurent Papers, MG2GL, vol. 220, file U-25-8.
49 Ibid.
50 Canada, House of Commons, *Debates*, 25 Mar. 1954, 3334.
51 DEA 50055-B-40, vol. 8, Canadian delegation, Geneva to DEA, 3, 6, 14, and 15 May 1954.
52 I am indebted to John Holmes for information regarding these discussions (interview and his *The Shaping of Peace*, vol. 2, 195).
53 Interviews with Arthur Menzies, John Holmes, and R.L. Rogers.
54 Personal letter, Heeney to Holmes, 31 Jan. 1955, cited in Holmes, *The Shaping of Peace*, vol. 2, 197.
55 DEA 50055-B-40, vol. 9, Memo for the Minister, 'Recognition of Peking,' 8 August 1955.

72 Reluctant Adversaries

56 In making this assessment about a potential shift in American policy, the Canadians were not alone; the French expressed similar optimism, (ibid., dispatch 367, Canadian ambassador, Paris to SSEA, 30 July 1955).
57 Interview with Arthur Menzies, John Holmes, R.L. Rogers, Peter Campbell, and Jack Maybee.
58 Ibid., Memo for the Minister, 'Recognition of Peking,' 8 August 1955.
59 DEA 50055-B-40, vol. 9, Memo for the Minister, 'Recognition of Peking,' 8 Aug. 1955.
60 Ibid.
61 Ibid., Memo for USSEA by Far Eastern Division, 24 Aug. 1955.
62 DEA, *Statements and Speeches*, 55/30, 25 Aug. 1955.
63 DEA 50055-B-40, vol. 9, Memo for the Minister, 'Editorial Comment on Recognition of Peking,' 2 Sept. 1955.
64 Ibid., SSEA to ambassador, Washington, 9 Sept. 1955.
65 Ibid., Memo to the Minister, 'Recognition of China,' signed by USSEA Leger, 6 Sept. 1955.
66 DEA 50055-B-40, vol. 10, SSEA to High Commissioner in London (repeated elsewhere), 1 Feb. 1956.
67 Ibid.
68 Canada, House of Commons, *Debates*, 31 Jan. 1956, 710–11.
69 DEA 50055-B-40, vol. 10, telegram 178, SSEA to Canadian High Commissioner in London, repeated to Paris, Brussels, New Delhi, and Tokyo, 1 Feb. 1956.
70 Ibid., vol. 8 secret memo for the Commonwealth Division 'Recognition of Communist China: Discussion during Nehru's Visit,' 18 Dec. 1956, by R.L. Rogers.
71 Interview with Basil Robinson, Dec. 1983.
72 Douglas A. Ross, *In the Interests of Peace; Canada and Vietnam 1954–1973* (Toronto: University of Toronto Press 1984).
73 House of Commons, *Debates*, 1 Nov. 1957, 654–5.
74 DEA, 500055-B-40, Sydney Smith to John Diefenbaker, 16 June 1958, and interview with John Holmes, June 1984.
75 DEA, 50055-B-40, Norman Robertson, USSEA, to Paul Martin, SSEA, 29 Aug. 1963. The memorandum was transmitted to the prime minister on the same day.
76 Department of External Affairs *Statements and Speeches*, 63/17, 24 Aug. 1963.
77 Quoted in John Holmes, 'Canada and China: The Dilemmas of a Middle Power,' in A.M. Halpern, ed., *Policies toward China: The Views from Six Continents* (New York: McGraw-Hill 1965), 120.
78 Ibid., 122.
79 See the discussion in ch. 4 (this volume) by Norman St Amour.

CHAPTER THREE

Don Page

The Representation of China in the United Nations: Canadian Perspectives and Initiatives, 1949–1971

Few cases better illustrate the variance between what a middle power may wish to achieve in a multilateral forum and what is possible, given its limited resources and the variables of international diplomacy,[1] than the twenty-two-year debate over the representation of the People's Republic of China (PRC) in the United Nations. While the enormity of the task was soon apparent to both the permanent Canadian delegation to the United Nations and the Canadian government, it did not prevent Canada from taking an active, though usually behind-the-scenes, role in trying to overcome the obstacles. Quite unlike the admission of other new members, it was a question of who should represent China. This was a far more complicated and drawn-out problem because the Nationalist government of the Republic of China (ROC) would accept no diminution of its status or position as a founding member of the United Nations and because it had the steadfast backing of a major ally, the United States. The long and often frustrating struggle that Canada had with both its friends and foes over the Chinese question is the focus of this essay.

Round One: 1949–1956

Months before the PRC came into being on 1 October 1949 officials at the Department of External Affairs were considering the various problems the Chinese situation could raise for the Canadian delegation which happened to be on the Security Council that year. The question of China's representation at the United Nations had first been raised on 27 January by Dr T.F. Tsiang, the permanent ROC representative on the Security Council, in conversations with George Ignatieff of the Canadian delegation.² As a result of Ignatieff's report, Ottawa was aware that any PRC effort to claim the single 'China seat' would be resisted vigorously by the Chinese Nationalists.

By October the question had to be faced head-on. Chou En-lai's demand that the United Nations immediately deprive the ROC of the right to represent the Chinese people in the U.N. and a rumour in the *New York Times* that the PRC might actually send a representative to the U.N. made it necessary to ponder Peking's precise intentions. Was the object of the Communists simply to discredit the Nationalist delegation or to signal their intention to be heard on the question of representation? Whichever, it was already clear that the United States delegation would not support Communist representation at that time and that a protracted debate would thus ensue.

Lester Pearson's objective was to avoid such a debate. If a challenge was to be made, Pearson wanted it referred to a special committee of the Security Council so as not to delay progress on the Indonesian and Kashmir questions.³ By the time the Soviet Union introduced a resolution to unseat the Nationalists in January 1950, Canada's two-year term on the Security Council had expired and its delegation was content to watch others shelve the issue as premature. As interpreted by Under-Secretary of State for External Affairs Arnold Heeney: 'The question of Chinese representation is not primarily a question of credentials to be decided by reference to the Rules of Procedure, but is a political question. It is difficult to challenge on constitutional grounds the right of each organization to determine who should represent China in its meetings. The results, however, of such a policy might be such as to discredit the United Nations as a whole and render it ineffective on major issues.'⁴ Canada would, nevertheless, still have to develop some yardstick for determining when to support the Soviet or a similar proposal when it came before the General Assembly. The delegation recommended that Canada support PRC representation when half of the United Nations was prepared to do likewise, though that policy would obviously have to be reviewed in the unlikely event that all the major powers came to recognize Peking without commanding a majority of votes in the U.N. Circumstances would have to be watched carefully in the knowledge that 'there are few things as important at present as keeping the Soviet Union in the United Nations.'

Tied to the question of representation in the United Nations was the uncertainty surrounding the possibility of Canadian recognition of the PRC.⁵ Although Canada had not recognized the new regime, through its offices in Nanking and Shanghai it was in touch with the Communist government. Not surprisingly, the Chinese Foreign Nationals Bureau soon asked Ottawa to support the acceptance of the Peking-appointed representatives to the United Nations. No reply was forthcoming. In view of the continued Canadian recognition of the Nationalists and the expected Canadian recognition of the Communists, Ottawa was not prepared to give a strong statement either way on the admission question. Should the credentials of the Nationalists be challenged, the Canadian delegation to the February meeting of the Economic and Social Committee (ECOSOC) was instructed to oppose the challenge, since Canada had not yet withdrawn recognition from Taipei.

A new twist was put on the question when the U.N. secretary general issued a memorandum stating that it should be possible for members to accept a representative of Peking in the United Nations without themselves having recognized that regime. A few days later, the U.N. Division of the Department of External Affairs (DEA) began work on a new set of instructions for Canadian delegations to international conferences that would come into effect after Canada had extended recognition. In these draft instructions it was acknowledged that 'the General Assembly should recognize as the representative of a member country the representative of a regime which has signified that it is able and willing to undertake to implement substantially all of the international obligations which have been incurred in the name of that country.'[6] Canadian delegations would be instructed to support any proposal to seat the Communists and to abstain on any proposal to unseat the Nationalists. While there was no doubt that the Nationalists were no longer in control of mainland China, in the absence of an acceptable alternative it seemed undesirable to force them out of the Assembly. In the specialized agencies, however, the Canadian delegate could vote them out on the grounds that the Nationalists were not in a position to carry out their obligations or, for that matter, pay their assessment.

Since implementation of this new policy was contingent on Canada recognizing Peking, decisions would have to be taken in the interval on the policy to be followed in specific international meetings. Initially, there was some confusion. The Canadian delegate to the Economic and Employment Commission of ECOSOC voted in favour of a chairman's ruling that it was beyond the competence of a functional commission to alter its membership, while the Canadian delegate on the UNICEF executive board voted that the board could alter its membership.[7]

The issue was deeper than a question of consistency within the United Nations. Decisions in institutions outside the U.N. could have important ramifications, as in the case of the Far Eastern Commission. Nations that were prepared to exclude the PRC from the U.N. might not act the same way on regional bodies dealing with the Pacific. With the Netherlands' recognition of Peking, there were now six states on the commission that did and seven that did not. If Canada changed its position it could be forced to cast the decisive vote to expel the Nationalists and open the door to Communist membership. This would have far-reaching effects, as the commission would also be determining the composition of the forthcoming Japanese peace conference.[8] It would also put pressure on the United Nations to change course. All that could be said to an American inquiry about the Canadian position was that it was still under review by cabinet but, in the meantime, there was no intention of according Peking immediate recognition. In issuing to a UNESCO delegation instructions to maintain the status quo, the American and Far Eastern Division reminded the U.N. Division that 'any gratuitously unfriendly action by us would render more difficult the somewhat unenviable task of the representative we send to Peking to negotiate with the new regime.'[9]

In the midst of this uncertainty and talk of an extraordinary session of the U.N. General Assembly to consider the Chinese question, the Soviet Union walked out of the Security Council in protest. On 30 March 1950 the much perturbed deputy under-secretary, Escott Reid, sent a memorandum to Pearson in which he argued: 'The present situation in the United Nations is so unsatisfactory and potentially so dangerous that I believe it warrants a new attempt to secure Cabinet approval for Canadian recognition of Communist China.'[10] As Reid had pointed out, the British were much concerned that the Soviet Union might use the present unsatisfactory situation as a pretext for permanently withdrawing from the United Nations. While Reid did not discount this as a possibility, more serious for him was the fact that the presence of the Nationalists was bringing the work of the United Nations close to a standstill at the very time when public opinion in both the United States and Canada was demanding an initiative to reopen dialogue with the Soviet Union. Proposals to hold a U.N. General Assembly in Moscow, to resume talks on atomic energy, or to invite foreign ministers to an extraordinary session of the Security Council had little chance of succeeding as long as the Chinese stumbling-block in the U.N. persisted. Reid concluded: 'In these circumstances it seems clear that the only positive action which the Canadian Government can itself take to create a more normal state of affairs within the United Nations and so to set the scene for a resumption of negotiations with the Soviet Union, is to announce its recognition of the People's Government in the hopes that such action would be followed by other governments and would result before many weeks in a change of Chinese representation within the United Nations.' Supportive of Reid's arguments was the U.S. State Department's perception that the Soviet Union's walkout would not last if more countries recognized China.[11]

While waiting first for Pearson and then cabinet to turn their attention to the subject, Reid suggested raising with the British, Americans, and French a compromise proposal whereby both the Nationalists and the Communists would be provisionally seated with a complicated formula for registering one vote. Divisional response to this 'ingenious' proposal was sceptical. The Legal and U.N. Divisions argued that it would frustrate the Security Council and would not be accepted by Taipei. The American and Far Eastern Division pointed out that Peking would not likely accept it either and that it would most certainly lead to propaganda diatribes that would result in little if any U.N. business being transacted. To complete the picture, the European Division argued that the Soviets could not accept the proposal and consequently it would not lead to their participation in the United Nations.[12]

All the while the situation was becoming more precarious. Chou En-lai was again seeking 'an early reply to the question as to when the sole legitimate delegation appointed by the Central People's Government ... can participate in the work of the United Nations,' in particular the Trusteeship Council which was scheduled to meet on 1 June, and why the Nationalists had not been expelled from the council as they had been from the Universal Postal Union.[13] On the same day the Hungarian and Czechoslovakian delegations walked out of UNESCO in protest over the defeat of a motion to expel the Nationalists. The U.N. secretary general returned from a mission to Moscow, where he learned that the Soviet Union had miscalculated by thinking that it would be a short walkout because several governments were on the point of recognizing China; nevertheless, there was little comfort to be had from the news that they intended to remain out until the Chinese representation question was settled. To make this point with as much fanfare as possible, the Soviet delegate to the Trusteeship Council announced that the Soviet Union would not accept as legal any decision taken while the Nationalist delegate was present, and promptly walked out of that body as well.

DEA was wedded to the idea of breaking the log-jam through recognition, but this was becoming a more distant prospect. At its meeting on 4 May 1950 cabinet could not come to a decision. By 14 June Pearson was able to report to cabinet that the Communists had indicated thay they would now welcome a Canadian representative to Peking. If France, Egypt, and Ecuador followed through with their plans to recognize, then matters would be brought to a head in the Security Council.[14] Cabinet discussed the issue but again deferred making a decision. A week later Pearson's even firmer proposal for immediate recognition was rejected, although Ronning was instructed to commence preliminary discussions related to procedural matters.[15] For Gardiner, and other cabinet ministers, the time for an easy acceptance of the recognition of the PRC had passed. There was no doubt that a move toward recognition would not be unanimously accepted in Parliament.[16]

While strident opposition from the Conservatives justified treading warily, it was international events that were responsible for halting any China initiative. On 25 June North Korean forces streamed across the border into the Republic of Korea with accompanying suspicions that Peking was behind the invaders. In these circumstances, DEA acknowledged, Canadian public opinion would not support negotiations with Peking. Just before the Korean War, the British government indicated that it would henceforth vote in U.N. agencies in favour of changing the China seat, and now Pearson told the Canadian high commissioner in London that 'given the present state of United States public opinion on this topic, it would plainly be quite unrealistic to attempt at this stage to bring pressure on the United States to bring in Communist China.'[17] Affirmation of this view was provided the next day when the State Department indicated that it would use every means short of the veto to prevent consideration of the China question in the U.N. so long as the fighting continued in Korea.[18] In New York Reid learned that the reason for this position was that the United States needed the Nationalists' voting support in the Security Council. Instead of sidelining consideration of the Chinese question, however, the Korean War brought the Soviet Union back into the United Nations, where it immediately raised Chinese representation as the first item on the agenda. While publicly admitting that there was much to be said for a Chinese voice in the U.N. at this time, Pearson also warned that 'the free people of the world are not to be browbeaten into a decision on this point by the tyrannical exercise of this kind of pressure.'[19]

Canada was finding it increasingly difficult to know what to do in view of divergent British and American policies. At meetings of the International Monetary Fund and the International Bank for Reconstruction and Development, the United States stressed that it expected Canada to vote with it against any challenge to the Nationalists, while the British had decided to vote for representation of the Communists unless the resolution was connected to Korea. Before leaving for New York, Pearson approved a recommendation to cabinet requesting that Canadian delegates be allowed to abstain rather than to vote against the Nationalists.[20] In cabinet, Prime Minister St Laurent argued that it would be illogical to keep the Communists out of the United Nations because it tended to drive them into the arms of the Soviets. Pearson's memorandum to cabinet also argued that

Peking ought to be heard before appropriate U.N. bodies in matters pertaining to peace in the Far East. Although strong arguments were heard from the minister of finance, D.C. Abbott, that Canada ought either to vote for the seating of the Communists or to abstain on the expulsion of the Nationalists, no decision was ultimately taken pending what might transpire when the General Assembly began. What was now certain, with the U.S. Seventh Fleet moving into the Straits of Taiwan, was that the Nationalist-Communist conflict would not simply disappear, as had once been expected.

When Commonwealth delegations met at the outset of the Fifth General Assembly in September it was obvious that major divisions existed. The Indian delegate proposed a resolution for seating the PRC. Pakistan supported it and the British were wavering pending another solution. The Australian and New Zealand delegations favoured putting off a decision, while the South Africans would oppose it. Pearson said that he would either abstain or support the Indian resolution depending on which way the debate developed. He also indicated that he was undecided on whether to vote in favour of seating the Communists, although in his report to Ottawa on the meeting he made no mention of this possibility.[21] British Foreign Minister Ernest Bevin, very conscious of what a division on this issue would do to the Commonwealth, expressed the hope that the Commonwealth might find some formula whereby the door would not be slammed shut on Peking at the opening of the Assembly. Taking his lead from Bevin, Pearson then proposed that a U.N. study of the Chinese question be undertaken while continuing to seat the Nationalists. Given the fact that the Indian resolution was bound to be defeated, Commonwealth and indeed all Western delegates could then unite around a resolution which would have the effect of demonstrating that they were prepared to consider the question on its merits.

The members of the Commonwealth were pleased with the Canadian initiative to create a seven-nation study committee that would report back before the end of the session, but the United States was not; it preferred that Pearson drop the subject but in the end suggested a minor amendment. As predicted, the Indian resolution was defeated 33 to 18 with 18 abstentions, including Canada's. Two Soviet resolutions for removing the Nationalists and seating the Communists were also defeated. Since Pearson had at this point already voted in favour of his own resolution, he voted against both Soviet ones. The British and American delegations divided on the Indian resolution but came together on the Canadian one, which passed with 42 for, 9 against, and 6 abstentions. Pearson was pleased with the line-up of supporters and told Ottawa that it established 'a procedure in regard to Chinese representation which does more than merely shelve the question indefinitely, as the United States delegation seemed to wish.'²² In spite of American views on the utility of the special committee, Pearson hoped that it would have more than a propaganda effect. That was not to be. The committee was so divided at its first meeting that it never met again except to decide to inform the Assembly that it had nothing to report.

Even more frustrating was the failure of informal talks to persuade friends in Washington that it was better to have the Communists in the United Nations, where they would be accountable, than to try to deal with them through ineffective ad hoc channels. The State Department was unmoved. Its officer responsible for Canadian affairs, Jack Hickerson, told the Canadian ambassador that the United States would work 'vigorously' to prevent the rallying of a majority in favour of Communist representation. Moreover, 'if they came into the United Nations in the near future, the United States would go out.'²³ From this it was quite clear that a scheme for a trade-off for admission of Italy and the PRC, being hatched by the Italians and Under-Secretary Heeney, had no chance of success. The entry of PRC forces into direct conflict with U.N. forces in Korea solidified hostile American opinion. By January 1951, when the United States Senate adopted a resolution against the admission of Peking into the United Nations, the handwriting was on the wall. There was no point in further trying to discuss the China question under these circumstances.

Events in Korea and discussions in Washington were so discouraging that Ottawa found it difficult to know what strategy to adopt. Under pressure from the United States, Canada had reluctantly voted to condemn China as an aggressor in Korea, although Pearson believed that such a move was premature and unwise because negotiations with Peking had not been exhausted. The next day he told the House of Commons that, 'They should not think that they can bludgeon or blackmail their way into recognition or into the United Nations.'²⁴ Canada tended to follow the U.S. line in voting to postpone debate on the China question without giving expression to its views. It also tried to maintain the position that the U.N. functional commissions were not competent to decide their own membership. Where the Canadians differed from the Americans was in the time limitation placed on postponement. The United States sought to defer the matter indefinitely; Canada wanted it left open for resolution as soon as there was change in Korea. In its instructions to an ECOSOC delegation, Ottawa reasoned that Peking could be represented as early as the summer and did not want to be constrained by having to wait for a decision from the General Assembly when it met in September.²⁵

In the specialized agencies, such as the World Meteorological Organization, DEA favoured seating the Communists as the de facto representatives who were in control of the territory affected by the organization, but Pearson changed this to abstention.[26] The difficulty in taking this position was that Ottawa did not always know in advance the precise terms under which the issue would be raised in the various U.N. bodies. Canadian delegations, which usually comprised technical experts from various departments, were thus advised to seek additional instructions from DEA, where inconsistencies and rationalizations were constantly being worked out. It was finally decided that consistency demanded that Canada not regard subsidiary organs of the specialized agencies as competent to admit the Communists if the Nationalists occupied the China seat in the parent agency. Changes in representation in these agencies would have to take place in a plenipotentiary conference or by a referendum.[27] In most instances Canada preferred that decisions be postponed and this gave rise to the perception that when the Korean War ended, it would support Peking's entry into the United Nations.

As events leading up to the armistice in Korea in 1953 unfolded, both President Eisenhower and Secretary of State Dulles, backed by Congressional resolutions and a decisive public opinion, made it clear that they did not want the Communists in the United Nations and would use their embassies to lobby against such a move. The British were torn between supporting the United States on a further moratorium and grappling with the issue. In Canada, spokesmen for the Conservative and Social Credit parties expressed their opposition to Communist representation. A public opinion poll in mid-February revealed that only half of the respondents knew that the Nationalists represented China in the U.N. and only half of those would disapprove of seating the Communists, while 37 per cent of the remainder would approve and 12 per cent had no opinion. Those writing letters to the government were overwhelmingly opposed to admission but had strong regional attachments which suggested organized campaigns.[28]

In these circumstances, Canada favoured the moratorium as the least divisive option but wanted to keep the issue under review. As the Far Eastern Division pointed out to the minister, Peking satisfied all the legal requirements for de jure recognition and there could be no real lessening of tension in the Far East without it. Furthermore, 'membership of Communist China in the United Nations would provide an opportunity for some of the tensions which must exist in the Sino-Soviet alliance eventually to be brought into the open where they might be exploited to the benefit of Canada and its allies.' Against PRC representation were placed American opposition and the fact that Taipei would not pay its substantial debt if it lost its place in the organization. 'On balance,' the division concluded, 'in the event of an armistice, the arguments in favour of recognition are overwhelming – recognition being understood to entail our derecognition of the Nationalist government and our support of Communist China for membership in the United Nations.'[29] It hoped that Peking could be persuaded to accept an interim solution on continuing Nationalist representation. In speeches in Eugene, Oregon, and Vancouver in late May 1953 when the truce negotiations at Panmunjom were drawing closer to a final agreement, Pearson indicated that was the route Canada would consider if the Chinese withdrew from Korea and refrained from aggression elsewhere in Asia.[30]

Through the U.S. chargé d'affaires in Ottawa, Eisenhower made it known that he did not want the issue discussed at the United Nations because of the deep hostility it would arouse in the American public. First from other capitals, and then from a Dulles press conference, Ottawa learned that the United States would change its attitude only when Peking demonstrated that it was no longer a puppet of the Soviet Union and was prepared to fulfil the obligations of the U.N. Charter. The most that the Canadian delegation could hope for was to limit any postponement of the issue in the expectation that it could then be raised immediately after an armistice settlement.

But the government had no solution to the problem should it be raised. It publicly justified its status quo policy on the basis of the PRC's inability to earn the right to full U.N. membership.[31] On the off-chance that the substantive question would come to a vote at the Ninth United Nations General Assembly, the Canadian delegation was instructed to abstain as a means of winning the Communists' support for the release of Canadian POWs, encouraging moderate elements in Peking, and demonstrating to Washington that Canada was not a supporter of the extreme pro-Nationalist cause.[32] By 1954 the American public was becoming even more set in its opposition to Communist representation. The Committee of One Million was gaining an impressive group of prominent backers for sustaining the Nationalists, and this growing public pressure had forced Dulles into agreeing to use the veto if necessary to keep the Communists out.[33] This was not, of course, required at this point because the majority in favour of postponement was gradually increasing at each year's assembly, but it did indicate the hardening of United States opposition to Communist representation, which was further exacerbated by the termination of the Korean conference.

As expressions of United States intransigence became more pronounced during the summer of 1954, the under-secretary advised Pearson that a change in Chinese representation was for the time being academic and that there was no point in considering unilateral Canadian action, though

Washington needed to be told in private that it should expect a change in the Canadian position at the appropriate time.[34] By the early summer of 1955 there were signs that Peking and Washington were at least willing to talk in Geneva, if not the United Nations, about minor bilateral matters. DEA interpreted this to mean that the United States might move faster than expected and sought to take advantage of this slight change in atmosphere to soften the moratorium resolution. Officials were anxious to demonstrate that the West was not intransigent on the China question and was willing to consider the position of the Asian countries that favoured Communist representation. Accordingly, the Far Eastern Division urged taking advantage of the improved conditions to state firmly that the Nationalist representatives spoke only for Taipei in the United Nations and that a report should be made by a U.N. committee with a view to coalescing support and demonstrating the West's desire to move beyond the moratorium.[35] No sooner had this course of action been proposed than the department learned that the State Department had rejected a British suggestion for revising the moratorium formula because it was convinced that it could still marshal a majority behind the old one.

Pearson was perplexed. India's Prime Minister Nehru, however, had been urging St Laurent to abandon the moratorium approach, yet there now seemed little chance of accomplishing anything more than upsetting the Americans by doing so. To raise the China question in Washington would only serve to rouse even further the right-wing opposition to Peking. Nor was he certain, in view of past responses, whether Canadian opinion would support a change of policy. To test the waters he decided to launch a trial balloon in a speech to the Women's Canadian Club in Vancouver on 25 August where he said that it was time to take a new look at recognition and to acknowledge that the de facto government of China had to be present for discussion of Far Eastern problems in the United Nations as a full participant.[36] DEA had decided that if the reaction to Pearson's speech was unfavourable, it would have to forgo its planned moves forward.

The initial response was surprising. Few people in Canada took any notice of it and the under-secretary described Washington's reaction as 'pretty temperate.' When the Belgian foreign minister subsequently endorsed Pearson's statement, however, they received a U.S. *aide-mémoire* stating that any new look 'would be embarrassing to the United States and damaging to the free world.'[37] Pearson concluded that to defy the United States might have the unfortunate effect of freezing its Far Eastern policies. Moreover, to introduce the China question at that time might jeopardize the initiative being taken by Canada to seat new members at that year's

U.N. General Assembly. Since a substantial majority of members would still support the moratorium, the Canadian delegation was instructed to do likewise. When the Canadian high commissioner to India suggested moving forward in another forum, the under-secretary replied: 'I do not think we can contemplate any solution which does not command the acquiescence, if not the support, of the United States or which does not flow from a decision of the General Assembly. The hard fact with which we are still faced is that public sentiment on this subject in the United States is still firmly opposed to Communist Chinese representation.'[38]

American opposition was confirmed when St Laurent and Pearson met Eisenhower at White Sulphur Springs in March 1956. The prime minister promised not to make any difficulty over this issue for the United States, at least until after the presidential elections. In the wake of a unanimous U.S. Senate resolution opposing Communist representation there appeared to be no other alternative. The encounter confirmed that representation in the United Nations would have to precede bilateral recognition if Canada was to avoid problems with its neighbour.

While Canada would continue its support of the U.S. position in the United Nations, DEA was determined to demonstrate its reluctance to do so by offering no advance commitment to further postponements. The Canadian permanent mission in New York thought that nothing would be achieved by this tactic. Given the coolness with which it had been treated by the Americans since the initiative taken by Canada over the admission of new members at the previous Assembly, the mission persuaded Ottawa to reserve its delaying tactic for something on which there was more likely to be a flexible U.S. response. Washington was to be told, however, that it should not automatically count on Canadian support next year.

In the midst of this quandary, DEA was embarrassed by a State Department suggestion that Canada should take the lead in persuading India not to press Chinese representation in UNESCO. Canada declined to be the 'chore-boy' for the United States and run the risk of losing credit with the Indians, but this incident did show how imperfectly the State Department understood the Canadian position. Perhaps this can in part be explained by External Affairs policy of presenting its contrary views to the State Department without trying to question Washington's perceptions. Nevertheless, as Pearson explained to the Canadian ambassador in Washington, 'it would not be appropriate for us to attempt to pull the chestnuts out of the fire for them.'[39] While Canada and Britain could agree at the Bermuda summit that the issue could not be avoided much longer, it seemed convenient for both nations to let it lie for the moment.

Round Two: 1957–1963

The change to a Conservative government in Canada brought about a new trading relationship with the Chinese but no change in policy regarding representation apart from perhaps a stronger concern with protecting the position of Taipei. In even more forceful terms than he had told St Laurent, Eisenhower informed Prime Minister Diefenbaker in July 1958 that the United States was opposed to PRC admission to the United Nations. According to one official, Diefenbaker told him that the president had threatened that regardless of motives, if Canada made a move toward admission, the U.S. would withdraw from the U.N. and 'kick' its headquarters out of the United States.[40] Although India had since 1956 taken over from the Soviet Union as the chief proponent of Communist representation, Canada still remained silent in the fear that any overt action or statement would retard the accceptance of more enlightened views beginning to percolate outside the White House. But if there was a sign of a substantial shift in votes at the 1958 U.N. General Assembly, the Canadian delegation was instructed to abstain on the Indian resolution against the moratorium as a means of promoting discussion. When the debate began, however, the minister, Sidney Smith, intervened to say that the discussion was inappropriate at a time of increased tension in the Formosa Strait and around the offshore islands.[41] Ironically, Canada had never been enthusiastic about the moratorium, yet appeared on this occasion as one of a handful of speakers supporting it.

After the 1960 U.N. General Assembly there were more compelling reasons for seeking a change in Canadian policy. Even some officials in the State Department were beginning to acknowledge that it made no sense to exclude the Communists from the recently formed Ten Member Committee on Disarmament. In spite of worsening Sino-Indian border relations, India still supported Communist entry into the United Nations, thereby destroying the old argument that Peking's aggressive behaviour warranted its exclusion. Moreover, the U.N. General Assembly's moratorium on discussion was losing ground. Not one of the new African states had been persuaded to support it. Those in favour had fallen from 44 to 42 and those against had increased from 29 to 34 with abstentions rising from 9 to 29. The results in the paragraph-by-paragraph vote were even closer, with the result that if five abstainers switched to a negative vote at the next Assembly, a debate would ensue on the substantive question of representation. While several officials thought that some states might seize this opportunity to switch to Peking, the under-secretary thought it more likely that there would be pressure by the Nationalists to declare Chinese representation an important question – which would require a two-thirds rather than a simple majority to pass. Consequently, the department was instructed by the minister, Howard Green, to make as a matter of 'high priority' the first major departmental study of problems involved in the representation of China in the United Nations.[42]

At the heart of this internal review was a lengthy study by the Legal Division which argued that there was no categorical answer as to whether Chinese representation was an 'important question' as defined by the U.N. Charter. It was open for a simple majority in the Assembly to make that decision. Nor was it certain that it was subject to a veto in the Security Council as there were ways of turning it into a procedural matter. What was clear was that the Assembly could not bind the Security Council on its members' credentials. The Legal Division also ruled that there was no prospect of pursuing the Far Eastern Division's idea for declaring both the PRC and the government in Taiwan successor governments to the former unitary Republic of China.[43] According to the head of the division, the issues involved, especially concerning procedural matters, were considerably more complicated than most officers realized.[44]

DEA learned it was on the right track when a sounding of various delegations convinced the State Department that the moratorium resolution was no longer a practical means of avoiding the issue. This was welcome news as it relieved Canada from having to choose between supporting an ally and voting the way it wanted. If Taipei was not abandoned and the West remained determined to resist Communist Chinese expansionism by all means at its disposal, Under-Secretary Norman Robertson informed Green, 'the experiment of giving Communist China an opportunity to measure up to United Nations norms of conduct might prove to be worth any risks it would entail for the West.'[45] The minister was advised to prepare the public for a change in policy. He was also told by the U.S. assistant secretary of state for U.N. affairs that Washington was now considering a two-Chinas approach which it was understood the Communists would not accept, but which would at least transfer the onus from the Western nations to the Communists themselves for remaining out of the United Nations. Ottawa was pleased to learn that the United States was finally considering a presence for the Communists in the U.N.

A Gallup poll taken in January 1961 indicated that for the first time in many years a majority of Canadians were now in favour of seating the Communists in the United Nations, but Green ordered this downplayed at a NATO meeting for fear that it would be seen as a reflection of government policy which had, in fact, not yet been decided. After formulating several possible alternatives to U.S. policy, all of which had their own inherent difficulties, officials were informed in June 1961 that 'the Minister does not want Canada to take any step to influence the United States position on Chinese representation at the United Nations.'⁴⁶

This position changed a few weeks later when the State Department invited DEA to share in the staff work of preparing a two-Chinas proposal. As part of this scheme the Japanese were unsuccessfully urging Canada and Australia to try to persuade Taipei to forgo its claim to represent mainland China. Ottawa soon learned, however, that President Kennedy had been forced to change direction. During a visit of the Japanese prime minister to Washington there had been a devastating leak about his flirting with a two-Chinas policy. This led to criticisms of the administration and Senate resolutions denouncing Communist representation. Under public pressure, the president had backed down and very soon afterwards brought the State Department back into line by announcing that he agreed with the ROC's vice-president that Peking should be kept out of the United Nations. Consequently the State Department informed Ottawa that it was going ahead with 'the important question' idea, and, to meet the president's concerns that this was too negative, this would be combined with a proposal for a study committee.

The committee idea had already surfaced in DEA as a possible fall-back position should the two-Chinas proposal fail to take hold. The possibility of making China an 'important question' had also been under review for some time. Indeed, there was little question that an issue that had received so much attention over the last twelve years in the U.N. General Assembly, and involved a permanent seat on the Security Council and the representation of a quarter of the world's population, ought to be considered as anything but important. Thus, the government decided to go along but rejected a U.S. suggestion that it co-sponsor the inscription of the important question on the agenda as this would curtail its freedom to manoeuvre.

More difficult to handle was U.S. insistence that Canada co-sponsor the study committee resolution. The permanent mission had at the outset been invited by the U.S. ambassador to join with five other states in a discussion leading to co-sponsorship. At this meeting they were assured that this was not a gimmick designed to postpone the issue further, but a sincere effort to develop recommendations that would also have the effect of conditioning the American public to accept a solution of the Chinese representation question. In a specially arranged meeting with Green, the U.S. representative to the United Nations, Adlai Stevenson, argued that even though it was known that Taipei did not support the idea, a committee was the only means of ensuring that the Nationalists remain in the U.N. while the subject was under review. While Green could sympathize with the dilemma facing the United States, he rejected co-sponsorship. Opinion in Canada was divided on the issue and the government did not want to be seen sponsoring a U.S.-initiated resolution. Nevertheless, Canada would by its vote and in debate support the initiative as a means of ensuring that Taiwan was entitled to self-determination and representation, that nations which were prepared to support the important question on condition that it not be shelved would in fact do so, and as a means of allowing time for Congressional and public opinion in the United States to accept a change in Chinese representation without insisting on any diminution of American support for the United Nations. Cabinet supported Green's stand but would not permit Canada to serve on the committee. By the end of November it was becoming clear that none of the original invitees would sponsor the committee and, as some Canadian officials had anticipated, American officials gave up the idea with few regrets.

While the U.S. delegation seemed confident that there would be a slight majority in favour of making it an 'important question,' DEA was concerned that the loss of the study committee could result in some wavering. Prime Minister Diefenbaker was warned by the under-secretary that there could be dire consequences if the United States was defeated; its financial support was needed to sustain the United Nations, in particular the U.N. Emergency Fund and the Congo exercises which were of concern to Canada.[47] On 8 December the vice-chairman of the Canadian delegation, Senator Brooks, delivered a vigorous defence of the Nationalists' right to self-determination, the necessity for making the United Nations universal, and the need for regarding Chinese representation as an important question. He also reiterated Canada's willingness to support any generally acceptable means to achieve an early solution of the Chinese representation question.[48]

This was the first time since 1950 that there had been a formal debate on the substantive issue of Chinese representation. Votes on related resolutions and amendments all went as Canada wished. On the main vote the important question was carried by 61 to 34 with 7 abstentions. In reviewing the debate, Canadian officials strongly objected to the belligerent way the Soviet delegate spoke of using force to 'liquidate the clique of Chiang Kai-shek.'[49] Over time, the arguments in support of protecting the Nationalists had grown, as much from expressions in Washington as from the persistence of Taipei's ambassador in Ottawa, who had the ear of Diefenbaker more than of his predecessor. Indeed, one reason why Green had refused to take an initiative on the study committee was out of deference to the Nationalists.[50]

Another result of the U.N. General Assembly's discussion in 1961 was greater public awareness of the China question. DEA now received more expressions in favour of Communist representation but its attention was increasingly riveted on disarmament questions which, at least in the initial stages, the minister did not feel required the presence of Peking.

Since the only realistic solution seemed to involve some variation of a two-Chinas formula, and neither side was willing to countenance that prospect, the issue was put on hold. At the United Nations, support for the important question held firm, and successive Canadian delegations were instructed not to take an active role in any debate on the issue when there were more important subjects requiring the attention of the delegates.

Round Three: The First Martin Initiative, 1963–1964

With the return of the Liberals to government in 1963 came a renewed desire to see a breakthrough on the Chinese representation question. This was somewhat surprising since the new secretary of state for external affairs, Paul Martin, had opposed Pearson's attempts at recognition of the PRC and representation in the 1950s. Now he was personally determined to bring about universality in the United Nations by finding a way out of the impasse. Having been instrumental in breaking the log-jam over the admission of new members in 1955, he regarded Peking's exclusion as unfinished business. Universality was, however, much easier to espouse than recognition, which could cost Canada something in its relations with the United States. In a much-publicized speech in August 1963, Martin questioned whether further isolation and containment of Peking would be prudent in light of the growing divergence in the communist world. While acknowledging that Canada's relations with the communist world should not be at 'wide variance' with those of its allies, it was, nevertheless, necessary to 'proceed forward with a realistic and yet progressive attitude.'[51]

But Martin could not persuade Prime Minister Pearson to allow him to bring the subject before cabinet. Pearson was concerned that it would raise unwarranted expectations, given past United States attitudes. In any event he was not given to having foreign policy debated in cabinet. He was, however, willing to let Martin sound out current views in Washington. There Martin learned to his chagrin that no initiatives could be expected this year from the Americans because of the war in Vietnam. Shortly thereafter he told the French ambassador that, consequently, none could be expected from Canada in the immediate future.

The China question suddenly took on a new prominence in January 1964 when the French announced that they were about to recognize the Communists. What was of greatest concern to Pearson and Martin was the effect such a move could have on NATO unity and the United Nations. Within

NATO councils, Canada argued unsuccessfully, against U.S. opposition, that the French action was not all that bad, as it provided a Western contact that ought to be exploited in working out a means of ending Peking's isolation. Yet Pearson made it known through an interview in *Le Monde* that Canada was not anticipating any fundamental change in its policy. Nevertheless, the U.S. secretary of state was dispatched to Ottawa to plead against any support for France at the United Nations as it could have a ripple effect among French-speaking African nations and would cause problems in dealing with the Viet Cong and U.N. deficits. What was not answered was whether a United States defeat would result in a walkout.

While DEA believed that the United States could hold its position at the 1964 U.N. General Assembly, this would be the last time and steps needed to be taken toward the development of a new policy. Within diplomatic circles Martin made it known that he was considering advancing some form of a two-Chinas solution. On hearing this, Secretary of State Rusk decided to call on Martin while in neighbouring Detroit. It was bound to be a difficult meeting. A media survey by Canadian posts in the United States confirmed that the public and administration were as one against any move forward. Undeterred and bolstered by Canadian polls that showed a slight majority in favour of Peking's admission, Martin was determined to convince Rusk that positive action was warranted. Rusk discounted Martin's concern with Canadian public opinion in the light of the all-pervasive spectre of a communist advance in Indochina. There could be no move in the United Nations until the United States brought that war to a successful conclusion, something Rusk thought would happen by the end of the year. As events unfolded in Indochina, U.S. policy would be kept under review and Rusk agreed to share the results of the review on condition that there be no rug pulling at the U.N. General Assembly. Both men agreed to keep the other informed of any move being contemplated.[52]

Precisely what move, if any, Canada should take at the Nineteenth U.N. General Assembly was the subject of considerable discussion in the department. With practically no support for and much opposition to a two-Chinas proposal forecast, the Far Eastern Division with the support of the U.N. Division had come up with the idea of a declaratory resolution which would register Canada's concern over the need to protect the rights of Taipei while signalling its desire to see a move forward. This two-Chinas solution in the U.N. General Assembly would be combined with a substitution of the Communists for the Nationalists in the Security Council. To get around the thorny issue of competing territorial claims, the resolution would adopt no position but refer the issue to the president of the U.N. General Assembly for investigation. It was, as Under-Secretary Marcel Cadieux admitted, a compromise which he supported because he wanted Canada to be ahead of any possible U.S. move, though he worried about its effect on American involvement in Indochina. The Economic Division and Deputy Under-Secretary Ed Ritchie were sceptical. To them it was a good idea but the wrong time for trying it out. They argued that such a resolution would not really help Taipei or later assist in obtaining better terms for recognition from Peking. Nor were there any national objectives to be achieved by following this route. On the international side it could have the effect of isolating the United States, which would not help the situation in Indochina or benefit Sino-American relations. The decisive argument for them was the detrimental impact it could have on U.S.-Canadian economic relations. Canada needed congressional and presidential goodwill to sustain oil and lumber exports and to secure all that it wanted in an auto pact. Any loss of trade with the United States could not be offset by an increase in trade with a foreign-exchange-poor PRC. Finally, to declare a position in advance would more likely lessen Canada's bargaining position on all fronts than earn it any credit. Ritchie argued that Canada's objective should be to help the United States move rather than irritate it by unilateral action. Unless there was an unexpected change in voting patterns at the United Nations, Canada could afford to wait it out while encouraging the minister to sound out Rusk on a Canadian initiative. If Ritchie had misjudged possible U.S. reactions, then Cadieux's move forward could be made.[53]

When Martin received this proposed plan of action he doubted Ritchie's arguments about the economic consequences outweighing the political gains. He was certain that, once a step had been taken toward Communist representation, other nations would climb on the bandwagon and by the next Assembly Peking could no longer be excluded. A change at the United Nations would then make it easier for Canada to withstand U.S. pressure and obtain better conditions when it came to recognition and the exchange of diplomats. For these reasons, Martin approved the declaratory resolution which would put Canada on the right side should the anticipated shift in votes begin. Martin was also agreeable to his officials accepting an Italian proposal for tripartite consultations with the Belgians on alternatives and tactics. Such discussions could provide the means for advancing a declaratory resolution with some chance of support at the U.N. General Assembly.

The final decision on what to do had been greatly influenced by news that the Communists had detonated a nuclear device. For the United States and its Pacific allies this action confirmed the desire to keep the Communists out. Peking would have to conform to United Nations standards before it could be accepted into membership. The response in DEA was the opposite, the view being that it was now all the more important that the PRC be made internationally accountable through membership in the United Nations.

Before Canada could advance along its chosen path, Martin's agreement to consult Washington had to be honoured. Martin thus instructed the ambassador in Washington to warn Rusk that because Canada was anticipating a slippage in votes on the Albanian resolution for a direct switch in Chinese representation and the 'important question,' the United States could be in for an embarrassing diplomatic defeat. While the United States could be assured of continuing Canadian support on the important question, its position would change if a clear majority came to vote against it. In any case, Canada intended to seek support for a two-Chinas declaratory resolution. Rusk made it known that he was not pleased, primarily because of Vietnam. He wanted no encouragement to be given to Peking whose recent activities did not speak well of its commitment to peace. He expressed dismay at the fact that there were countries so anxious to move toward recognition that they were soft-pedalling their complaints against the Communists.[54]

With the ambassador's report in hand, Martin called on the State Department to explain that he wanted to move ahead and now had the support of cabinet members and significant public groups in Canada who were demanding a change in policy. If the U.S. would give some indication of a desire to move on the issue then it could avoid defeat. The State Department was just as convinced from its soundings, however, that the status quo could be held for at least the current General Assembly and that there was no urgency requiring a move forward at this time.

From Washington, Martin went on to the United Nations where he met with Rusk, who confirmed DEA's assessment. Not only would Rusk refuse to see the problem from Martin's perspective, he grew impatient at Martin's refusal to view the China questions through the perspective of Vietnam where, he reminded Martin, the United States rather than Canada was carrying the burden.[55] While there was clearly no acceptance for Canada's position, there were no threats of economic retaliation either. Probably none were needed as Rusk must have known by then that Martin was having trouble in getting co-sponsors for his proposed declaratory resolution.

After lengthy negotiations to find acceptable wording for the proposed declaratory resolution, the original co-sponsors withdrew their support. The Belgians were concerned about the possible loss of allied support for their activities in the Congo, while the Italians backed off in fear of American retaliation. In addition, neither the Communists nor the Nationalists had encouraged Canada to believe that its initiative would be welcomed.

In the end, the Chinese question did not get beyond the general debate at the Nineteenth U.N. General Assembly, as there was an agreement to raise no issue which would force a vote until the question of payment for past peacekeeping operations had been settled. As the State Department had predicted all along, there would be no appreciable slippage in votes in that year's U.N. General Assembly, and even Canada would vote as usual.

Round Four: The Second Martin Initiative, 1965–1966

Following the failure to move ahead in 1964 there was somewhat less desire to try other alternatives the next year. The government had called an election to try to win a majority of seats in the House of Commons. Although the Chinese question was not on the agenda, the government was leery of trying too much in New York. It was not interested in an Italian effort to resurrect a study committee proposal and was happy that it had not been asked to join with the United States and its Pacific friends in promoting what Canada had now come to regard as a stalling tactic. While estimates varied on the support the American position was likely to command at the Twentieth U.N. General Assembly, there was considerable uncertainty as a result of Indonesia's withdrawal from the United Nations and problems in Africa. Canadian diplomats around the world as well as in New York kept a close watch on possible movements, carefully passing on to Washington any rumours of changes in the hope that they would encourage the Americans to re-examine their position.

A further attempt to find co-sponsors for the declaratory resolution was no more successful than the earlier one. DEA therefore recommended, and cabinet approved, asking the president of the General Assembly to explore with Peking possible terms of entry. The idea was shelved when on 29 September 1965 the PRC's foreign minister, Chen Yi, made what Ottawa regarded as impossible demands for representation in the United Nations. External Affairs took these denunciations of the United Nations' role in Korea, its charter, and 'puppet' members more seriously than most foreign offices. In Parliament, Martin blamed the Communists for the stalemate. 'In the view of the Canadian Government,' Martin said, 'it is not for the United Nations to accommodate itself to the views of a single nation, however powerful or populous. It is for Communist China to make that accommodation. Much to the regret of the Canadian Government there is no present evidence that she is ready to do so.'[56] Martin then went on to express his displeasure at Peking for forcing the postponement of an Afro-Asian conference because it could not dominate it and pushing its attitude on Indonesia and Vietnam, which bespoke the doctrine of armed revolution. Although Canada still sought universality, it felt compelled to vote against the Albanian resolution.

Early in 1966 Martin was encouraged by U.S. advocacy of a NATO study as long as it was not to be used as a delaying tactic. Rusk then invited Martin to Washington, where they discussed ways of bringing Peking in without hurting the United Nations. Martin told Rusk that because the U.S. line could not be held any longer, Canada was now prepared to support any progressive and equitable solution which would make the Communists more accountable for their actions, even if it did not meet all of Taipei's objections. Martin left this meeting convinced that the United States would now be moving ahead, though in what direction and how far remained in doubt.[57]

Subsequent rumours of differences in opinion in the State Department encouraged DEA to believe that by playing its cards right, it might lend some assistance to the progressives. Pearson was to pave the way with an address at Columbia University and the U.S. ambassador to the United Nations was invited to Ottawa in order to convey Canadian views to his friend the president before the prime minister made direct representations. Martin even wanted his emissary to Hanoi, Chester Ronning, to go via Peking where he could sound out the Communists on their real attitude toward the United Nations. Over the next several months numerous proposals were discussed before it became evident that worsening circumstances in Vietnam and strong support from Pacific allies against any Canadian move were making Rusk more determined than ever to hold firm. Furthermore, there was nothing encouraging from Peking to share with the Americans because Ronning had failed to obtain an audience with the Communist leaders.

Meanwhile, Martin was using every opportunity to sound out other foreign ministers and DEA was trying to work out a position in a series of studies on the possible effect on the United Nations of various courses of action. Martin was convinced that Canada should at the very least abstain on the Albanian resolution as a means of demonstrating the need to move forward. While Pearson did not object to this, he was unwilling to abandon Taipei to its own fate as long as it seemed to be calling so much of the tune in Washington. 'Surely peace with Washington is more important than praise in Peking,' was Pearson's rejoinder. 'Our policy should not depart too radically from the position established over the years by the U.S. and its allies,' he concluded.[58] He would, in the end, reserve judgment on Martin's proposal until its impact on Canada-U.S. relations could be assessed at the time of the vote. Pearson's preference was for an Albanian-type resolution without reference to Taipei, thereby reducing the strain on Washington.

At the same time as it was looking for allies to help to carry a Canadian initiative against anticipated U.S. objections, DEA also began assessing domestic support for such a move. Journalists and academics had freely been using their various platforms to criticize the government's status quo. Could the critics suggest a way out? At a much publicized Banff Conference on World Affairs in August, Martin pointed out 'that those who urge a radically different position on us sometimes neglect the thornier aspects of the problem.'[59] While he was frustrated by the impasse over the two-Chinas solution, there were pitfalls in following the critics' suggested courses of action. In the end, he had little to take away from the conference beyond a consensus report endorsing immediate recognition of Peking to be followed by unspecified efforts to have it seated at the United Nations.

In October 1966 a Liberal party conference approved a resolution calling for the immediate recognition of Peking and its admission to the United Nations. There were other pressures as well to recognize and leave the U.N. conundrum to be sorted out later. Still, there were practical difficulties in recognizing Peking before representation in the United Nations paved the way, and Martin decided on one last multilateral approach before the bilateral avenue was explored. If for no other reason than to satisfy the public demand, there would have to be some demonstrable change in policy. 'The cumulative effect of the Government's statements,' Far Eastern Division told Cadieux in reviewing the alternatives, has been 'such as to convince that section of the Canadian public which thinks about these matters that the Canadian position is about to move in a direction designed to try to bring about the seating of Peking representatives in the United Nations.'[60]

After exploring several alternatives to meet the wishes of the prime minister and minister, officials decided to recommend a proposal calling for an interim two-Chinas solution without prejudice to the eventual settlement of the disputed territorial claims of both parties. Since neither party would accept the interim solution as permanent, the president of the Assembly would investigate with both of them the means of finding a permanent solution. By putting forward such a resolution Canada hoped to force Washington to abandon the status quo. As a lever to get support for this proposal and to persuade the United States to move ahead before it was defeated at the United Nations, Canada would threaten abstention on the Albanian resolution. Such a step would appeal to Martin because his domestic critics could not accuse him of merely following the United States, and it would also meet Pearson's concerns since the United States was bound to protect the rights of the Taiwanese in anything it had to offer as an alternative. The government approved and the department set about preparing the way for its introduction.

Notice of Canada's intention was, unfortunately, delivered to the State Department on the very day that Peking tested an atomic missile. The event served to highlight the differences between Ottawa and Washington. Ambassador Ed Ritchie argued that the test demonstrated the need for bringing the Communists into the United Nations, while the State Department argued that it confirmed their determination to kept the trouble-maker out. Canada did not ask for U.S. support, only its quiet acquiescence in return for no Canadian lobbying against the U.S. position. The State Department was also told that if this minimum move forward was not accepted, there were those in the cabinet who would force the issue of abstention.[61]

Rusk had not been present to receive Ritchie, but his reply was not long in coming. A move forward at this time would encourage the hardliners in Peking. Moreover, the Canadian proposal would render the Security Council ineffective for the settling of disputes if the bellicose Communists were admitted. The interim solution would tend to become permanent in the absence of any agreement between the contending parties. In no uncertain terms, Rusk made it clear that the United States would use every ounce of its influence to ensure defeat by the widest possible margin and this open split with its old friend would have serious repercussions on bilateral relations. Instead, he suggested that Canada sponsor a study committee which the United States would agree to support. Canada agreed to participate in discussions to determine if Rusk was serious, but it was not prepared to give up on its own resolution.

Could it use its threatened abstention and introduction of an interim solution to get the United States to move any further? That depended on the support other nations would give to the proposal. After completing soundings, only four nations indicated their support and another was willing to consider it with amendments. No amount of fiddling could produce a more acceptable resolution as the non-communist members lined up behind the Italian study committee resolution.

Meanwhile, four prominent Liberal members of Parliament, including the prime minister's parliamentary secretary, Pierre Trudeau, were urging Martin that if Western nations would not accept the Canadian proposal with reasonable modifications, then he ought to reject the study committee proposal as a delaying tactic and announce Canada's intention to abstain on the Albanian resolution in the hopes of starting a trend. Rejection of the invitation to co-sponsor the study committee resolution was easy enough because it did not meet the minimum requirements laid down by the government: a committee based on instructions to chart a viable solution to the impasse. More difficult was the decision on how to vote now that the Canadian proposal was dead.

Canada's delegation at the United Nations decided to recommend to Martin that there be no change in the voting that year because they believed that they had already created enough enemies by their forceful advocacy of the resolution. For this and other reasons, Cadieux was also advocating the status quo as the path of least resistance. En route to the General Assembly, Trudeau learned of the intention of the officials and strenuously pressed Martin to abstain on the Albanian resolution. Martin pondered both sides. It was a difficult decision to make, with his officials and church hierarchy on one side and some political colleagues and his conscience on the other. An early morning call to Ottawa promised cabinet support for abstention but, according to Martin, no one in New York knew which way he would vote until he actually pushed the button for abstention.[62]

What caught Ottawa by surprise was the mild reaction it provoked in Washington. In fact, one U.S. official at the General Assembly privately congratulated Martin. While the State Department generally resented having little advance warning of Canada's intention, it seemed unconcerned about the actual vote. Its main concern was that its allies might think that Washington had put Ottawa up to such a manoeuvre in order to obtain support for the study committee proposal. This was plainly not the case and an independent-minded minister was quick to disabuse the allies of any such plot. After all the speculation about possible U.S. reaction and economic retaliation, it was clear that the minister had a more accurate perception than did his officials. In his subsequent speech to the General Assembly on 23 November 1966 Martin made public the interim solution that Canadian diplomats had unsuccessfully been working toward.[63] The decision to make such efforts known to Canadians back home would silence those critics who accused the government of doing nothing.

Martin had decided, after seeing his proposal rejected as a non-starter, to put aside the multilateral approach in favour of bilateral recognition. The multilateral approach had always seemed to be the easiest approach to lessening U.S. opposition to a Canadian bilateral move as long as a majority of other countries were unwilling to make it more acceptable by also taking that route.

The decision having been taken, no action followed. Another hindrance had appeared. Neither Martin nor Pearson was prepared to move on either the multilateral or bilateral front as long as the Cultural Revolution was placing foreign diplomats in Peking in such precarious positions, and other nations refused to join hands in an initiative. When questioned about Canada's attitude prior to the 1967 U.N. General Assembly, Pearson replied: 'This does not seem to be a very good moment to repeat the initiative we took last autumn without success.'[64] Canada did, however, vote against a resolution attempting to make the Italian study committee an important question requiring a two-thirds majority vote. Despite Canadian support for the main resolution for a committee, it was once again struck down.

Round Five: 1968–1971, the Switch to Bilateralism

Given these well-known international difficulties, DEA was surprised during the spring of 1968 to hear Pierre Trudeau, soon to be Pearson's successor as prime minister, declare his intention to recognize the Communists. His objective of having the PRC 'occupy the seat of China in the United Nations, taking into account that there is a separate government in Taiwan,'[65] prompted a major interdepartmental study of the possible road to recognition. But there seemed little place to go at the United Nations. A subsequent parallel departmental study on Canada's policies at the U.N. concluded that the current stalemate on Chinese representation would continue. In the likelihood that Peking would continue to impose impossible conditions on entry, it was thought best to await the outcome of bilateral discussions on a diplomatic exchange before attempting any move on the U.N. front.[66] To avoid offending the Communists, now that serious thought was being given to bilateral negotiations with them on recognition, Canada ceased talking about a two-Chinas policy, which everyone in DEA now recognized as an impossibility that would only lead to severe complications in discussions with the Communists. Canada abstained when the study committee resolution was again put to the vote at the next U.N. General Assembly. It was not prepared to go further at this stage. In conversation with the secretary of state for external affairs, Mitchell Sharp, Rusk once again threatened that the United States would leave the U.N. if the Communists were admitted. Sharp listened but, like Martin, realized this was a bluff and was not deterred from pressing on with the Stockholm talks leading to bilateral recognition.

At the first Stockholm meeting the Communists placed three principles for recognition on the table. Canada was asked to recognize the PRC as the sole and lawful government of the Chinese people, to recognize Taiwan as part of Chinese territory, and to support its claim to the China seat in the United Nations and all its organs. Ottawa made it clear that it would be prepared to support the seating of the Communists at the U.N. once the bilateral negotiations had been successfully concluded. By this move, the U.N. question was effectively sidelined at Stockholm. At no time did Peking insist that Canada alter its vote at the United Nations as the price of recognition. Had it been pressed on this issue, however, the government was prepared, as a last resort, to recommend voting for the Albanian resolution while continuing to uphold it as an important question.

With a change in administration in Washington there was greater appreciation of Canada's position and the fact that Canadian policy at the U.N. General Assembly would have to be consistent with bilateral moves with the Communists. There was no longer any talk of the United States leaving the U.N. over Communist representation. All that was asked was that Canada not drop its traditional support for regarding the Chinese issue as an important question. Ottawa was willing to give assurances on the matter as long as it was not used as a procedural means of frustrating the will of a majority in the U.N. General Assembly. Meanwhile, Canadian diplomats took a back seat on this issue at the General Assembly. Being unwilling to give out any information on the Stockholm negotiations, they avoided raising the subject with their diplomatic colleagues.

After the successful completion of the Stockholm negotiations in 1970, the PRC insisted that continued Canadian support of the important question would be contrary to the new spirit of Sino-Canadian relations and would be regarded as part of the U.S. plot to deny or impede its representation. The response, which was taken quite mildly by the Communists, was that Canada would support the will of the majority in the General Assembly but would itself switch from abstaining on the Albanian resolution to supporting it. Washington took note of the change but made no comment. Its concern seemed to lie more with retaining a majority on the important question. Henceforth, Canada was prepared to follow a one-China policy and would, consequently, not support an effort by Ghana to detach Taipei's expulsion from the Albanian resolution.

As it turned out, the Canadian shift on the Albanian resolution coincided with it receiving majority support. It lost, of course, as an important question which Canada, along with a decreasing number countries, upheld. In explaining its vote, however, Canada made clear that any further shifts would spell the end to its support for the important question.[67]

Change was in the air. In the few months following Canada's recognition of Peking, ten other countries followed suit. And equally as important for the U.N. context, the Communists were assuming a more active and realistic role in international affairs. When it came time for the next General Assembly, Canada was not interested in supporting a U.S. effort to salvage a losing position by promoting a questionable compromise in the unworkable form of dual representation. By then, its position was well understood in Washington. Ottawa was not asked to support the U.S. position, only to refrain from lobbying against it. This Ottawa was prepared to do, though it would inform its allies of the position it would be taking and proceeded to announce well in advance that it would no longer support the important question position. From its survey of probable voting patterns, DEA was convinced that the United States was in for a defeat and Sharp did not hesitate to say so in public.

While there was no formal U.S. reaction to Canada's position, there were appeals to past friendship. With the possibility of defeat looming in Vietnam, it was not the time to desert their ally at the United Nations. Allusions were drawn to the worst possible scenario of an American retreat into isolationism. While there were never any threats raised, it was pointed out that Canada-U.S. economic relations were already in difficulty over protectionist 'Nixonomics'. The reply was always the same; Canada would not lobby for its position but nor would it alter it. In vain, Washington and its Pacific allies looked elsewhere for support that in the end was not forthcoming. After years of predicting it, Canada quietly expressed its pleasure when the PRC finally inherited the 'China seat' in October 1971.

Conclusion

'We must not exaggerate the importance of the role Canada can play. But we must do our best to ensure that Canada plays as important a role as she is capable of playing.'[68] That was Escott Reid's admonishment to the 1968 University of Guelph Conference on 'Contemporary China' and the central question of this essay. In the circumstances of the time, did Canada do its best to secure Peking's representation at the United Nations? In the intellectual climate the Reid found himself in, the answer would have been a resounding no. Many Canadian academics with a radical student following saw Canada's failure unilaterally to extend recognition to the Communists and to vote for their representation in the United Nations as yet another example of Canada's dependence on the United States. Being caught up in the rhetoric of domination theories, few academics sought to understand the real context of the dilemma that Canada found itself in.

At the outset there were fundamental reasons why the government did not vote in favour of Peking's representation, of which only one, and certainly not the most important, was U.S. opposition. Even if the diplomatic arguments for such a vote had been acceptable, this would not have been enough to overcome the political opposition in both Parliament and cabinet, which was rooted in strongly held public attitudes against the Communists. The participation of the PRC in the Korean War intensified that opposition, which returned Canadian missionaries supported with first-hand descriptions of Communist persecution in mainland China. It was this public opposition, with powerful spokesmen in Parliament, that prevented cabinet from endorsing the line which St Laurent and Pearson and their officials were anxious to pursue.

Subsequent attempts by Canada to initiate a movement against a position held so tenaciously by the United States failed, because there was insufficient support by other countries. Unless there was a reasonable prospect of achieving that objective, it seemed best to mark time. To have done otherwise would have raised problems for the government in Washington and among the Canadian public without any compensating advantages for Canada, either domestically or externally. By waiting for a majority move, Canada could at least use its position as a bargaining lever to persuade Washington and its Pacific allies, and to a lesser extent other countries, to take account of a gradually changing attitude on Chinese representation.

When international events forced the representation question more to the forefront in the mid-1960s, neither civil servants nor politicians were agreed on what should be done and when. Martin and his officials advanced various proposals, even to the point of conspiring with like-minded senior officials in the State Department to change the views of Rusk, before retreating to the less bold decision in 1966 to abstain on the Albanian resolution. As minor as this may seem in retrospect, it was, nonetheless, the first substantive change in Canadian policy since 1949. No amount of lobbying by pro-Peking groups in Canada could force the government to go further along what it quite realistically regarded as a functionally unmanageable route. Moreover, there was no evidence that a unilateral Canadian move in the sixties would have led others to change their votes at the United Nations. It was this inability to begin a substantive movement, more than direct American opposition, that in the end always deterred Canada.

Although the Trudeau government took a more definite stand on recognition and representation in the United Nations, it set no timetable for completion. The political climate had changed and the new U.S. administration was willing to tolerate, if not endorse, Canada's bilateral moves. At this juncture, Sharp's decision to persist at any cost had the support of his prime minister and cabinet colleagues in a way that Martin's initiatives never had.

While it might be argued that Canadian diplomats and statesmen could have done more to speed up the process, there was no guarantee that their efforts would have been rewarded with an earlier success. What capabilities, skills, and credibility they had were best marshalled for the crucial Stockholm negotiations regarding recognition. In the end, recognition was the key that broke the impasse at the United Nations. In this, Canada had forged the way for other countries which soon used its formula to follow suit, thereby making Peking's representation in the United Nations inevitable. But in the final analysis, the PRC took possession of the 'China seat' not because of Canadian lobbying or leadership, but because a majority of members, including Canada and most Canadians, now wanted it within the precincts of the United Nations.

Notes

1 In the literature on influence Kal Holsti has written: 'In general, the successful wielding of influence varies with (1) the quality and quantity of capabilities at a state's disposal, (2) skill in mobilizing these capabilities in support of the goals, (3) the credibility of threats and rewards, (4) the degree of need or dependence, and (5) the degree of responsiveness among the policy makers of a target country' (*International Politics: A Framework for Analysis*, 2nd ed. [Prentice-Hall, Englewood Cliffs, New Jersey, 1978] p. 166). The framework for multilateral diplomacy carried on in an international institution is similar since the emphasis is on bilateral bargaining for votes rather than on the strength of public oratory, though the nature of the bargaining concessions may be quite different.
2 DEA file 5475-EJ-40, vol. 1, Ignatieff to SSEA, 28 Jan. 1949.
3 Ibid., Permanent Mission to the U.N. (PERMISS) to SSEA, 8 Dec. 1949.
4 Ibid., J. Holmes to A.D.P. Heeney, 3 Feb. 1950.
5 For thorough treatments of the early recognition problem, see Stephen Beecroft's essay in this volume (ch. 2), and F. Soward, 'A Survey of Canadian External Policy' (unpublished DEA–Historical Division manuscript), 15–78.
6 Ibid., 'Action proposed to be taken by Canadian representatives at international meetings after Canada has granted recognition to the Central Government of the People's Republic of China,' 13 Mar. 1950.
7 Ibid., J. Holmes to SSEA, 23 Mar. 1950. There was, of course, as Holmes pointed out, a difference between the commission and the board, but this did not mask the confusion surrounding Canadian policy.
8 Ibid., E. Reid to SSEA, 28 Mar. 1950.
9 Ibid., AFE Division to U.N. Division, 2 May 1950.
10 Ibid., 30 Mar. 1950.
11 Ottawa learned that most officials in the State Department regarded the Soviet walkout as a means of pressuring countries to extend recognition rather than breaking up the U.N. In any case, Washington expected it to be resolved by the autumn when it would probably accept a majority decision to seat the Communists. Trinity College Archives, Ignatieff Papers, vol. 1, file 1,

Ignatieff to D. Le Pan, 2 Mar. 1950.
12 Ibid., E. Reid to A. Menzies, 18 May 1950.
13 U.N. Press Bureau, Press Release TR/428, 31 May 1950, 'Cable from Chou En-lai on Chinese Representation in Trusteeship Council.'
14 PAC, Privy Council Office Papers, Series 18, vol. 139, Cabinet Document 166–50, 13 June 1950.
15 Ibid., Cabinet Conclusions, 21 June 1950; and see Beecroft, passim.
16 House of Commons, *Debates*, 3 Mar. 1950, 459–96.
17 DEA file 5475-EJ-40, SSEA to High Commissioner, 13 July 1950, and Heeney to Pearson, as drafted by the U.N. Division, 25 July 1950.
18 Ibid., Wrong to SSEA, 14 July 1950.
19 DEA, *Statements and Speeches*, 50/26, 14 July 1950.
20 DEA file 5475-EJ-40, 'Memorandum to the cabinet: Asian questions before the General Assembly,' 11 Sept. 1950.
21 Ibid., Pearson to St Laurent, 20 Sept. 1950. For the contrast with what was actually said, see the 'Record of Meeting of Heads of Commonwealth Delegations, September 19, 1950.' Two months later the chief Canadian delegate told Pearson that at the beginning of the Assembly he had personally been in favour of accepting Peking (ibid., 21 Nov. 1950).
22 Ibid. Rusk seemed pleased with the outcome, which to him meant that 'the issue can be more or less shelved in the Committee's hands until after the elections here and the end of North Korean resistance' (as reported by Wrong to Pearson, 20 Sept. 1950).
23 Ibid., Wrong to Hickerson, 19 Dec. 1950.
24 House of Commons, *Debates*, 2 Feb. 1951, 55.
25 DEA file 5475-EJ-40, SSEA to PERMISS, 30 Mar. 1951.
26 Ibid., Heeney to Pearson, 3 Mar. 1951. Similar discussions ensued at this time over instructions to delegations to meetings of the Universal Postal Union, the International Children's Fund, and the Administrative Council of the International Telecommunications Union.
27 As an example, see ibid., U.N. Division to AFE Division, 9 Feb. 1951. In particular, the two divisions were debating the probable effects of withdrawing recognition from Taipei without concurrent extension of recognition to Peking (ibid., 8 June 1951). See also Heeney to Pearson, 8 Mar. 1951, and, for the final policy ruling, a memorandum of 30 May 1951.
28 See Paul Evans and Daphne Taras, 'Looking (Far) East: Parliament and Canada-China Relations, 1949–1982,' in David Taras (ed.), *Parliament and Canadian Foreign Policy* (Toronto: Canadian Institute for International Affairs 1988), and Evans and Taras, 'Canadian Public Opinion on Relations with China: An Analysis of the Existing Survey Research' (Working Paper No. 33, University of Toronto–York University Joint Centre on Modern East Asia

1985). Between 25 November 1950 and 5 January 1951 DEA received 61 letters in favour of admission of the PRC and 258 against. Those in favour came primarily from Regina, Saskatoon, and Vancouver and those opposed from Roman Catholics in Toronto.

29 DEA file 5475-EJ-40, FE Division to SSEA, 15 May 1953.
30 *Statements and Speeches*, S/S 53/26, 25 May 1953, and S/S 53/29, 27 May 1953.
31 *Debates*, 31 Mar. 1954.
32 Commentary for the Canadian Delegation to the Ninth UNGA, 1954.
33 DEA file 5475-EJ-40, 'Chinese representation in the United Nations,' 7 Apr. 1954, included in the minister's Handbook, 1953-4. Dulles's position was spelled out rather thoroughly on 9 July 1954, Department of State Press Release No. 376, 'Chinese Representation in the United Nations.'
34 DEA file 5475-EJ-40, Mackay to Pearson, 14 July 1954.
35 Ibid., USSEA to SSEA, 15 Aug. 1955.
36 *Statements and Speeches*, S/S 55/30, 25 Aug. 1955; see also Pearson to USSEA, 12 Sept. 1955. PAC, Pearson Papers, vol. 20, file 14.
37 Quoted in C. Ronning to USSEA, 30 Mar. 1965, DEA file 20-China-14.
38 DEA file 5475-EJ-40, Leger to Reid, 27 Mar. 1956.
39 Ibid., Pearson to Canadian Embassy, Washington, 26 Sept. 1956, and Leger to Pearson, 28 Sept. 1956.
40 DEA file 20-China-14, Ronning to USSEA, 30 Mar. 1965. This story cannot, however, be confirmed in such categorical language from reports filed at the time.
41 DEA file 5475-EJ-40, draft instructions to the Canadian delegation, 27 May 1958, and DEA Press Release No. 2, 22 Sept. 1958.
42 Ibid., Campbell to USSEA, 17 Mar. 1961.
43 Ibid., Legal Division to FE Division, 10 Feb. 1961.
44 Ibid., Murray to Jay, 7 Apr. 1961. The U.N. Division had never been as optimistic as the Far Eastern Division that the presence of the Communists in the U.N. would be all that beneficial.
45 Ibid., Robertson to Green, 22 Mar. 1961.
46 Ibid., Campbell to FE Division, 23 June 1961, and Robertson to SSEA, 20 June 1961.
47 Ibid., Robertson to PM, 5 Dec. 1961.
48 DEA Press Release No. 23, 3 Dec. 1961.
49 DEA file 5475-EJ-40, FE Division to U.N. Division, 29 Dec. 1961.
50 Ibid. For Diefenbaker's statement on the rights of Taipei to be protected, see House of Commons, 20 Sept. 1961, 8592.
51 *Statements and Speeches*, S/S 63/17; see also Martin's address to the Canadian-American Relations Seminar at the University of Windsor, 7 Nov. 1963, and in the House of Commons debates on 28 Nov. 1963, 5194. Martin's

attitude was also confirmed in the author's interview with him on 13 October 1982 in Windsor.
52 Martin interview.
53 DEA file 20-China-14, Cadieux to SSEA, 29 Sept. 1964. On the presumed economic consequences, see Economic Division to Far Eastern Division, 30 Sept. 1964. The final recommendation to the minister was arrived at during a meeting in the under-secretary's office, the results of which appear in notes taken by D. Molgat, 29 Oct. 1964.
54 DEA file 20-China-14., C. Ritchie to DEA, 16 Nov. 1964.
55 Ibid., Martin to DEA, 1 Dec. 1964.
56 *Statements and Speeches*, S/S 65/28, 17 Nov. 1965.
57 Ibid., Martin to C. Ritchie, 15 Feb. 1966, and Cadieux to file, 21 Feb. 1966.
58 Ibid., Pearson's comment on Martin to Pearson, 28 June 1966. This was also the line he took just before his retirement in justifying his refusal to act in an interview with the *United Church Observer*: 'When you have a division of public opinion inside your own country and there is no great impelling urgency, morally or politically, to take action, then your relations with your neighbor, with the United States, become important in respect of that issue' (15 Apr. 1968, 16).
59 *Statements and Speeches*, S/S 66/34, 26 Aug. 1966.
60 DEA file 20-China-40, Goldschlag to USSEA, 7 Oct. 1966. A public opinion poll conducted at the beginning of the 1966 General Assembly indicated that those favouring Communist representation had gone up slightly but still represented only 55 per cent, with 15 per cent undecided.
61 Ibid., DEA to C. Ritchie, 3 Nov. 1966.
62 Interviews with Cadieux, 29 June 1979; Martin, 13 Oct. 1982; and the Head of Far Eastern Division, Pamela McDougall, 17 Sept. 1982.
63 *Statements and Speeches*, S/S 66/47, 23 Nov. 1966.
64 *Debates*, 25 Sept. 1967, 2434, and 11 Dec. 1967, 5262.
65 *Statements and Speeches*, S/S 68/17, 29 May 1968.
66 Ignatieff Papers, Box 5, 'United Nations Policy Review,' 15 Feb. 1969.
67 Statement by Yvon Beaulne, DEA Press Release No. 35, 13 Nov. 1970.
68 E. Reid, 'Canadian Policy on China,' *Contemporary China* (Toronto: Canadian Institute of International Affairs 1968), 134.

CHAPTER FOUR

Norman St Amour

Sino-Canadian Relations, 1963–1968: The American Factor

The victory of Lester Pearson's Liberal party in the national elections of April 1963 sparked expectations of a change in Canadian policy toward China. The time seemed ripe for something new. Immense in size and population, and developing a nuclear capability, the People's Republic of China (PRC) was emerging as the dominant military power in East Asia and an important strategic force in international affairs. Yet the country remained diplomatically isolated, recognized by few Western governments, and denied representation in the United Nations. American policy, strangled by the Cold War rhetoric of the Dulles years, maintained an implacable bulwark around the contagion of Chinese communism.

By the summer of 1963 this wall was beginning to crack. The rift separating Peking and Moscow had finally shattered the myth of a monolithic communist menace – a myth which, while never prominent in Canada, had paralysed American thinking on China since McCarthy. President Kennedy's own views revealed a careful evolution away from his early criticisms of the Truman administration's 'loss' of China. Delivering the commencement address at American University in June 1963, Kennedy called for a re-examination of attitudes hardened by tensions and fears of the Cold War. Two months later, at a press conference on 1 August 1963, he told reporters he wanted to take steps to lessen the ominous prospect of confrontation with a Communist China possessing nuclear weapons.[1]

This evolving American attitude appeared to offer opportunity for an improvement in Sino-Canadian relations. Although convinced that the PRC's continued isolation only encouraged 'recurring crises,' Pearson approached the situation cautiously. Concerned about the escalating conflict in Vietnam (where membership on the International Commission for Supervision and Control gave Canada special responsibilities) and questioning the wisdom of a policy that ignored the political realities in East Asia, Canadian policy makers did enter the forefront of a mounting effort to reach a pragmatic accommodation with Peking. Despite a series of policy initiatives, all of which proved futile and were ultimately abandoned, there was no dramatic improvement in Canada's diplomatic relations with the PRC during the Pearson years.

Critics of Pearson's China policy have argued that his caution reflected undue concern with, even a humiliating subservience to, the United States.[2] Certainly Canada's proximity to and unique relationship with the United States meant that Pearson was always particularly aware of the American position on Canadian actions likely to prove controversial in Washington. Yet Pearson's whole approach to the China issue was shaped by his conviction that there was no compelling reason to recognize the PRC. Canada's bilateral relations with mainland China, principally in the realm of trade, were developing satisfactorily despite the absence of formal diplomatic ties. The Chinese were, for example, about to sign a second major long-term wheat purchase agreement with the Canadian Wheat Board. Given this progress, an explicit initiative to recognize the PRC, while running the risk of angering the United States, appeared to serve no significant Canadian national interest. For Pearson, at least, changes in China policy were consciously designed to serve other ends.

Speaking to a Toronto audience on 24 August 1963, Secretary of State for External Affairs Paul Martin revealed the factors constraining Canadian China policy. Bound as it was by tradition, treaty obligations, and national interest to the NATO alliance, it was neither possible nor desirable for Canada's relations with the PRC to differ widely from those of its closest allies. Yet within the limits imposed by these constraints, there were opportunities for Canada to pursue its interests while also serving the larger interests of the alliance. It was time, Martin told his audience – in a remark obviously meant also for American ears – 'to ponder very carefully whether an answer to the rising power of Asian communism is to be found in its further isolation and containment, or whether it lies in broadening contacts at a variety of levels in an endeavour to penetrate the curtain of ignorance and blunt the edge of ideological differences.'[3]

In late August 1963 DEA completed its own internal review of China policy, the first major review since 1958.[4] Under-Secretary of State Norman Robertson, assuming that recognition of the PRC had by now become merely a question 'of timing and of techniques,' advocated the adoption of a two-Chinas policy linking Canadian support for Peking's seating in the United Nations with the establishment of informal Sino-Canadian contacts to discuss recognition. Robertson was confident that American opposition could effectively be mitigated; first, by keeping the Kennedy administration fully informed of Canadian intentions and, second, by supporting the right of Chiang Kai-shek's government to a separate seat in the U.N. General Assembly as representatives of an independent Taiwan.[5] Pearson did not share Robertson's confidence. American officials, convinced that Western contacts with the PRC would have little moderating influence on Chinese policies or attitudes, opposed any initiative encouraging Communist China's leaders in their pursuit of an aggressive and destabilizing foreign policy in Southeast Asia. Although supported by Paul Martin, Robertson's proposal was quietly shelved.[6]

In the aftermath of the assassination of President Kennedy, rumours of a major shift in American China policy persisted. Speaking to the Commonwealth Club of San Francisco on 13 December 1963, Assistant Secretary of State for Far Eastern Affairs Roger Hilsman sought to lay the foundation for a series of new policy initiatives that had been fermenting within the working ranks of the State Department since 1961.[7] His speech embodied the Kennedy style, easing the rhetoric of the Cold War but offering little of substance. Six years earlier John Foster Dulles had confidently told another San Francisco audience that communism was only a 'passing phase' of the Chinese revolution. Hilsman now acknowledged that China's 'Marxist puritans,' as he termed the current leadership, were a permanent fixture of the political landscape. Echoing an earlier theme in Sino-American relations, he could only promise that the United States would keep the door open to an improvement in Sino-American relations when a more pragmatic second echelon of Chinese leaders someday assumed power.[8]

President Johnson, in office only three weeks, was angered by the speculation that Hilsman's speech raised. Rumours of a major departure in American China policy cast doubts upon his administration's commitment to an active presence in Southeast Asia, thereby undermining the confidence of America's allies throughout the region. Chiang Kai-shek, citing the Canadian press as a major source of these rumours, was particularly concerned. In Taipei, American Ambassador Jerald Wright reported that many Kuomintang leaders feared 'trends in US-China policy increasingly divergent from [their] aspirations' and recommended 'such means of reassurance as may be available and appropriate.'[9] American officials in Taipei, Saigon, Bangkok, Tokyo, and other Asian capitals denied that any change in China policy was being contemplated by Washington. In a late

December interview broadcast over Japanese television, Secretary of State Dean Rusk specifically reaffirmed the Johnson administration's commitment to the security and defence of Taiwan. In Washington, members of the Canadian embassy were repeatedly told that the Hilsman speech was 'not intended to indicate any current or future change in USA policy towards Communist China.' Ambassador Charles Ritchie, reporting back to Ottawa, concluded that the speech was little more than an effort to redefine existing American policy in more sober and moderate terms.[10] Events, however, were gathering their own momentum.

In January 1964 France recognized the PRC. French relations with Taiwan were left intentionally ambiguous, prompting speculations within DEA that de Gaulle was attempting to implement his own two-Chinas policy. Pearson, intent on maintaining the integrity of the NATO alliance, flew to Washington, urging Johnson to respond to this latest example of Gaullist impudence with caution and restraint. A hostile reaction would only further the damage done to American China policy, already widely viewed as stubbornly perverse. Johnson now had the opportunity, Pearson argued, to adopt a more realistic policy: while working to preserve a separate seat in the U.N. General Assembly for Taiwan, he could use French recognition as the rationale for accepting the PRC's entry into the United Nations. If this opportunity was ignored, Pearson feared that Taiwan would quickly be reduced 'to an island fortress protected by the United States Seventh Fleet and almost completely lacking in international status.'[11]

Facing an election in November 1964, Johnson was not prepared to initiate any fundamental change in Sino-American relations. Publicly he managed to contain his anger. Privately, however, many members of the administration were furious, convinced that de Gaulle was severely handicapping, if not intentionally sabotaging, American policy in Asia. Dean Rusk was particularly annoyed, in one conversation with Paul Martin asking how long NATO could possibly survive. Fearing that Canada might follow France's lead, the State Department conveyed its firm opposition to any Canadian move.[12]

At the top levels of the Johnson administration, as involvement in Vietnam escalated, attitudes towards the PRC were hardening. China policy was becoming the proving ground for the Johnson administration's larger commitments in Southeast Asia. It was important, therefore, that the United States not allow itself to be manoeuvred into situations where policy setbacks could be interpreted as retreats or defeats. Rusk was convinced that only a policy of firmness would substantiate American resolve in Asia and force the PRC to moderate its bitter anti-American hostility. Walt Rostow, the president's national security adviser, argued that until the United

States 'demonstrated that the game of "Wars of National Liberation" is not viable and that the borders of China and Vietnam are firm, the acceptance of Communist China within the world community and in the UN ... would signal to those on the spot that we have granted Chinese Communist hegemony in Southeast Asia.'[13] The Johnson administration intended to stand firm in the area of China policy.

Most Canadian policy makers, convinced that the continued isolation of the PRC was both dangerous and self-defeating, did not share this attitude. But with State Department warnings still fresh in mind, Pearson was not prepared to follow France's example and recognize the PRC. Attention instead focused on the United Nations.[14] Although initial Canadian fears that French recognition would lead to Taiwan's expulsion from the U.N. had subsided, the Far Eastern Division warned 'that potential supporters of what we consider an equitable solution [to the problem of Chinese representation] will be driven towards extreme position in 1965 if the supporters of the status quo exhibit no flexibility in 1964.'[15]

Hoping to avoid this polarization, DEA began to work on a one-China, one-Taiwan declaratory resolution. Paul Martin expected opposition from Washington as well as from both the PRC and Taiwan, and recognized that there was little chance of this resolution gaining support in the General Assembly. He nevertheless felt that it had considerable value. Canada, having gone on record supporting Taiwan's right to continued representation in the United Nations, would then be in a position to recognize the PRC. 'In the end,' one official concluded, 'the best outcome is also the likeliest, that we attempt a one-China, one-Formosa solution and fail to achieve it because of the refusal of both Chinese governments to cooperate. The U.S. diplomatic defeat would then at least be mitigated, since the Americans could say they had done their best for their Nationalist allies, who were too stiff-necked to accept the help offered ... And Peking would be in the U.N.'[16]

Not everyone at the DEA shared Martin's enthusiasm for his one-China, one-Taiwan formula. Critics argued that the resolution was a 'stab in the back for the Americans,' primarily intended to get Canada 'off a moral hook' so that the PRC could be recognized 'with an appearance of virtue.'[17] Martin, hoping to resolve this conflict and arrive at a definitive policy prior to the upcoming General Assembly session, convened a departmental meeting in late September 1964. In a key memorandum, the Economic Division warned that any Canadian initiative on China could have a serious impact on bilateral trade relations with the United States. Peking lacked foreign reserves and offered little prospect for significant increase in trade. Canadian companies, because of their subsidiary relationships to

American corporations, were not free to exploit those opportunities for Sino-Canadian trade that already existed. Even where there were no direct corporate links, companies dependent on American markets 'would be reluctant to face possible blacklist there as the price of access to rather hypothetical market opportunities in China.'[18]

In Washington, Ambassador Charles Ritchie also felt a Canadian initiative was dangerous. In the aftermath of the August 1964 Tonkin Gulf incidents and the escalation of hostilities in Vietnam, the Johnson administration would actively oppose any initiative undermining its position in Asia or Taiwan's status in the United Nations. The declaratory resolution, Ritchie concluded, locked Canada into a policy where the risks clearly outweighed the potential benefits. Paul Martin was unable to convince Pearson that these risks were worth taking and abandoned plans for any Canadian initiative at the upcoming Assembly.[19]

Communist China's explosion of an atomic bomb in October 1964 forced a sudden reassessment of this decision. Reports from the United Nations indicated that several African countries were now likely to support admission of Peking. Italy and Belgium were pushing for consultations with Canada to co-ordinate a common initiative 'with the particular object of persuading the Americans to accept that a negative policy could not ... be pursued indefinitely.'[20] Martin was convinced that if Canada merely adhered to its past policy, it would be accused of 'knuckling under' to American pressure. Seizing the opportunity to augment Canadian pressures upon the Johnson administration's China policy, he revived the declaratory resolution as the basis for joint discussions with Italy and Belgium. Privately, Martin advised Pearson that Canada should recognize the PRC if it was seated at the 1964 session of the United Nations.[21]

The PRC's successful nuclear test was viewed by the Johnson administration as yet another attack upon the international prestige and confidence of Chiang Kai-shek's government; 'confidence,' one American diplomat wrote, 'which we wish to maintain in view of Free World security interests in Taiwan and the Far East.'[22] Yet American officials remained officially optimistic, characterizing initial world reaction to the Chinese test as 'entirely satisfactory' in conversations with members of the Canadian embassy. Those countries on the periphery of the PRC, including Taiwan, were concerned but showed no signs of panic. The State Department, recognizing that Taiwan's support in the United Nations was eroding, nevertheless did not expect the 1964 vote on Chinese representation to be seriously affected. Fearing that any change in American China policy might lead to an uncontrollable rush by other countries to 'get on the bandwagon,' U.S. support for Taiwan remained firm. Privately, however, some members of the administration felt that the fight was already lost. Harlan Cleveland, the State Department's assistant secretary for international organizations, warned that America's traditional approach to the Chinese representation issue, 'which has (remarkably) served us well for a decade-and-a-half, is eaten away at its very foundations. Our major allies ... are hanging on only for fear of what it could do to their relationship with us if they were to let go.'[23]

Ambassador Charles Ritchie met Dean Rusk in mid-November to prepare him for a possible change in Canadian China policy. Instructed to speak frankly, he told Rusk that DEA did not accept the State Department's optimistic assessment of the upcoming United Nations debate on Chinese representation. A majority of the Canadian public viewed the PRC's continued diplomatic isolation as both unrealistic and incompatible with the Pearson government's professed interest in furthering disarmament talks and the resolution of international tensions. Internationally, Canada's reputation among the non-aligned nations for objectivity and independence was being adversely affected. It was time to move forward on this issue. Hoping to prevent a serious diplomatic defeat for the United States, DEA was exploring the possibility of sponsoring a declaratory resolution advocating some form of two-Chinas policy. If the PRC was admitted to the U.N., then Ottawa, not wanting to go through the agony of another long policy debate, would be inclined to view this as amounting to recognition.[24]

Rusk was clearly annoyed. Speaking with what Ritchie described as an unusual measure of emotion, Rusk warned that the policies being followed by the Chinese were leading directly toward war in the Pacific. On 18 November 1964 Harlan Cleveland flew to Ottawa. The American attitude toward China, Cleveland told Martin, was determined by Vietnam. Given the critical situation there, any accommodation with the Chinese Communists would only reward their aggressive policies, further threatening the security of Southeast Asia. Surely, he argued, the PRC should first be made to conform to the requirements of U.N. membership before being welcomed into the family of nations. Neither Rusk nor Johnson could understand DEA's sense of urgency on this issue. Hinting that the United States would support the creation of a study committee at the 1965 General Assembly to examine the issue of Chinese representation, Cleveland indicated that a major policy review was already under way at the State Department – but change could not be expected overnight. Maintenance of the status quo would be the greatest help Canada could give the Johnson administration in bringing about a significant change in American China policy.[25]

These arguments had little impact on Martin. Meeting with Dean Rusk in New York on 30 November 1964, he agreed that the PRC's admission into the United Nations would not lead to any immediate improvement in its policies or behaviour. But Canada considered that this issue was coming to a resolution regardless of American desires or actions. The United States was facing a serious diplomatic defeat if it rigidly adhered to present policies in the one area of the China problem where the West could afford to display flexibility. Canada believed that its resolution was a genuine move forward, in the best interests of both the U.N. and the United States. Martin did agree to continue supporting the U.S.-backed important question resolution. In return, he wanted 'a very specific promise at the highest level of a new look in American attitudes towards the China problem.'[26]

Events at the United Nations left Canada without an effective course of action. The State Department was adamantly opposed to any Canadian initiative. Initial Belgian and Italian support for the declaratory resolution evaporated, owing in part to American pressure. Italy, for example, now believed that the resolution was dangerous unless it was assured the support of a significant majority in the General Assembly, including Washington and Taipei. This support simply did not exist. At a meeting on 22 December 1964, the Canadian cabinet decided not to table the declaratory resolution when the debate on Chinese representation commenced at the United Nations. Having raised expectations of a change in policy, DEA was saved embarrassment by a fortuitous set of circumstances. The General Assembly, unable to resolve a dispute between the United States and the Soviet Union over the funding of peacekeeping operations, recessed without debate on 18 February 1965. Canada was, at least for the moment, off the horns of its dilemma.[27]

The failure of the declaratory resolution left DEA searching for the threads of a coherent policy. In April 1965 PRC officials suggested to Peter Roberts, Canada's trade commissioner in Hong Kong, that the two countries exchange permanent trade offices. There would be little commercial advantage from such an exchange. The PRC's lack of foreign exchange reserves meant there were few Canadian products that the Chinese were willing or able to purchase. Yet Roberts personally felt that the establishment of a Canadian trade office in Peking could be used 'as a long step in the direction of recognition,' serving as an alternative to the United Nations as a 'venue in which to work out [a] solution to the problem of our relations with China.'[28]

Other voices within DEA, again concerned about the possible reaction in Washington, were more cautious. Any sign of a Sino-Canadian rapprochement, warned Deputy Under-Secretary Ed Ritchie – soon to be appointed ambassador to the United States – particularly given the present intensity of the conflict in Vietnam, could seriously damage relations with the

Johnson administration. While the Americans might close their eyes to a Canadian trade office in Peking, they could hardly ignore a PRC office in Ottawa. This risk would be acceptable only if trade offices could be tied to a final decision regarding relations with Taiwan, to a change in Canadian policy at the United Nations, and to a definite timetable for recognizing the PRC. Ritchie knew such a timetable did not exist.[29]

The situation at the United Nations remained uncertain. The PRC suffered a series of setbacks in the summer of 1965 which undermined its support among the Afro-Asian nations. A number of African states accused Peking of subversion and supporting armed insurrection in Africa. There was also widespread resentment of Chinese attempts to dominate the preparatory meetings of the Second Afro-Asian Conference (Bandung II), and to inject extraneous ideological and political issues into the conference agenda at the expense of Afro-Asian interests and solidarity. When many moderate African states refused to attend the conference, scheduled for late June in Algeria, it was postponed until November and then abandoned.[30]

Communist Chinese officials seemed intent on campaigning against themselves. Continuing their attacks on the United Nations as a submissive tool of American imperialism, they called for the formation of a rival revolutionary organization dominated by and serving the interests of the Afro-Asian nations. The climax came on 29 September 1965 when Foreign Minister Chen Yi, in a rambling four-hour news conference taunting the United States, escalated the conditions that had to be met before the PRC would agree to enter the United Nations. They included cancellation of the U.N. resolution condemning China as the aggressor in the Korean War; condemnation of the United States as the aggressor; reform of the U.N. Charter, giving the Afro-Asian nations greater influence; the inclusion of all independent states; and, in an obvious reference to Taiwan, the expulsion of 'all imperialist puppets.' Although Chen Yi's speech left many puzzled, including Dean Rusk and the State Department, the United States was quick to react. Admitting the PRC to the United Nations now, American Ambassador Arthur Goldberg told the General Assembly, 'would be tantamount – in light of Communist China's belligerent attitudes – to yielding to undisguised blackmail.'[31]

Despite Goldberg's impassioned rhetoric, Canada's U.N. Mission predicted that a resolution calling for the Albanian resolution might well gain a simple majority. This would represent a serious psychological and diplomatic defeat for both the United States and its allies in Southeast Asia. Pearson, facing a federal election in early November, was reluctant to make any firm policy commitments. Although Martin instructed the Canadian delegation not to participate in the debate on Chinese representation, PRC belligerence allowed him to take the high ground. Canada was prepared to welcome the PRC into the United Nations, but only 'on terms which are common to all members.' Debate ended on 17 November 1965. With the election safely past, Canada quietly voted for the important question resolution and against the Albanian resolution. The results of this vote confirmed Canadian warnings and American fears. The majority in favour of the important question resolution was a slim 56 to 49; the Albanian resolution produced a tie vote, 47 members of the United Nations favouring the seating of the PRC and 47 opposed.[32]

In Ottawa, Martin moved to placate domestic critics expecting a change in Canadian policy, telling a news conference that Peking had set an unacceptable price for its admission. In a revealing comment, he noted that Chinese representation was 'not an issue which can be considered in isolation. It must be part of any independent policy judgement that Canada assess the total impact of the seating of Communist China on its other relationships and on the United Nations itself.'[33]

American officials at the U.N. shared Martin's concern that the PRC would gain a simple majority in 1966 and enter on its own terms. In December 1965 Ambassador Goldberg recommended to President Johnson a serious reconsideration of American policy and tactics to 'avoid a major defeat in the [General] Assembly next year.'[34] Goldberg's recommendation was undoubtedly a significant factor in the State Department's easing of restrictions on travel by Americans to the PRC. Although this was largely a symbolic gesture – the PRC consistently refused to issue visas to American citizens – it was a small victory for moderates in the State Department which both surprised and pleased Canadian officials searching for any signs of American flexibility. Martin tried to push the Johnson administration further, suggesting to Rusk in January 1966 that Chester Ronning serve as an informal American emissary to Peking and Hanoi. Rusk was reluctant to accept this offer, unable to refuse without appearing unreasonable and yet fearing that Ronning would find himself 'engaged in discussion, especially in Peiping, of the problems relating to Chinese representation and even ... questions of recognition.'[35] This was, of course, precisely the reason Martin suggested the Ronning mission. Rusk's fears eventually proved unfounded. Despite Ronning's past friendships with top Chinese Communist party officials, he too was refused a visa.

The spring and summer of 1966 were a landmark in the development of American China policy. An ongoing debate within the Johnson administration was producing strong differences of opinion. Dean Rusk remained the principal obstacle to any significant liberalization of policy. Canadian officials, through their contacts at the State Department and in New York, were kept informed of the broad outlines of the debate. Flying to Washington in February 1966 for additional talks with Rusk, Martin again pressed the case for a relaxation of American policy as the only viable response to the deteriorating situation at the United Nations. He left Washington convinced that Rusk had modified his position on Chinese representation, American policy was under review, and the United States was now ready to take meaningful steps to improve relations with the PRC. Martin was wrong.[36]

The signals emanating from Washington remained confusing. In March 1966, J. William Fulbright's Senate Foreign Relations Committee held a series of public hearings examining China policy. A host of American academics and China specialists, led by professors A. Doak Barnett and John King Fairbank, called for a change in policy, 'from one of containment plus isolation to one of containment without isolation.' Testifying before the House Committee on Foreign Affairs one week later, Rusk acknowledged the dangers inherent in 'assuming the existence of an unending and inevitable state of hostilities between ourselves and the rulers of Mainland China.' Yet it was just as essential, he argued, in a manner reminiscent of the Dulles years, 'to "contain" Communist aggression in Asia as it was, and is, to "contain" Communist aggression in Europe.'[37]

DEA watched the unfolding Senate and House Committee hearings intently. The reaction of both the Congress and the American public was restrained, almost complaisant, much of the boilerplate rhetoric of earlier administrations having dissipated. The China Lobby had declined as a salient factor in American politics, with senators like Jacob Javits of New York calling for a new China policy and making a point of publicly repudiating their membership in such organizations as the Committee of One Million. Public opinion was running ahead of administration policy, thus giving President Johnson an opportunity to rationalize Sino-American relations. Yet as one member of the State Department shrewdly pointed out to Ambassador Ritchie, although the American people would acquiesce to any change in policy if President Johnson provided firm leadership, there was no real pressure upon him to implement such a change. The congressional hearings nevertheless indicated to Ritchie an evolving attitude and flexibility that had important implications. 'It is now open to third countries, especially Canada,' he concluded in a dispatch home, 'to include in their calculations the possibility, even probability, that changes in their attitudes will hasten the process of change in that of the United States.'[38]

Expectations of a change in American policy left Chiang Kai-shek and other ROC officials disturbed, reawakening fears that the Johnson administration was prepared to abandon its commitments in Southeast Asia and sacrifice the interests of Taiwan for a settlement in Vietnam. The foreign ministry in Taipei, delivering an *aide-mémoire* to the American ambassador on 16 May 1966, strongly objected to Rusk's statement before the House Foreign Affairs Committee that Chinese Communist control of the mainland was secure. His statement gave the PRC a legitimacy damaging to the Kuomintang's claim to be the sole representative of the Chinese people, and created the impression that the United States was prepared to accept a two-Chinas policy. A CIA Intelligence Report completed in May 1966 warned that Chiang was becoming 'less responsive to American suggestions and increasingly rigid and uncompromising in international relations.' Any additional moves, particularly by the United States, which could be interpreted as further threats to the status or prestige of Taiwan might well prompt him to walk out of the United Nations.[39]

American policy was under review. Moderates in the State Department were indeed pushing for precisely the policies Chiang Kai-shek feared and opposed. In late April 1966 the State Department's Policy Planning Council recommended a three-phased course of action leading to the creation of a two-Chinas policy. The real leadership behind this effort came from Assistant Secretary for East Asia William Bundy and Assistant Secretary for International Organization Affairs Joseph Sisco, with the strong support of Ambassador Goldberg at the United Nations. Meeting with Dean Rusk on 6 May 1966 they recommended that the United States support the efforts of countries like Canada who were trying to implement a two-Chinas policy at the upcoming session of the United Nations. The meeting ended with a memorandum to President Johnson asking for authorization 'to acquiesce in a two-Chinas approach by third parties at the 21st General Assembly.'[40]

Rusk remained sceptical, still not convinced that the situation at the United Nations required a new policy. Bundy and Sisco appealed to Canada for help, telling Pearson and Martin that they now had the opportunity to exert real influence on the administration's China policy by stressing the probability of change in Canadian policy and indicating a willingness to consult with the United States on new tactics to deal with the problem of Chinese representation. This quiet co-operation was successful. Flying to Ottawa on 16 May 1966 at the expressed desire of President Johnson, Goldberg and Sisco discussed with Martin the possibility of Canada introducing a two-Chinas resolution in the upcoming General Assembly. The president, they promised, would use his influence with Chiang Kai-shek to try to prevent Taiwan's bolting from the United Nations.[41]

Martin was prepared to go further than even Bundy or Sisco anticipated. In a memorandum to Pearson he argued that Canada's primary objective 'should be to bring the PRC into the United Nations as quickly as possible.' Despite the State Department's review, the best thing that could be expected from the Johnson administration was some form of study committee resolution or two-Chinas initiative. Canadian participation in this type of initiative would only be seen as another delaying tactic prompted by American pressure. Martin proposed a major departure from past policy, recommending that Canada abstain on the Albanian resolution at the 1966 U.N. General Assembly session. While a Canadian abstention would undoubtedly provoke a strong American reaction, it would also aid the progressive elements in the Johnson administration. Pearson still had doubts. 'Surely peace in Washington,' he noted in the margins of Martin's memorandum, 'is more important than praise in Peking.'[42]

The reaction of the United States remained an overriding concern for Pearson, at the same time that American policy, in a state of flux, was becoming harder to fathom. Speaking before the American Alumni Council on 12 July 1966 President Johnson called for a 'reconciliation of nations,' telling his audience that a 'misguided China must be encouraged toward understanding of the outside world and toward policies of peaceful cooperation.'[43] The rhetoric had clearly changed, from containment to containment without isolation, and now reconciliation. 'Our problem in the months ahead,' James C. Thomson Jr noted, 'is what kind of substance, and at what pace, to pour into this new rhetorical container.'[44] Dean Rusk met with Chiang Kai-shek in July 1966, seeking to prepare him for a possible alteration in American tactics at the United Nations. Stressing the basic similarity of both American and ROC policy objectives, Rusk warned that initiatives by countries like Canada might create circumstances that would require careful tactical planning if a defeat on either the Albanian or important question resolution was to be avoided. Chiang remained adamantly opposed to any change in tactics, arguing that countries like Canada were wavering precisely because of the Johnson administration's refusal publicly and explicitly to oppose the seating of the PRC in the United Nations. If the United States stood firm, then he was confident of victory.[45]

Rusk, not sharing this optimism, returned to Washington with stronger doubts about the need for a change in China policy. The political turmoil and confusion that accompanied the outbreak of the Cultural Revolution in August 1966 underlined his conviction against PRC representation. On 16 September 1966 interested governments were informed 'that there had been no change in U.S. policy: the United States would strongly oppose an Albanian-style resolution, would seek reaffirmation of the "important question" resolution, and was seeking support for these positions.'[46] In a series of conversations with Paul Martin, Rusk tried to forestall a Canadian initiative, arguing that the PRC's presence in the United Nations would only prove divisive and paralyse effective action. Canada, having no direct involvement or interests in the Far East, was getting a 'free ride' on the issue of Chinese representation. Rusk could see no point in hurting those governments who did have responsibilities in the region simply for the sake of public opinion in Canada and Western Europe.[47]

In fact no final decision on Canadian policy had been made, much to the annoyance of Canada's ambassador to the U.N., George Ignatieff, who was growing impatient with all the 'dilly-dallying in Ottawa.' Martin still felt that only an abstention on the Albanian resolution would break the stalemate. Pearson feared that a Canadian abstention would aid passage of the Albanian resolution, leading to Taiwan's expulsion from the United Nations and damaging relations with the United States. DEA recommended that Canada resurrect a modified one-China, one-Taiwan resolution that would specifically grant China's seat on the Security Council to the PRC. Canada could transform its continued opposition to the Albanian resolution into at least 'passive acquiesence' on the part of the Americans toward the Canadian resolution. After considerable debate, cabinet approved this resolution on 21 October 1966, one month before the scheduled U.N. debate on Chinese representation. An abstention on the Albanian resolution would be reconsidered only if unforeseen circumstances prevented the tabling of the resolution.[48]

On 3 November 1966 Ambassador Ritchie gave the State Department a draft copy of the proposed Canadian resolution. Touring the Far East, Johnson and Rusk returned to Washington the next day, 'absolutely dumfounded,' according to William Bundy, to be confronted 'with this belated and rather scatter-shot Canadian initiative.'[49] Immediately contacting Martin, Rusk argued that the Canadian resolution was both unnecessary and unacceptable, particularly in awarding China's Security Council seat to the PRC. It might well cause Chiang Kai-shek to walk out of the United Nations. Although hoping to avoid an open fight, the United States would be forced actively to oppose the resolution. In a personal letter to Pearson, Rusk was even more explicit. 'I need not tell you,' he wrote, 'the depth of our conviction on this subject ... If your resolution is introduced, we shall not merely have to oppose it, but [shall] have to go to great lengths to see that it is defeated by the heaviest possible margin. I need not underscore the seriousness of such a split between our two nations.' Although Rusk's warnings disturbed Pearson, Martin successfully argued that Canada would lose all leverage over American policy if it quietly abandoned its own initiative. Pearson's reply to Rusk was non-committal, stressing the need for some forward movement on the issue of Chinese representation and concluding that the Canadian resolution represented a carefully thought out, balanced, and realistic solution to the problem.[50]

The State Department, facing a resolution that it feared would cost Taiwan badly needed support in the United Nations, concluded 'that the best hope for a favorable outcome lay in diverting the Canadian initiative into a less damaging direction by offering a counter-draft that would avoid the "two Chinas" implication.'[51] Called to a meeting with Under-Secretary Katzenbach, Joseph Sisco, and William Bundy on 8 November, Ambassador Ritchie was given an alternative draft resolution calling for the formation of a study committee that would make appropriate recommendations to next year's General Assembly for an equitable and practical solution to the problem of Chinese representation. Sisco in particular appealed for co-operation, noting that the study committee resolution was 'a long step forward,' capable of gaining broad backing and having a 'considerable impact' on the United Nations.[52]

In New York, Canada's U.N. Delegation encountered the full weight of American opposition. Arthur Goldberg, hoping to avoid a direct confrontation, initiated consultations with Canada, Belgium, Chile, Italy, and other interested governments to generate support for the American proposal. He was not able to convince Ignatieff, who argued that the study committee was simply another delaying tactic designed to dilute Canada's own resolution. Without some authentic move forward, Canada would find it difficult to continue opposing the PRC's seating in the United Nations. Belgium, Chile, and New Zealand had expressed an initial interest in supporting a modified one-China, one-Taiwan resolution. This support was now rapidly eroding. In conversations with both the Italian and Belgian representatives, Ignatieff tried to reach a compromise that would meet Canadian needs and still be acceptable to the United States.[53] This proved to be impossible. On 21 November 1966 the study committee resolution was tabled in the General Assembly, with Italy, Belgium, and Chile all agreeing to serve as co-sponsors. In a letter to the ROC's foreign minister, Rusk noted that the United States had used 'the tactic of a study committee to head off Canada's dangerous initiative ... This step has now succeeded.'[54]

Canada's initiative was, for all practical purposes, dead. The tabling of two competing resolutions would only leave the General Assembly divided and confused and might actually aid passage of the Albanian resolution. George Ignatieff, fearing that Canada had weathered enough opposition for one year, recommended that Martin vote against the Albanian resolution. Back in Ottawa, Pearson expressed the hope that Canada would now vote for the study committee resolution. Yet a number of the younger members of Martin's entourage at the United Nations, including Pierre Trudeau, argued vigorously for an abstention as the least that the Canadian public would now accept. Canada's efforts on behalf of the one-China, one-Taiwan resolution had generated expectations of a change in China policy. Not meeting those expectations would cost the government both domestic and international credibility, and prestige.[55]

The vote on Chinese representation was scheduled for 29 November 1966. No one knew which course of action Martin would recommend to Pearson. Three times on 28 November and again the following day Dean Rusk called the Canadian delegation but Martin refused to talk with him. Early on the morning of the vote, in a telephone call back to Ottawa, Martin persuaded Pearson that only an abstention would disarm domestic critics of the government's China policy and lend credence to Canada's stated desire to end the PRC's isolation. As soon as Arthur Goldberg entered the General Assembly, Ignatieff informed him of the Canadian decision to abstain on the Albanian resolution. But the decision would be kept secret so as not to influence the outcome of the vote. The important question resolution passed with a comfortable majority (66 for, 48 opposed, 7 abstentions); the Albanian resolution was easily defeated (46 for, 57 against, 17 abstentions); and the study committee proposal, which Canada reluctantly supported, went down to an unsurprising defeat (34 for, 64 against, 25 abstentions). The PRC was thus excluded from the United Nations for yet another year.[56]

Martin, finally returning Rusk's telephone calls, was invited to Washington for lunch the next day. During the quiet meal at the State Department, no mention was made of the Canadian vote. When questioned by a surprised Martin, Rusk expressed little concern. A decision that had been taken with such caution, indeed trepidation, in Ottawa, one that was seen as an important first step leading to a new Canadian China policy, was rather capriciously received in Washington. Although DEA turned again to the possibility of bilateral recognition, the Cultural Revolution forestalled any further Canadian move. On 31 March 1968 a weary Lyndon Johnson, defeated by Vietnam, announced that he would not seek re-election. One week later Lester Pearson turned over leadership of both the Liberal party and Canada to a relatively unknown Pierre Elliott Trudeau.[57]

Conclusion

John Holmes has noted that 'the fact of U.S. policy ... has determined the framework in which relations with China are conducted.'[58] For Pearson, as for most members of DEA, changes in Canadian policy had to occur within the confines of this framework. This reflected a caution, critics have argued a fear, at publicly dissenting over a policy fraught with emotional and symbolic value for the United States but having little intrinsic importance for Canada. Intent on maintaining the perceived influence gained through 'quiet diplomacy,' Pearson embodied this caution. 'I have always taken the view,' he told a CBC interviewer in 1965, 'that if there is a division of opinion in your own country on a particular item of foreign policy, such as recognition of Red China ... then it seems to me the reaction of the United States becomes even more important. If you can't make up your own minds ... then you should be very careful about not getting into trouble with your friends.'[59] There were a few Canadian policy makers, notably Chester Ronning, Escott Reid, and, to a lesser extent, Paul Martin, who were willing either to ignore or directly to challenge American policy in Asia. Motivated by ideology, a sincere disagreement over policy, or personal ambition, they pushed for the dramatic breakthrough that would lead to the normalization of Sino-Canadian relations. Both Ronning and Reid, however, were increasingly on the fringes of power by the mid-1960s. And while Martin's counsel was clearly more influential, it was more circumspect and even then not always heeded.

Pearson's China policy was shaped by his perception of the likely American reaction it would produce. DEA feared that any initiative directly undermining the U.S. position would lead to a retaliatory response affecting other areas of Canada's bilateral relations with the United States. This concern was sufficient to limit both the scope and implementation of Canadian policy. When necessary, the Johnson administration could efficiently, almost ruthlessly, oppose those Canadian initiatives it perceived as threatening its strategic interests in East Asia. There is, however, no evidence that American officials considered linking this opposition to concrete economic or trade sanctions directed against Canada. Yet fear of this 'linkage' existed in the minds of Canadian policy makers, playing a critical role in the options considered and the policy adopted by Pearson. Of course, there were other forces at work as well. The PRC's unrelenting hostility to both the United States and Canada certainly inhibited the development of diplomatic relations. But the limits placed on Canadian policy were largely self-imposed.[60]

For both the United States and Canada, China policy acquired a symbolic value that outweighed the importance of any improvement in bilateral relations with the PRC. Few American officials, for example, believed the fiction that Chiang Kai-shek represented the government of China. Even fewer, however, were willing to publicly to challenge it. The Johnson administration was responding to its own set of pressures. Faced with an escalating conflict in Southeast Asia demanding even higher commitments and exacting even higher costs, Johnson and Rusk were determined to stand firm. Their commitment to Taiwan, a commitment that Chiang was adept at manipulating, served as a symbol of the administration's larger commitments in Asia – to Vietnam in particular, but also to Japan, Thailand, the Philippines, and those other Asian allies whose doubts constantly needed to be assuaged.

Canadian China policy encompassed two contradictory goals. For large segments of both the Canadian public and foreign policy community, that policy symbolized a subservience to the United States. Canada's China initiatives were undertaken despite the certain assurance that they would be rejected by Washington and both Chinese governments because they allowed Pearson to articulate a logical and defensible policy. This policy was designed in part to silence domestic critics by demonstrating an independence from the United States. Paul Martin captured something of this sentiment when he told Dean Rusk at the 1966 United Nations session that above all 'Canada must not be considered by anyone as a U.S. satellite.'[61]

Yet Canadian policy was never merely a reaction to American pressure. The policy process contained a much more important dynamic. Pearson was genuinely concerned about the threat that an isolated China posed to world peace and the integrity of the post-war collective security system embodied in the United Nations. The PRC's continued isolation limited the ability of the U.N. to deal effectively with such crucial issues as disarmament, nuclear proliferation, and the continuing crisis in Vietnam. This concern, however, was always secondary to the more urgent effort aimed at preventing an American diplomatic defeat on the issue of China – a defeat which would have had profound and disturbing implications for America's global leadership.

Pearson was convinced that the Johnson administration's unreasoning rigidity helped undermine the moral and political authority of the United States, especially in its role as linchpin of the Western alliance. Working quietly behind the scenes in Washington, New York, and other world capitals, he sought to push American policy forward, hoping this would broaden the framework within which both American and Western relations with the PRC existed. This involved a delicate and frustrating balancing of priorities that ultimately proved futile. And in this sense, at least, Pearson's China policy was not really about China at all. Like the progressive elements in the Johnson administration, he was as much concerned with preventing the isolation of the United States as he was with ending the isolation of the PRC.

Notes

1 Commencement Address at American University, 10 June 1963, *Public Papers of the Presidents: John F. Kennedy, 1963* (Washington, DC: US Government Printing Office 1964), 459–64; The President's News Conference, 1 Aug. 1963, ibid., 616. For Kennedy's views on the Truman administration's China policy, see Victor Lasky, *J.F.K.: The Man and the Myth* (New York: Macmillan 1963), 583–6.
2 Chester Ronning became the most persistent, if not the most effective proponent of this argument within DEA. See Brian Evans's essay in this volume (chapter 6), and Memorandum, Chester Ronning to USSEA, 29 Mar. 1965, DEA File 20-China-14, vol. 9, as well as 30 Mar. 1965 (in same file).
3 Press Release, 'Advance Text of Speech ... by Paul Martin,' 24 Aug. 1963, DEA file 20-China-14, vol. 1.
4 A fuller discussion of the 1958 and 1963 reviews can be found in Evans's Epilogue to ch. 2.
5 Norman A. Robertson, 'Memorandum for the Minister,' 29 Aug. 1963, DEA file 50055-B-40, vol. 15.
6 Memorandum, D/USSEA to Far Eastern Division [hereafter FE Div.], 10 Sept. 1963, DEA file 20-China-14, vol. 1.
7 Roger Hilsman, *To Move a Nation: The Politics of Foreign Policy in the Administration of John F. Kennedy* (Garden City, NY: Doubleday 1967), 344–50.
8 Roger Hilsman, 'United States Policy toward Communist China,' Department of State *Bulletin* 50 (6 January 1964), 11–17; Dulles's statement can be found in ibid. (15 July 1957), 91–5. Who actually cleared the speech remains somewhat of a mystery. See James C. Thomson Jr, 'On the Making of U.S. China Policy, 1961–9; A Study in Bureaucratic Politics,' *China Quarterly* 50 (Apr./June 1972), 230–1, and Hilsman, *To Move a Nation*, 350–7.
9 Telegram 490, Taipei to Department of State (hereafter DOS), 17 Dec. 1963, 'China Cables, vol. 1,' National Security File, Country File, China, Box 237-38, LBJ Library (hereafter NSF China with appropriate box number).
10 'Secretary Rusk Discusses the Outlook for 1964 over Japanese Television,' DOS *Bulletin* 50 (13 January 1964), 40–6; Telegrams 4160 and 4161, Washington to DEA, 18 Dec. 1963, DEA file 20-China-14, vol. 1.
11 Memorandum for the Prime Minister, 20 Jan. 1964, DEA file 20-China-14, vol. 2; see also John A. Munro and Alex I. Inglis, eds., *Mike: The Memoirs of the Right Honourable Lester B. Pearson*, vol. 3 (Toronto: University of Toronto Press 1975), 126–32.
12 Telegram 332, Washington to DEA, 27 Jan. 1964, DEA file 20-China-14, vol. 2; Telegram 268, Washington to DEA, 22 January 1964, ibid.; Telegram 440, Washington to DEA, 4 Feb. 1964, DEA file 20-China-14, vol. 3; Telegram 161,

Paris to DEA, 24 Feb. 1964, DEA file 20-China-14, vol. 3; Telegram 449, Washington to DEA, 4 Feb. 1964, DEA file 20-China-14, vol. 3.
13 Memorandum, W.W. Rostow to Dean Rusk, 17 Apr. 1964, 'China Memos vol. 1,' NSF China, Box 237-38, LBJ Library; Memorandum , R.W. Komer for the President, 16 Mar. 1964, Declassified Documents Reference System [hereafter DDRS] (77)195 A.
14 The details of various Canadian initiatives on the U.N. representation issue after 1964 are discussed in more detail in the essay by Don Page in this volume (ch. 3).
15 Memorandum, FE Div. to A/USSEA, 24 Apr. 1964, DEA file 20-China-14, vol. 4; [Memorandum], Chinese Representation – Effect of French Recognition on Developments at the United Nations, 2 Apr. 1964, DEA file 20-China-14, vol. 4.
16 No. Letter 64-171, Canadian Government Trade Commissioner – Hong Kong to DEA, 26 Aug. 1964, DEA file 20-China-14, vol. 5; see also Telegram 997, Permanent Mission of Canada to the United Nations [hereafter, PerMisNy] to DEA, 26 June 1964, DEA file 20-China-14, vol. 5.
17 Memorandum, U.N. Div. to FE Div., 10 Aug. 1964, DEA file 20-China-14, vol. 5. The U.N. Division in particular did not believe the time was ripe for Canada to introduce any resolution at the United Nations. See Memorandum, U.N. Div. to FE Div., 23 July 1964, DEA file 20-China-14, vol. 5.
18 There were a number of specific concerns: Congress was investigating the export of Canadian automotive parts as a violation of the Countervailing Duties Act; west-coast lumbermen were mounting a campaign to restrict imports of Canadian lumber; and the oil industry was challenging Canada's exemption from import quotas on oil shipped to the U.S. Memorandum, Economic Division to FE Div., 29 Sept. 1964, DEA file 20-China-14, vol. 5; see also [Memorandum], Talking Points: Communist China–Canadian Policy, 29 Sept. 1964, ibid. And see the essay by Don Page in this volume (chapter 3).
19 Telegram 3632, Washington to DEA, 15 Oct. 1964, DEA file 20-China-14, vol. 6; For the FE Division's response to these criticisms see Memorandum, FE Div. to USSEA, 20 Oct. 1964, ibid.
20 Telegram 979, Rome to DEA, 21 Nov. 1964, DEA file 20-China-14, vol. 7; Memorandum for the Minister, 30 Oct. 1964, 20-China-14, vol. 6; Telegram 1475, PerMisNy to DEA, 12 Oct. 1964, ibid.
21 Draft Memorandum for the Minister, 19 Oct. 1964, DEA file 20-China-14, vol. 6; Memorandum, SSEA to the Prime Minister, 10 Nov. 1964, DEA file 20-China-14, vol. 7.
22 Visit of Prime Minister, 7–8 Dec. 1964, Briefing Book – Background Paper,

126   Reluctant Adversaries

'FE Regional Paper,' 2 Dec. 1964, 'PX Wilson Visit Briefing Book, 12/64,' NSF UK, LBJ Library.
23 Memorandum, Harlan Cleveland for the Under-Secretary, 31 Oct. 1964 [with attachment] The Taming of the Shrew: Communist China and the United Nations, DDRS (77)218C; see also Telegrams 3516 and 3710, Washington to DEA, 2 and 22 Oct. 1964, DEA file 20-China-14, vol. 6. As early as August 1964 the Johnson administration was aware of a survey report commissioned by the Council on Foreign Relations revealing 'that the presence of the Nationalists as an alternative Chinese government was not a salient reality for most Americans.' Although this study was not released until after the American presidential election in November, Canadian officials also knew the details of this report. See Memorandum, James C. Thomson Jr to Mr Bundy, Mr Komer, 21 Aug. 1964, DDRS (78)55C.
24 Telegram Y-809, DEA to Washington, 13 Nov. 1964, DEA file 20-China-14, vol. 7; Telegram 3992, Washington to DEA, 16 November 1964, ibid.
25 Telegram Y-831, DEA to Washington, 19 Nov. 1964, DEA file 20-China-14, vol. 7; Telegram 3970, Washington to DEA, 13 Nov. 1964, ibid.
26 Memorandum, USSEA to the SSEA, 23 Nov. 1964, DEA file 20-China-14, vol. 7; see also Memorandum, FE Div. to U.N.. Div., 20 Nov. 1964, ibid.
27 Memorandum, FE Div. to A/USSEA, 19 June 1965 [with attachment] Nineteenth Session Provisional Agenda: Item 91 – The Question of Chinese Representation in the United Nations, DEA file 20-China-14, vol. 8; Telegram Y-879, DEA to Rome, 3 Dec. 1964, ibid; Telegram Y-890, DEA to PERMISS, 8 Dec. 1964, ibid.
28 Telegram TC-108, Trade and Commerce Hong Kong to Trade and Commerce Ottawa, 29 Apr. 1965, DEA file 20-China-14, vol. 9.
29 Memorandum, [A/USSEA] to USSEA, 3 June 1965, DEA file 20-China-14, vol. 9.
30 For a detailed account of PRC subversion in Africa and developments affecting the Second Afro-Asian Conference see United States Information Agency, Research and Reference Service Reports R-160-65 and R-165-65, 16 Nov. 1965, 'Office Files of Bill Moyers: Red China,' Office Files of Bill Moyers, Box 82 (1392), LBJ Library, and CIA Office of Current Intelligence Memorandum, OCI No. 1804/65, 10 May 1965, DDRS (77)1B.
31 United States Information Agency, Text: Ambassador Goldberg's Remarks on Chinese Representation in the U.N.., DEA file 20-China-14, vol. 10; for a transcript of Chen Yi's press conference see *Peking Review* 41 (8 Oct. 1965), 13–15.
32 Telegram Y-778, DEA to PerMisNy, 1 Nov. 1965, DEA file 20-China-14, vol. 10; see also Memorandum, A/USSEA to the USSEA, 28 Oct. 1965, ibid., and Telegram Y-685, DEA to Rome and Brussels, 16 Sept. 1965, ibid.

33 Press Release, Statement by the Honourable Paul Martin, 17 Nov. 1965, DEA file 20-China-14, vol. 10.
34 Memorandum, Arthur J. Goldberg to Lyndon B. Johnson, 22 Dec. 1965, 'IT 47-8 General Assembly,' WHCF Confidential File, IS 1-47-9, Box 58, LBJ Library.
35 George C. Herring, ed., *The Secret Diplomacy of the Vietnam War: The Negotiating Volumes of the Pentagon Papers* (Austin: University of Texas Press 1983), 173–4, and for a discussion of the Ronning mission see pages 163–207 passim as well as the essay in this volume by Brian Evans (ch. 6).
36 Memorandum, FE Div. to the USSEA, 15 Feb. 1966, DEA file 20-China-14, vol. 11; Memorandum for File, 21 Feb. 1966, ibid.
37 Statement of A. Doak Barnett, *U.S. Policy with Respect to Mainland China*, Hearings before the Committee on Foreign Relations, United States Senate, 89th Cong, 2nd Sess, 3–16; Rusk's statement can be found in Department of State *Bulletin* 55 (2 May 1966), 684–95.
38 No. Letter 648, Washington to DEA, 4 May 1966, DEA file 20-China-14, vol. 11; Telegram Y-210, DEA to Washington and PerMisNy, 3 Mar. 1966, ibid.; Telegram 782, Washington to DEA, 18 Mar. 1966, ibid.
39 CIA, Intelligence Memorandum No. 0820/66, 17 May 1966, 'China Memos vol. 6,' NSF China, Box 240, LBJ Library; see also Memorandum, William P. Bundy to the Secretary, 14 Mar. 1966, 'China Cables, vol. 6,' ibid., and for the official Kuomintang reaction to Rusk's testimony and the American response: Telegram 1290, Taipei to DOS, 17 May 1966, DDRS (83)2446 and Telegram 1286, DOS to Taipei, 7 June 1966, DDRS (83)2453.
40 Memorandum, Dean Rusk to Lyndon Johnson, 14 May 1966, quoted in *Department of State Administrative History*, Chapter X – The United Nations, Part B, Institutional and Financial Problems, Section 5. The Question of Chinese Communist Representation: 19, LBJ Library and see pages 13–20 passim.
41 Transcript, William P. Bundy Oral History Interview, 26 May 1969, Lyndon B. Johnson Library, Tape 1, 21–4; Peter Stursberg, *Lester Pearson and the American Dilemma* (Garden City, NY: Doubleday 1980), 282–5.
42 Memorandum, SSEA for the Prime Minister, 28 June 1966, DEA file 29-China-14, vol. 12; see also ibid., 21 July 1966; Memorandum, FE Div. to A/USSEA, 5 July 1966, ibid.
43 Lyndon Baines Johnson, 'Four Essentials for Peace,' Department of State *Bulletin* 55 (1 Aug. 1966), 158–62.
44 Memorandum, James C. Thomson Jr to Walter Jenkins, 25 July 1966, DDRS (79)413A.
45 *Department of State Administrative History*, Chapter X, 19–24; see also Telegram,

128   Reluctant Adversaries

McConaughy to DOS, 1 July 1966, 'China Cables, vol. 6,' NSF China, Box 239, LBJ Library.
46 DOS *Administrative History*, Chapter X, 28.
47 Extracts of Telegram 2181 of Jul 26/66, DEA file 20-China-14, vol. 12; Stursberg, *Lester Pearson and the American Dilemma*, 282–3.
48 Memorandum, FE Div. to the USSEA, 7 Oct. 1966, DEA file 20-China-14, vol. 14; Chinese Representation: Notes on Three Possible Courses of Action, 20 Oct. 1966, ibid.; Memorandum, USSEA for the SSEA, 24 Oct. 1966, ibid.
49 Quoted in Stursberg, *Lester Pearson and the American Dilemma*, 283–4; see also Telegram Y-754, DEA to Washington, 3 Nov. 1966, DEA file 20-China-14, vol. 15.
50 Quoted in Paul Martin, *A Very Public Life*, vol. II, *So Many Worlds* (Toronto: Deneau Publishers 1985), 521–2; see also Memorandum, SSEA to the Prime Minister, 4 Nov. 1966, DEA file 20-China-14, vol. 15; Telegram 3361, Washington to DEA, 7 Nov. 1966, ibid.; Telegram 2010, Moscow to DEA, 11 Nov. 1966, ibid.; Letter, Lester Pearson to W. Walton Butterworth, 11 Nov. 1966, ibid.
51 Airgram A-518, Taipei to DOS, 21 Jan. 1967, DDRS(79)70D; see also DOS *Administrative History*, Chapter X, 33–5.
52 Telegram 3394, Washington to DEA, 9 Nov. 1966, DEA file 20-China-14, vol. 15; Telegrams 3390 and 3391, Washington to DEA, 8 Nov. 1966, ibid.
53 Telegram 2482, Canadian Delegation, New York [hereafter CanDelNy] to DEA, 10 Nov. 1966, DEA file 20-China-14, vol. 15; Telegram 486, Wellington to DEA, 7 Nov. 1966, ibid., Telegram 785, Brussels to DEA, 8 Nov. 1966, ibid.; Telegram 494, Wellington to DEA, 10 Nov. 1966, ibid.; Telegram 2473, CanDelNy to DEA, 10 Nov. 1966, ibid.
54 Telegram 2374, White House Situation Room to the President, 26 Nov. 1966, 'China Cables, vol. 8' NSF China, Box 240, LBJ Library. For an example of the type of pressure exerted by the United States on wavering delegations see Message from Ambassador Ralph Dungan in Santiago, Chile, 29 Sept. 1966, 'China Memos, vol. 7,' NSF China, Box 240, LBJ Library.
55 Martin, *So Many Worlds*, 523–6; author's interview with Pamela McDougall, 31 Oct. 1985; for Trudeau's role at the U.N. see also Peter Dobell, *Canada's Search for New Roles* (Toronto: Oxford University Press 1972), 10–12.
56 Memorandum, USSEA to the Prime Minister, 29 Nov. 1966, DEA file 20-China-14, vol. 16; Telegram 2910, CanDelNy to DEA, 29 Nov. 1966, ibid.
57 Martin, *So Many Worlds*, 526–7; Memorandum, USSEA to the Minister, 9 Dec. 1966 [with attachment] Memorandum: Canadian Recognition of the People's Republic of China, 9 Dec. 1966, DEA file 20-China-14, vol. 17; see also Letter, Pamela McDougall to Arthur Menzies, 29 Dec. 1966, ibid.
58 John W. Holmes, 'Canada and China: The Dilemmas of a Middle Power,' in

A.M. Halpern, ed., *Policies toward China: Views from Six Continents* (New York: McGraw-Hill 1965), 118.
59 [Lester B. Pearson Interview], 'Men and the Issues', 3 Nov. 1965, CBC TV and Radio, DEA file 20-China-14, vol. 10; see also his interview in the *United Church Observer*, 15 Apr. 1968. This was almost identical to the assessment he made three years earlier. See the quote in the essay by Don Page in this volume (ch. 3) n. 58.
60 Richard Gwyn, *The 49th Paradox: Canada in North America* (Toronto: McClelland and Stewart 1985), 103–6.
61 Martin, *So Many Worlds*, 525.

SECTION III

The Policy Makers

CHAPTER FIVE

John English

Lester Pearson and China

China bothered Canadian Methodists. To a church that at the dawn of the twentieth century still bore the enthusiasm of its founders, but that was shifting its energies from the salvation of the individual soul to the regeneration of a corrupted society, China presented the greatest missionary challenge. One of the most prominent Canadian Methodists, Newton Wesley Rowell, asked in 1907 how the foreign mission effort should be assessed. 'The least result,' Rowell argued, 'is the number of converts added to the church. The larger and more important results are the great changes wrought in the whole social and intellectual life and character of the people.' Nowhere was it more important that the universal dominion of the Lord be established than in China 'where more than one-fourth of the human race is awakening from the sleep of ages.' In the imperialist fashion of the day, Rowell cited the judgment of Sir Robert Hart, inspector general of the Chinese customs service, that 'China is today the greatest menace to the world's peace unless she is Christianized.' Canada, Rowell calculated, should be responsible for the uplift of no less than forty million Chinese.[1]

Lester Pearson's early life as a child of a Methodist manse must have made him very familiar with the missionary mind as it was being applied to the Chinese challenge. As a boy of nine in 1906, Pearson saw a freshly ordained cousin proceed, much honoured, to the exotic mission field of Ren-Shou in Szechuan province.[2] The tales of the China missions spun out by the returned missionary or through missionary letters broke through the monotony of the Methodist Sunday in southwestern Ontario. They at least had some of the flavour of the Henry and Kipling which the young imperialist so adored.[3] Pearson's contact with China endured after his return from the war and Oxford. At Victoria College, where he served his brief academic career in the mid-1920s, Pearson saw bright young students such as James Endicott as well as a young woman who had caught his eye, Mary Austin, go off to West China just as his cousin had two decades before. The missionary was still much honoured in the 1920s. When Victoria bestowed an honorary degree upon his father in 1927, two missionaries, Rev Charles Carscallen of Szechuan and Rev William Cragg of Kobe, were similarly honoured.[4] And 'China' was a compulsory subject for all those who were truly serious. In his first published work, a light-hearted look at Canada's growing fascination with sports (one which Pearson certainly shared), Pearson jocularly deplored a situation where 'Millions who have never heard of the nationalist movement in China hang on to the last sentences of a Mr. "Swede Risberg"' (a figure in the Chicago Black Sox scandal).[5]

And yet one suspects Lester Pearson was hanging on to the last sentences of Swede Risberg more tightly than on to the news from China. Although it is tempting to expatiate upon the Methodist influence on Pearson, it would be misleading. China continued to touch upon Lester Pearson's life long after he left the Methodist confines, but like so many of the Methodist enthusiasms, the fascination, not to say obsession, with China was one toward which Pearson cast a wary glance. From his earliest university days, Pearson had kept his distance from the theological debates which pervaded Victoria College and which so disturbed his relative and Victoria's chancellor R.P.Bowles. 'China' and what it meant was often central to these debates in which he declined to join, not because of intellectual incapacity but rather because of an aversion to the immoderation which marked them. 'China' was a theological question in his early years, subject to the gusts of fierce extremes. Later he would not be surprised that it remained so in his later years when new religions were political, and the partisans ranged from the Endicotts, on the one side, to the Dulleses, on the other. He shared the religious background of both, but the passion had left him.

China, thus, never troubled Pearson in the sense that it did Newton Rowell, John Foster Dulles, or James Endicott. Yet it did concern him. Pearson's diplomatic education came in the 1930s, and it was marked by futile disarmament conferences, broken promises, ranting dictators, and international instability. He received his education in Europe and believed that Europe remained the most significant actor in the world system. When its threads became untied, world-wide discord followed, as it had done since the seventeenth century when European world hegemony had been established.[6] By the 1930s, the pillars which had supported European hegemony were atrophying. Unlike some others, Pearson welcomed this process, not least as it occurred with China. He may have cast aside much Methodist baggage in his later years, but he remained convinced, as he put it much earlier, that 'a beneficent government and a good educational system [would] regenerate' a 'backward' people.[7] The problem was the establishment of that government and education as Europe's enforcement of order in distant continents became more difficult.

With China Pearson had some hopes in early 1930, but the Japanese abruptly punctured these with their attack. Pearson's sympathies, unlike those of some other Canadian diplomats, were fully with the Chinese. The Japanese not only threatened the collective system he had come to believe was the essential replacement for European hegemony but also drastically affected China's chances for the development of a 'beneficent government.' Here again lay a Methodist residue: China's salvation seemed possible not through Christianity but through democracy and education. Nevertheless, Pearson granted that indigenous definitions of what those concepts were appeared satisfactory in the case of China with its proud past. In 1936, when Pearson and the members of the naval conference toured a Chinese art exhibition in London, he wrote in his diary: 'I hope it made the Jap soldiers feel sufficiently humble.'[8]

China, then, was not at the centre of Pearson's diplomacy. Nor did China ever seem the greatest opportunity for a religious or social experiment: it warranted special attention in the 1930s because its instability threatened the collective system which Pearson believed was essential to world order. Japan, nevertheless, was the major culprit in East Asia, and it was the Japanese who attracted Pearson's strongest condemnation. Their refusal to negotiate was simply intolerable, a deep wound to the process of building the essential collective system.

Pearson approached China with a Eurocentric vision, but one whose perspective derived from the belief that it was Europe which remained the greatest threat to global order. This was the perceptual lens through which Pearson viewed the dramatic events of the 1940s in East Asia. In August 1942, for example, Pearson attended his first meeting of the Pacific Council at the White House along with British, Dutch, Australian, and New Zealand representatives and Dr T.V. Soong. He reported to Ottawa that 'I am afraid that I was as much interested in the appearance and personality of the President as I was in the discussions themselves ...' There was no mention of the substance of the discussions.[9] By 1945, however, Pearson, now ambassador to the United States, was showing considerably more interest in East Asia than he had earlier. This no doubt partly derived from his Washington vantage point from which events in the Pacific loomed large. He also became Canada's representative on the Far Eastern Commission, although he rarely attended meetings and passed the responsibility to Herbert Norman in 1946. He recognized that passions and biases were already deeply affecting American judgment on Asian affairs, and he followed with genuine interest the differences of views between the pro-Chiang Victor Odlum, and the pro-Communists Chester Ronning and James Endicott about what should and would occur in China after the Japanese defeat. One gathers that Pearson shared more of Endicott's and Ronning's hopes than he did Odlum's doubts.[10] Nevertheless, the three, unlike Pearson, were *parti pris* as were so many of the Americans Pearson encountered in Washington.

Pearson returned to Ottawa in 1946 deeply concerned about East Asia in two respects. First, he saw that a peace settlement which would bring stability to the area was unlikely to happen quickly. Second, he feared the intensity with which the Americans took sides about the Chinese civil war. Within the Canadian government, DEA had lost a cabinet battle to C.D. Howe who emphasized long-term economic advantage in granting a sixty million dollar Mutual Aid credit for China in 1946.[11] When Howe tried to push further to sell off wartime surplus to China, Pearson, strongly supported by Escott Reid and Arthur Menzies, opposed the plans. Despite strong opposition, Howe got his way and Canadian planes arrived in China to assist a collapsing Kuomintang.[12]

The story of Canada's hesitant steps toward non-recognition of China and Pearson's part therein are dealt with elsewhere.[13] By the late fall of 1950, Canada and China were at war, and recognition was, in Pearson's view, impossible until hostilities ceased. Pearson the politician recognized that his role was to convince Canadians that the war was worth fighting. As a result his rhetoric did not reflect the more measured analyses of East Asia's future that one found in DEA. In public addresses, Pearson excoriated Chinese communism which, he declared, must never be allowed to 'shoot its way' into the United Nations.[14] The Communists had brought a totalitarianism which Pearson despised. Privately, however, he fretted about the consequences of American obsessions about China and shared the fear of his External Affairs advisers that the Americans were too provocative towards China. Not even publicly would he commit Canada to the American policy of containing China and of linking too casually the Korean effort with the interests of the Nationalists on Taiwan.[15] In the American refusal to compromise, he saw elements of the same arrogance that he had condemned earlier in the case of Japan. Writing in March 1950 to Dean Acheson's close friend and Canada's ambassador to the United

States, Hume Wrong, Pearson summarized his fears about Acheson's latest statement on East Asia. Acheson, Pearson suggested,

> took a step of major consequence to us all when he drew or seemed to draw the line of western defence firmly across the southern borders of China and hinted that some kind of Pacific Association should be formed for the purpose of holding this line. Is he really thinking in terms of a Pacific Pact? ... I for one have very grave doubts whether at the moment an alliance or grouping of this nature would be practicable, and I have even greater doubts about the willingness of the Canadian people to participate in such an alliance ... and I would need a lot of convincing that we were not simply being asked to repeat in South East Asia, through an international instrument, policies which the United States had followed with such unhappy consequences in China; and which are not working out too well in Korea.[16]

There would be many American 'experiments' in the Pacific in the remainder of Pearson's public life and, for better or worse, Canada felt their results.

For Pearson, the settlement in Korea should have been part of a broader Asian solution, one which would involve the participation of China.[17] For Canada Pearson made it clear that recognition was merely postponed, not put off indefinitely as the Americans had done. He emphasized this to Dean Rusk in March 1950, but Rusk equally firmly disagreed, arguing that halting the recognition of the PRC and its representation at the United Nations were essential 'for encouraging the anti-Communist forces on which [American] policy depends.'[18] Despite Pearson's views, participation in the Korean War acted to limit Canada's options. As Denis Stairs has shown, 'the identification of Canada with the American-dominated "sub-system," which was apparent much earlier, became as a result of the Korean experience much more fully entrenched. The external setting of Canadian foreign policy grew more narrowly defined and more tightly bound.'[19] In the case of China, the binding felt especially tight because American public opinion had hardened considerably.

The end of the Korean War and the death of Stalin in 1953 reopened the question of China in the minds of Pearson and his prime minister, Louis St Laurent. St Laurent had earlier been cautious when the cabinet considered the recognition of China, but subsequent events and the influence of Pearson and of Nehru, with whom his relationship was good, made him more aware of the dangers of Chinese isolation. Both St Laurent and Pearson, upon whom he relied more than ever, feared that the United States was unnecessarily provocative in its China policy. In an article published in 1953 which Douglas Ross claims was 'a minor landmark' in Canadian Indochina policy, Pearson responded to Dulles's Asian policy by warning that 'Our policy in Asia must be more than a policy of mere opposition to Communism. It must be constructive.' St Laurent in his Asian tour a few weeks later tried to be constructive by pointing out that Canada could not refuse recognition of Peking indefinitely. A strong reaction, especially from the Roman Catholic church, forced St Laurent to moderate his public statement, but he did not change his view. The same was true of Pearson when he connived with the Australian foreign minister, R.G. Casey, to test the limits, but he found that the Americans would regard Canadian recognition of the PRC as offensive.[20]

The price, loss of influence in Washington, was too high, especially when the offshore islands question seemed dangerous. As Pearson told Molotov in Moscow in October 1955, Canada did not agree with 'all of US policy on China ...' but it was 'not going to get into any unnecessary difficulties with our American friends over this problem.'[21] In Pearson's view China was not central to Canadian interests. Nor was a moral stand worth taking if its political and economic price was high, especially if it destabilized institutions of central interest to Canada such as NATO and even the United Nations. Moreover, Canadian opinion was divided, and probably most of those who felt strongly opposed recognition.[22] Finally, there was the problem of what to do with Taiwan. Upon these obstacles Canada's initiative faltered.

In January 1956 Pearson and his opposition critic John Diefenbaker both condemned mainland China. But in Pearson's view diplomatic recognition was separate from the question of the 'cruelties and tyrannies of the Peking regime.' Perhaps in the future this yoke of oppression would be lifted and, Pearson predicted, China and the Soviet Union might clash. Diefenbaker was harsher. Speaking for the Conservative party he declared that 'so long as communist China remains an undisciplined bankrupt in the field of diplomacy and in the field of aggression, so long can there be no justification for the legal recognition of that country.'[23]

Diefenbaker, of course, did not recognize the PRC but during his tenure as prime minister, Canada-China relations thawed considerably and public support for recognition grew. Pearson as opposition leader moved left, calling in 1959 for Canada to work with other governments which had not recognized the PRC to break the impasse.[24] Although Pearson held back from advocating recognition, his leading adviser Walter Gordon, who had toured mainland China for a month in 1959, strongly urged that Canada recognize the PRC whatever impact such an action might have upon the Americans.[25]

The Liberals won the 1963 election, and Walter Gordon became finance minister in the new government. Paul Martin, the new secretary of state for external affairs, had not favoured recognition in the 1950s, but he was a leading advocate of universality within the United Nations. In August 1963 Martin publicly asked whether it was in the interests of Canada and its allies to have China isolated now that Moscow and Peking were openly bickering. Martin, who hoped to succeed Pearson as Liberal leader, knew that his prime minister had accomplished much and won acclaim through his diplomatic initiatives in the 1950s at the United Nations. He understandably wanted to follow the path Pearson had trod towards leadership. But the situation was different. As prime minister Pearson was much more cautious in his willingness to undertake bold initiatives in foreign policy. Moreover, Pearson's eminence in diplomacy made him hesitant to become involved in such initiatives. Martin did not have the advantage Pearson had in St Laurent, nor was his department the self-confident department it had been in its so-called golden age.[26]

By the time Pearson returned to office in 1963, the United States was becoming entrapped in another Asian war which would bedevil Pearson's and Martin's attempts to clarify the Sino-Canadian relationship. Dean Rusk was now secretary of state, and his opposition to increased Western links with the PRC remained as adamant as it had been when Pearson dealt with him in 1950. After conversations with Rusk in 1963 and 1964, Pearson and Martin concluded that expansion of Canadian-PRC bilateral relations through recognition would offend the Americans deeply. While Martin and Pearson welcomed French recognition of China, Rusk deplored it and sought Canada's assistance in minimizing its effects.[27] Whatever benefits Canada might derive in the areas of trade and information, these would be greatly outweighed by the impact such an action would have upon Canada's major ally and trading partner. Recognition, then, was not considered, yet China policy remained a test for Canadians of the independence of Canadian foreign policy, and for Martin and Pearson, a political problem that would not disappear.

DEA accordingly began to work on a declaratory resolution which would express a belief that Taiwan and the PRC should both be members of the United Nations. Canadian officials simultaneously began to prepare other countries, including the Republic of China (ROC), for their change of stance. This preparation began with a warning that PRC representation was inevitable, perhaps a year or two away. It would be better to present a compromise now which, however unsatisfactory, at least offered some consolation to the ROC on Taiwan and its allies. Canada had no intention of promoting this so-called two-Chinas compromise unless the compromise found reasonably widespread support among U.N. members. In 1964 and early 1965 such support was not found and, with the United States, opposition soon appeared.[28]

Canada's ambassador to the United States Charles Ritchie pointed out to Dean Rusk in the winter of 1965 that the PRC owed nothing to anyone and that Chinese interference in the Vietnam War might be reduced if recognition or U.N. admission were used as a bargaining tool by the West. Isolation of the PRC had achieved nothing; it had only resulted in the loss of Third World support and political difficulties for many of America's allies. Rusk was not convinced, and he reiterated his view that recognition of any kind meant reward.[29] In 1966, the American attitude became even firmer, partly because of the disruptions of the Cultural Revolution and partly because of American determination to seek a military improvement in Vietnam before any negotiations in which the PRC might prove useful. The rapid change in East Asian politics in 1965 and 1966 – the intensification of the Vietnam War, the fall of Sukarno in Indonesia, and the beginning of the Cultural Revolution – also confused the Canadians, and their hesitation became apparent to the public as well as to their allies.

Faced with decreasing domestic support for America's Asian policy but even more afraid of Johnson's reaction to any Canadian initiative, Pearson and Martin were puzzled where to lead. They sought guidance, dropping strong hints that Canada was reconsidering its own policy toward PRC admission to the United Nations. They suspected that Pearson saw advantages in declaring this publicly. Yet when the U.N. general assembly opened in the fall, no new path was taken. In his address on 24 September 1965 Martin merely spoke in general terms about the need for 'universality of membership.' In the debate on Chinese representation, the Canadian delegation remained silent. In its voting the delegation followed past practice: it voted with the Americans in declaring Chinese representation 'an important question' – hence requiring a two-thirds majority – and it voted against the 'restoration of the lawful rights of the People's Republic of China.'[30]

Pearson was particularly disturbed by the demand that Taiwan be excluded. Pearson at this time was perplexed by domestic problems and particularly wary of external initiatives. No longer was the U.N. forum so congenial for him, and his mood was more querulous than ever before. Others, especially some new Liberal MPS, were not so pessimistic: they believed that concern about Taiwan should not continue to bar the PRC from world councils. After the Martin statement was issued, cabinet considered whether in fact the right course had been followed at the United Nations. Just before Christmas 1965 the cabinet decided that the notion of a declaratory resolution should be dropped until attitudes in Washington and Peking changed. The wait was not to be a long one.

In February 1966 Paul Martin met Dean Rusk and, to his surprise, found him more flexible on PRC admission than ever before. The Taiwan-PRC proposal that had not been made in 1965 'interested' Rusk, who promised to speak to Martin about it again when William Bundy returned from discussions with the Taiwanese about their future. Martin, encouraged by Rusk's attitude, asked his department to consider changing Canada's China policy in 1966. At the same time, William Bundy and Joseph Sisco, who were convinced that PRC representation in the United Nations was inevitable, sent a joint recommendation to the secretary of state urging that a means be found 'to cushion the shock' of admission. The Canadians, it was thought, should be encouraged to introduce a compromise resolution along the lines of their earlier proposal of a Taiwan-China declaratory resolution. On 16 May Arthur Goldberg, with President Johnson's permission, suggested this course to Pearson who agreed it should be followed.[31]

There is some indication that this new American flexibility derived from a suspicion of Canadian motives and from a strategy designed to prevent wide divergence between Canadian and American policy. In January 1966 Martin proposed that Chester Ronning, a retired Canadian diplomat sympathetic to the Chinese revolution, should visit Hanoi and Peking to discover what might bring peace in Vietnam. The United States approved of this mission because, in the words of the Pentagon Papers, 'there seemed no proper response other than encouragement.' Privately, there was much dissatisfaction with Canadians' 'meddling.' American Ambassador to Canada W.W. Butterworth reported to Washington that 'ever since he became Minister for External Affairs two and a half years ago Martin has had the idea of using Chester Ronning, who was born in China and went to school with Chou En-lai, to help bring about recognition of the Chinese Communists by the UN or by Canada or both.'[32] Furthermore, Butterworth claimed that Pearson shared some of the American doubts: 'Pearson confirmed that the Ronning mission was Martin's idea, that it entailed greater dangers than Martin had perhaps appreciated and that he had "scared the hell out of Paul about it last night."' This evidence of division between the prime minister and his foreign minister may have led to a warning Rusk issued to Martin on 4 February. Rusk said that he was 'seriously concerned at the possibility that Ronning may find himself engaged in discussion, especially in Peiping, of the problems relating to

Chinese representation at the UN and even, if I understand your last conversation with Walton Butterworth correctly, questions of recognition.' Rusk continued, 'I think we shall both have a great deal of thinking to do on this subject in the months ahead and I hope that in the first instance we can do it on a very confidential basis between ourselves. I have therefore welcomed the indication that you are not discussing the Ronning trip with any other government, and I would end by repeating my hope and assumption that he will be listening *only* [in Peking] as to matters other than Vietnam.' In any case, Rusk's hopes and assumptions were untested, for in late February Peking refused Ronning's visit, citing the Canadian government's support for the United States as the reason for the rejection.[33]

Martin and Pearson had begun to share doubts about Canada's course not long after Goldberg had left them in May. The declaratory Taiwan-China resolution seemed a fruitless venture which would only offend Taiwan and the PRC. It might also lead to suspicion of its sponsor's motives. Something more direct was appropriate. The failure of the Ronning visits to Hanoi in March and June and the U.S. refusal to limit bombing of North Vietnam during and after the visit had angered and frustrated Martin. It is, perhaps, not surprising that Martin went further than first intended and recommended that Canada should abstain on the so-called Albanian resolution that called for the restoration of 'China's legal rights.' But what should Canada do on the 'important question' vote? Surely Chinese representation remained an important question, and Canada would declare its belief through its vote. And yet if Chinese representation was deemed an important question, it would require a two-thirds majority, and this would not occur. Pearson was troubled by the apparent contradictions in the recommended Canadian stand. How, he asked, could Canada state that it hoped to keep Taiwan in the United Nations when its action on the Albanian resolution tacitly accepted the ROC's expulsion? He also wondered whether the Americans should be told or whether Canada should keep its silence until the eve of the vote.

In fact the Americans themselves had been silent since the Goldberg visit in May. There was some indication in its rhetoric that administration attitudes toward Peking were hardening. Although there were many in the State Department and the administration who still favoured an 'opening' to the PRC, the president and the secretary of state were sceptical.[34] Pearson, having noticed the 'hard line' rhetoric, told Johnson at their Campobello meeting on 21 August 1966 that Canada might have to consider a change in its position on Chinese representation at the United Nations. This test of Johnson's reaction produced no outburst. Indeed Johnson recognized an advantage in having Peking in the U.N., although he questioned whether the

PRC would accept U.N. membership if it were available. Both leaders agreed to consider the problem and to consult in the future.

Pearson told Johnson that Canada had not decided what it would do at the United Nations in the fall. This was technically true, but in fact Martin and Pearson had already agreed that some new action must be taken. After the Johnson-Pearson meeting, Martin at the Banff Conference on World Affairs seemed to signal a new China policy. 'We consider,' Martin declared, 'that the isolation of Communist China from a large part of normal international relations is dangerous.' Canada was now 'prepared to accept the reality of the victory in mainland China in 1949.' Taiwan remained a problem, and the 'two-Chinas' solution was impossible so long as both Taiwan and mainland China denounced it. And yet, under questioning, Martin admitted that Canada had taken an initiative on the problem in the fall of 1965. The 'matter' remained 'very much on our minds.'[35]

It was also on Dean Rusk's mind, and he continued to be disturbed by the direction Canada appeared to be moving. Thus, during a September meeting he warned Martin that the PRC's international behaviour and its internal turmoil made admission and recognition impossible. Martin pointed to domestic pressure in Canada and within the Liberal party and argued that mainland Chinese exclusion from international councils could only prolong the bloodshed in Vietnam. Rusk curtly replied: 'Let me be rude. If Canada had troops in Vietnam, I would be more sympathetic to your dilemma. But the fact is that Canada has no risks to bear in the situation.' The United States no longer wanted even the third-party initiative that they themselves had suggested to the Canadians in March. Circumstances had changed; even the Soviets did not want what they saw as those unpredictable, possibly maniacal, Chinese Communists in United Nations. If Canada sponsored an initiative, the United States would tell its allies – and Canada's allies – that they opposed it.[36]

What followed need not be traced in detail here. Despite Rusk's warning, Martin proceeded with his plan to introduce a one-China, one-Taiwan resolution. Rusk objected strenuously to Pearson and promised active opposition to Canada's efforts. International support soon evaporated. Nevertheless, domestic support for Martin's initiative was significant, although not from John Diefenbaker who declared that China should not gain U.N. admission until it turned 'its back upon its past to repudiate its wrongdoing and tyranny.' Pearson defended Martin's initiative and warned that Canada would consider bilateral recognition if the 'log-jam' remained solid.[37] Pearson, however, was still unwilling to expel Taiwan. Once again the Canadian delegation at the United Nations was instructed to vote against the Albanian resolution which would give the seat to Peking and expel Taipei. Martin disagreed with these instructions as did Pierre Trudeau who was also in New York with the delegation. Pearson relented and Canada abstained on the Albanian vote. The American reaction was surprisingly muted.

On 15 August 1967 Pearson indicated that 'the situation in China at the moment is such as to make it very undesirable to revert to those proposals [of 1966] at this time.'[38] There was some expression of disagreement, but the Cultural Revolution had broken the momentum. Canada once again abstained on the annual Albanian resolution and offered the same explanation as in 1966. This time scarcely anyone noticed.[39] Canadian recognition plans gathered dust until the Cultural Revolution slowed, and by that time the Pearson government had also come to an end.

In the 1960s, Pearson's approach was marked by caution. He acted as a restraint upon Martin's initiatives even though he fully shared Martin's concern that the PRC's isolation should end. For Pearson and, in his view, for Canada, the China question had moved from the periphery but not to the centre. Damaging Canada's already weakened influence with the United States was too high a price. Moreover, if the United States withdrew its support from the United Nations as a result of PRC admission, the price would be paid world-wide.

Finally, Pearson shied away from China because he distrusted the emotionalism which suffused all debate upon the subject. Those who most vigorously participated in these debates too often ignored what for him was the central implication of the contemporary international relations: in the words of Denis Stairs, the understanding that 'in a world of endless diversities and perpetual disagreements, the only principle of political action which in the end is consistent with the pursuit of self-interest is the principle of give and take.'[40] In the mid-1960s the principle was honoured neither in Washington nor in Peking. It was a time that made a diplomat who loathed extremes especially uncomfortable – and sad. Many years earlier, Mary Austin Endicott sent Pearson a copy of her pamphlet *My Journey for Peace* with a letter which asked for his support. 'Mike,' she wrote, 'I don't want ever to stand by a grave in a foreign land and know that it contains the bones of your son or of mine and that we did not shed our last drop of blood and sweat to save them.' 'History' she warned Pearson was not on Washington's side. He should join her 'on the side of people who want a better life.' Pearson, in declining to join her side, replied: 'It is not very comfortable to be in the middle these days.'[41] But it was the place which he chose and where he remained. He could do no other. For China, this meant he stayed on the outside.

Notes

1 N.W. Rowell, 'Foreign Missions: Our Privilege and Responsibility,' an address at Parkdale (Toronto) Methodist Church, quoted in Margaret Prang, *N.W. Rowell, Ontario Nationalist* (Toronto: University of Toronto Press 1975), 65–6. Rowell was, in that year, made a founding governor of West China Union University which became the focus of Methodist–United Church missionary activities.
2 The cousin was Newton Ernest Bowles (see H.J. Morgan, *Canadian Men and Women of the Time* [Toronto: William Briggs 1912], 128).
3 On the 'missionary mind' and the influence of the missionary upon public opinion, a recent study of the American situation is useful (see James E. Reed, *The Missionary Mind and American East Asia Policy* [Cambridge, Mass.: Harvard 1983]; also Peter Mitchell, ch. 1 in this volume).
4 J.C. Hopkins, *The Canadian Annual Review for 1926–1927* (Toronto: University of Toronto Press 1927), 322.
5 L.B. Pearson, 'The Game's the Thing,' *Words and Occasions* (Toronto: University of Toronto Press 1970), 3.
6 This attitude, of course, pre-dated the 1930s as one can see in Pearson's extant lecture notes for the mid-1920s (see Pearson Papers, MG 26 N8, vol. 2).
7 He wrote this in respect to some Macedonian villagers he encountered during the first World War (Pearson Diary, Pearson Papers, MG 26 N8, vol. 2).
8 Ibid., 13 Jan. 1936 (MG 26 N8, vol. 2, Diary 1936–41). He respected the exhibition but was not charmed. 'I fear I was not in an "arty" mood, as I had dined most successfully at the Services Club. Hence, I insisted on treating the priceless Mings, Changs and Tons [sic] with unseemly indifference and at times most unbecoming frivolity.'
9 Pearson to Norman Robertson, 12 Aug. 1942 (Pearson Papers, MG 26 J1, vol. 331.
10 See Pearson to James Endicott, 21 Nov. 1946 (DEA, file 11578-B-40); also Kim Nossal, 'Business as Usual: Canadian Relations with China in the 1940's,' (Canadian Historical Association Papers 1978), 139–47, and Stephen Endicott, *James G. Endicott: Rebel Out of China* (Toronto: University of Toronto Press 1980), 217–18.
11 See Nossal, 'Business as Usual,' and J.W. Pickersgill and D.F. Forster, *The Mackenzie King Record*, vol. 3 (Toronto: University of Toronto Press 1970), 160.
12 DEA, file 11044-B5-40.
13 See the discussions in the essays by Beecroft, Evans, St Amour, and Page in this volume; see as well Chester Ronning, *A Memoir of China in Revolution* (New York: Pantheon Books 1974), ch. 12.

14 Standing Committee on External Affairs and Defence, 21 Mar. 1952, 21–6, 663; see also W.E.C. Harrison, *Canada in World Affairs 1949 to 1950* (Toronto: Oxford University Press 1975), 164–8, 302–3.
15 House of Commons, *Debates*, 31 Aug. 1950, p. 94, and 2 Feb. 1951. On his private concerns, see, for example, Pearson to R.G. Casey, 29 June 1951 (Pearson Papers, MG 26 N1, vol. 2).
16 Pearson to Wrong, 24 Mar. 1950 (Pearson Papers, MG Z6 N1, vol. 1).
17 L.B. Pearson, *Mike: The Memoirs of the Right Honourable Lester B. Pearson*, vol. 2 (Toronto: University of Toronto Press 1973), 168.
18 Pearson to St Laurent, 17 Apr. 1950 (St Laurent Papers, MG 26 L. vol. 174. Ralphe Bunche and Andrew Cordier, however, were much more sympathetic to the Canadian view.
19 Denis Stairs, *The Diplomacy of Constraint: Canada, the Korean War, and the United States* (Toronto: University of Toronto Press 1974), 332–3.
20 See Beecroft, ch. 2 in this volume; also L.B. Pearson, 'Don't Let Asian Split the West' *Statements and Speeches* 53/50 and Douglas A. Ross, *In the Interests of Peace: Canada and Vietnam 1954–1973* (Toronto: University of Toronto Press 1984), 55ff. Pearson to Casey, 15 June 1955 (Pearson Papers MG 26 N1, vol. 20). The public trial balloon was launched by Pearson in August 1955 (DEA, *Statements and Speeches*, 55/30 D).
21 Pearson, *Mike*, vol. 2, 195.
22 Standing Committee on External Affairs and Defence (SCEAND), 25 Apr. 1950 (no. 1), 27 and 31 Jan. 1956 (22–3), 710; also F. Conrad Raabe, 'The China Issue in Canada: Politics and Foreign Policy' (unpublished PhD thesis, University of Pennsylvania, 1970).
23 SCEAND, 31 Jan. 1956, 710–20.
24 Ibid., 26 Feb. 1959 (24–2), 1413.
25 See Walter Gordon, *A Political Memoir* (Toronto: McClelland and Stewart 1977).
26 Paul Martin, *A Very Public Life*, vol. II *So Many Worlds* (Toronto: Deneau 1985), passim.
27 Much of what follows derives from confidential papers, interviews, and Paul Martin, 'At the Right Hand' (draft manuscript; portions of the manuscript were incorporated in *A Very Public Life*); also see Page (ch. 2) and Beecroft (ch. 3) in this volume.
28 See Page (ch. 3) and St Amour (ch. 4) in this volume.
29 On Pearson's 1964 conversation with Johnson, see *Mike*, vol. 3, *1957–1968* (Toronto: University of Toronto Press 1975), 119–20. Pearson and Johnson apparently did not discuss the subject in 1965 although China was on the agenda. The relevant External Affairs file is DEA file 20-China-14.
30 *Commentator* (Sept. 1965), 2; and *Canadian Annual Review 1965* (Toronto 1966),

272. See St Amour, ch. 4 in this volume, and Andrew Boyd, *Fifteen Men on a Powder Keg: A History of the U.N. Security Council* (London: Methuen 1971), 340–5.
31 Interview with William Bundy, 6 Oct. 1976; see *Canadian Annual Review 1966*, 205; also Paul Martin, 'At the Right Hand' (draft manuscript).
32 Butterworth to William Bundy, 28 Jan. 1966, quoted in *United States–Vietnam Relations 1945–1961* (diplomatic section *Pentagon Papers*, 'Ronning Mission' section; mimeographed copy in possession of author).
33 Ibid., Butterworth to Rusk, 31 Jan. 1966; State to Butterworth for Martin, 4 Feb. 1966; and, on Chinese rejection, State to American Embassy, Saigon, et al., 24 Feb. 1966; see also Charles Taylor, *Snow Job: Canada, the United States and Vietnam* (Toronto: Anansi Press 1974), ch. 3.
34 China's 'hard line' on Vietnam affected Johnson's and Rusk's attitude (see Herbert Schandler, *The Unmaking of a President: Lyndon Johnson and Vietnam* [Princeton: Princeton University Press 1977], chs. 2 and 3).
35 *Statements and Speeches*. 66/34, 26 Aug. 1966.
36 Interview with Paul Martin, Apr. 1976; interview with William Bundy, 6 Oct. 1976; interview with George Ignatieff, 12 Feb. 1978 (Ignatieff was Canada's U.N. ambassador at the time); Martin, *A Very Public Life*, vol. 2, 519.
37 House of Commons, *Debates*, 24 Nov. 1966, 10283; and Martin, *A Very Public Life*, vol. 2, 521.
38 Quoted in John Saywell, ed., *Canadian Annual Review 1967* (Toronto 1968), 250; also *Globe and Mail*, 16 Aug. 1967 (Anthony Westell).
39 If the cabinet decided that action had to be taken for domestic political reasons, DEA recommended that unilateral de jure recognition be the approach. Negotiations would be impossible. A unilateral act would be the only action which would be more than mindless futility.
40 Denis Stairs, 'Present in Moderation: Lester Pearson and the Craft of Diplomacy,' *International Journal* 19.1 (Winter 1973–4), 145.
41 Endicott to Pearson, 20 Apr. 1951, and Pearson to Mary Austin Endicott, 30 Apr. 1951 (Pearson Papers, MG 26 NI, vol. 1).

CHAPTER SIX

Brian Evans

Ronning and Recognition: Years of Frustration

In the two decades following the Communist victory in China, one name in particular came to be associated with the question of Canada's recognition of the People's Republic of China, that of Chester Alvin Ronning.[1] As chargé d'affaires in Nanking, and later at the United Nations, Geneva, and New Delhi, Ronning was deeply involved in diplomacy relating to China. From Nanking in 1949 he urged the early recognition of the new government, but as that and subsequent opportunities slipped away, he became more and more frustrated with Canada's position. Convinced of the justice of the case for recognition, Ronning appointed himself its champion. Upon retirement from the Department of External Affairs in 1964, he became a more outspoken advocate of recognition, a point of view he was able to put with greater effect following his appointment as a special envoy to Hanoi in 1966.

Ronning came to diplomacy late in his life – he was fifty-one in 1945 when he entered DEA – and the method of his recruitment was, as Ronning described it, somewhat unorthodox and casual. 'I was asked to examine in Chinese candidates for the Canadian Embassy in Chungking. I failed them all, so in the end External asked me if I would go ... I had received no training whatsoever as a foreign service officer except that I was hastily and properly inoculated.'[2] One wonders now whether DEA really appreciated what it was getting.

A tall, rangy man, Chester Ronning delighted in his Chinese heritage. Like several other members of DEA, he was the son of China missionaries, but not of Canadian missionary stock. He was born 13 December 1894 in Hopeh province, at Fancheng where his father and mother had established an American Lutheran mission in 1891. Chinese, with a Hopeh accent, was Ronning's first language and, apart from a family visit to Norway and Iowa (1899-1901), he remained immersed in a Chinese milieu until 1907 when his mother died. A boy of thirteen, he returned to the United States one year before his family moved to Alberta to homestead. For the next eight years Ronning was a young homesteader, farmer, and cowboy in northern Alberta before his father, discerning that Ronning was a natural teacher, encouraged him to become one. In 1917 Ronning enrolled as a student at the Camrose Normal School and taught agriculture at the newly created Camrose Lutheran College. He later followed in his brother Nelius's footsteps and enrolled at the University of Alberta. In 1918, after a short stretch in the Canadian Engineers, Ronning returned to his homestead for 'harvest leave,' married, and transferred to the Royal Flying Corps to begin training at Toronto. The war over, he returned to Edmonton where he taught school for two years before taking a special course in education at the University of Minnesota.[3]

Although the Ronning family was now Canadian, it had not cut its ties with the Lutheran mission in China. It was anticipated that the eldest son would return to China to teach in the school founded by his parents at Fancheng, but Nelius drowned in 1921 on the eve of his departure. Thus, Chester became the candidate to return to China. It was a journey he relished but one that proved daunting to his wife, who had been born and raised in a small Norwegian community in northern Alberta.[4] The Ronnings went first to Peking where Ronning studied classical Chinese and Mandarin – his Hopeh accent was never fully erased – before moving to Fancheng. They remained there until 1927.

The years from 1922 to 1927 were important ones in consolidating Ronning's Chinese identity and in sharpening his appreciation of Chinese nationalism. He became an avid witness to the growing revolution and he would never again be able to look on China with the eyes of an outsider. Ronning's earliest commitment was to China and to the changes that would modernize it, not to any specific group promoting those changes. As a young boy in his father's school at Fancheng, he had shared in the excitement aroused among his Chinese schoolmates by the many revolts to bring down the Manchus. He had been greatly impressed by the senior students who were involved in the movement headed by Sun Yat-sen. In the 1920s, as a teacher in that same school, Ronning understood the enthusiasm of his students for the promise of the Kuomintang and its northern expedition. At Fancheng, Ronning and his family were only 350 km from Wuhan which, in the spring of 1927, was to become the temporary seat of the new government and the scene of bitter struggle between the members of the Kuomintang and its temporary allies – the Chinese Communist party and Soviet advisers.

Yet with the rising tide of nationalism came threats to the physical well-being of foreigners. Ronning, on the firm advice of the British Consulate at Hankow, began the evacuation of his wife and three children in the spring of 1927. The trip was made by boat down the Han River to the safety of the Lutheran mission home at Hankow. En route Ronning witnessed the new nationalism at full boil and nearly became its victim. He quelled a riot of which he appeared to be the cause, by leaping atop a table and proclaiming in full Hopeh accent that he too was against imperialism. His potential attackers collapsed in laughter to hear a Fancheng accent coming from the mouth of a tall, lanky, foreign devil. In Hankow, Ronning learned of the anti-left purges carried out by Chiang Kai-shek. He also heard of the death of a friend and fellow teacher who had been a supporter of Sun Yat-sen. With other foreigners, the Ronnings were evacuated down the Yangtze, through Nanking, to Shanghai. They returned to Canada, Ronning having been invited to become principal of the Lutheran College located at Camrose, Alberta.

Back in a more peaceful environment Ronning taught, took a Master's degree, and entered into the politics of Depression, Alberta, first as a MLA for the United Farmers of Alberta and later as the first provincial leader of the Canadian Commonwealth Federation party (CCF). It was a time when to the average Albertan the term 'Red China' could only mean Medalta pottery from the works near Medicine Hat, but Ronning was attacked separately for being too Chinese, and for being too socialist. Meanwhile he was kept informed on events in China by his younger brother Tolbert, now a missionary there.[5] By the outbreak of the war in the Pacific, Ronning was a unique commodity: a Westerner, a social democrat with a deep understanding of China and a feel for its politics, a teacher of great and persuasive talent, and trilingual (Chinese, Norwegian, and English). He had many of the same qualifications of Canadian 'Mish Kids' (sons and daughters of China missionaries), but he was not one of them, an attribute that was to become more important later as Canadian missionary opinion on China tended to be polarized by Rev James G. Endicott. Endicott, an inspiring and persuasive speaker, was first a supporter of Chiang Kai-shek and later a supporter of the Chinese Communists. These activities led to his subsequent resignation from the church.[6]

Ronning was not part of the United Church or the Anglican mission network. He had not crossed the threshold of Victoria College or of the Canadian Academy at Kobe. He even spoke a different dialect than Ralph Collins, Arthur Menzies, John Small, or James Endicott. An invitation to join the RCAF discrimination unit monitoring Japan took Ronning to Ottawa in 1942. He became known there beyond the range of CCF politics. When DEA had exhausted its list of available Chinese-speaking officers willing to serve in the Chungking embassy under General Victor Wentworth Odlum, Ronning was inducted as a likely, short-term recruit. Odlum, Canada's first ambassador to China, was by all accounts a difficult man to serve under. He had been born in Japan and had learned a little of the language in his childhood. Although he had long since lost the facility to speak Japanese, he assumed this earlier skill to be the reason why Mackenzie King had asked him to serve in China. A newspaper publisher, a successful Liberal candidate in British Columbia, and a high commissioner to Australia, Odlum took the greatest pride in his military career. Above all, he admired military virtues. By the time Ronning arrived in Chungking in late 1945, Odlum had already been smitten with Chiang Kai-shek, of whom he would hear no wrong. He was so attuned to the Nationalist regime that he agreed with Freda Utley, an American journalist, that anyone who described Chen Li-fu, a minister in the Nationalist government, as a reactionary or a fascist was talking 'nonsense.'[7] Although he saw China differently, Ronning developed a working relationship with Odlum. Odlum grew in his adulation of Chiang, but Ronning, while admiring some members of the Kuomintang, found in the Communists, particularly Tung Pi-wu and Chou En-lai, the qualities of dedication that were needed to solve China's problems. Odlum was proud to have told Mao Tse-tung that the reason there was no crime in Yenan was because there was nothing there to steal; Ronning was elated to have defeated Madame Chiang at checkers. Odlum diplomatically lost at checkers to the generalissimo; Ronning as an interpreter softened some of Odlum's blunt language directed at Chou En-lai. Odlum, the military commander, delighted in the company of Chiang Kai-shek; Ronning, the missionary's son, revelled in the people of the street. Each of them liked the Rev James Endicott, but Odlum thought Endicott's advocacy of the Communist position nearly irrational and difficult to reconcile with the reverend's Christianity. While admitting that Endicott might be politically naive, Ronning did not reject his message.[8]

In T.C. Davis, Odlum's successor, Ronning found a more compatible soul, but conditions in China were deteriorating and Canadian policy was being brought more in line with American. The Chinese, however, chose to ignore outside suggestions on how to resolve their internal differences, and American policy was in disarray. When Davis left in mid-October 1949, Ronning became chargé d'affaires. The main issue which he confronted turned out to be the question of recognition. As the People's Liberation Army marched into Nanking, Ronning could not help but feel some hope for the future and for the prospect of long-delayed reforms being instituted. As a young boy he had witnessed scenes of the dying years of the Manchu empire. As a young teacher he had sympathized with the revolutionary Kuomintang, only to witness the destruction of the hopes that many of his Chinese friends had placed in it. As a foreign service officer in Chungking he had seen the worst of the failing Nationalist regime, and in Nanking he had observed its inability to tackle major problems. Thus, he was happy to act as interpreter for the remarks of Huang Hua, speaking on behalf of the new regime, when Huang invited foreign representatives at Nanking to recognize the Communist government proclaimed in Peking on 1 October 1949.[9]

Despite his optimism for China's future, Ronning soon began to feel frustrated when he realized that those foreigners who had supported reform in China were now going to reject the opportunity for change through their misunderstanding of the role of ideology in the relations between the Soviet Union and China. The assumption that not only was Chinese communism the same as Soviet communism, but that this common belief would override all conflicting national interests, was, to Ronning, highly suspect. He was eventually proved correct since ideology kept China and the United States apart much longer than it kept China and the Soviet Union together. Ronning's attempts to convince Ottawa of the importance of recognizing the new regime sooner, rather than later, were based on the belief that delay would only diminish possible benefits to Canada. Ottawa was more cautious.

By 1950 Canadian policy toward Asia was neither well developed nor bold. From the outset of this century Canadian policy makers had to consider Japan. This was partly because Britain's acceptance of Japan as an equal partner in the alliance of 1902 made Japan available, and partly because the rapidly modernizing Japanese economy and the expanding Japanese empire offered the best settled area in Asia with which Canada could expand trade. As loyal as Canada might be to Britain, however, the Anglo-Japanese alliance was an impediment to Canadian relations with the United States, particularly in the event of conflict between Japan and America. The fact that during the First World War the alliance enabled British Columbia to be protected by Japanese warships against a German attack was not reassuring: it only emphasized the threat. Moreover, the alliance made for immigration problems. Although Ottawa played a part in the ending of the Anglo-Japanese alliance, a comprehensive Canadian policy toward Asia was not developed. As the missionaries established transpacific links, successive governments in Ottawa played to both sides of the Canadian-Asian equation by responding sympathetically, as far as possible, to the narrow racism of seemingly beleaguered whites, and by seeking to develop profitable economic links.

Before Pearl Harbor, Canadian policy toward Asia was self-interested, but not very enlightened. Although the British Columbian economy was becoming increasingly locked into Asia – Japan at least – no serious efforts were made to bring greater understanding to the voters of British Columbia, or to the rest of Canada, of this fact. Canadians chose instead to enlighten Asia about their ways of doing things. The establishment of a legation in Japan in 1929 grew out of these pragmatic interests, just as did the reluctance to establish one in Nanking. Canada wanted Asia to accept it on its terms, and the terms were, perhaps inescapably, imbedded in a Eurocentric view. Canadians continued to believe in a world in which Asia was to be dictated to by Western colonial powers and to adhere to a system that worked against Asian national interests. Even though the Pacific war and the Chinese civil war made Asia's nationalist aspirations apparent, Canada was but a naive and uninformed player on the Pacific stage. Lumping the European and Asian theatres of war together into the one concept of the Second World War only encouraged Canadians to continue to look at Asia in terms of European experience. The Cold War and the triumph of the Chinese Communists consolidated that view. Some Canadians like George Drew, leader of the Conservative party, were influenced by the opinion, very popular in the United States, that the new Chinese regime was simply a puppet of Moscow. Having spent the war convinced that the enemy was fascism and that a new world would dawn with the defeat of Germany and Japan, Canadians now learned that they could not relax. The real enemy all along had been Soviet communism. In a world made so much more uncertain by the atomic bomb, Canadians became aware of the spread of Soviet influence. To the internationally paranoid, what could be more dangerous than 'the Yellow Peril covered in red lacquer'? John Blackmore, a Social Credit MP from southern Alberta, expressed this concern frequently and fervently. Senator Joseph McCarthy was not without his echoes north of the border.

Canadians could be forgiven their ignorance of China – they had chosen to ignore it. The people who did know China, the missionaries, were divided on the issue, and in the late 1940s, James Endicott, the most vocal advocate of the benefits of Chinese communism, only seemed to inspire people to doubt his message. After all, he was the person who had spoken with enthusiasm about Chiang Kai-shek in the early 1940s. If Canada was to have a policy toward the new Chinese government, it would have to take into account the ignorance of Canadians on the issue and their fears of communism. Having followed Britain's lead in Asia to the late 1920s and America's since then, Canada was not likely to produce an innovative China policy. Indeed, speed was not of the essence. Despite Odlum's infatuation with Chiang, Canada was not wedded to that regime. Odlum's blueprint for post-war Canada-China co-operation most certainly could wait.[10]

Ronning might have appreciated this, but he was still new to the Canadian diplomatic game; he had been hired to help Ottawa understand China. When he was appointed to DEA, Ronning (and likely the department) regarded himself as a one-trick pony. He was brought in to help with Chinese matters and he did not anticipate much beyond a year or two's involvement. His wife did not like the prospect of returning to China, but an offer to make Ronning ambassador to Norway, if he stayed on, made the diplomatic life and China more attractive. It is clear, however, that Ronning would have liked nothing better than to become ambassador to China. But personal ambition was not what drove him. Rather it was his growing conviction of what was the correct China policy. Ironically, the more his understanding of China grew, the less his views were accepted in Ottawa as a basis for policy. In turn, and to his frustration, the delays in the formulation of a Canadian policy made him increasingly less credible to the Chinese.

In the period between the Chinese Communist occupation of Nanking and the eve of the Korean war, Ronning became an important source of opinion on China from the inside. It is debatable whether he felt greater frustration with Ottawa or with Washington. Frustration with Ottawa was over timing, missed phone calls, and the question of whether to go it alone or under some umbrella such as the Commonwealth. Frustration with Washington for Ronning was of a different nature. Like many Western Canadians, Ronning was of American origin and, although he was by now thoroughly Canadian, his family continued to have deep roots in the United States and in the American Lutheran mission movement in China. Two of his daughters were to marry Americans, one a navy man, the other a rising reporter for the *New York Times*. For Ronning, the failure of America to do the correct thing in China was a personal hurt. He believed that there was no reason why China should be a source of friction between Canada and the United States as long as the United States saw the issue clearly. The problem was that they did not. Unfortunately for Ronning, American opinions became stronger, robbing him of credibility in Ottawa. For example, after the outbreak of the Korean War, Arnold Heeney, the under-secretary of state for External Affairs, identified Ronning's isolation in Nanking without his family and away from the seat of the new government in Peking as a possible reason for his lack of balanced argument.[11]

When the question of possible PRC intervention in Korea arose, Ronning's support for Peking's case came to look more like simply co-option, verging on the incautious advocacy of James Endicott. During the summer of 1950 Ronning sought ways of maintaining recognition as a live issue, but with the PRC's entry into the Korean War in October and the United Nations' condemnation of Peking as an aggressor, there was little hope. Ronning was withdrawn from Nanking and he returned to Ottawa via Hong Kong and Camrose in the spring of 1951. His departure from China was made difficult by police harassment and a thorough search by customs lasting nine hours.

Korea had given Canada a China policy of sorts. Rather than a one-China policy, or a two-Chinas policy, Canada had a modified no-China policy. Like the proverbial arrow, in 1951 our last representative in China had been shot into the air and had landed, as far as the Nationalists and Communists were concerned, they knew not where. If either side had been polling, Canada would have been put down as a definite maybe. Meanwhile on Taiwan, the memory of the Canadian missionary George Leslie Mackay remained strong, and on the mainland the legend of Norman Bethune burned beacon bright.[12]

One of the many stories about Chester Ronning that circulate in Alberta concerns the time when Ronning was principal of the Camrose Lutheran College. In the days of the Depression, the school faced closure if donations did not come in from the community. Ronning toured the district selling the idea of education and its importance during hard economic times. He hit on one family of several brothers, one of whom adamantly refused to donate money. Ronning challenged him to wrestle. If Ronning won, the man would donate; if he did not, Ronning would cross him off the list. Ronning, a skinny schoolteacher, won even though the farmer was husky and strong. Against the five-dollar donation, Ronning had to set his torn new shirt, and three broken ribs.[13] Whether or not Ronning approached Ottawa in 1951 with the same spirit, one can only guess, but he was determined to collect on DEA's promise of a posting to Norway. But, to use his own words, 'When I got to Ottawa no one remembered the promise. As the Norwegians say: "If someone goes so far as to make a promise, you can't expect him to keep it too!"' Instead, for the next two years Ronning was assigned to the Far Eastern Division in Ottawa and to the United Nations. Against him in Washington was Dean Rusk who was a staunch proponent of the isolation and containment of Communist China. Ronning was later of the view that the difference of opinion between himself and Rusk came home to roost a decade or more later when he undertook his special missions to Hanoi.[14]

If Korea left Canada with a no-China policy of sorts, it did help in the formation of a Canadian attitude toward China and in a Chinese attitude toward Canada. Through the United Nations, Canada was able to make it clear that although Canadian policy might appear to outsiders to be synchronized with that of the United States, Canadians were not sycophantic. This was particularly important to Ronning, who knew in his bones that the United States was wrong on the China issue: China had to be explained to the United States, not the United States to China. This was extremely difficult at a time when the United States was destroying its China experts and sinophiles, and when one of the most articulate pro-Peking ones in Canada, James Endicott, appeared to self-destruct. Moreover, another External Affairs Asian expert, Herbert Norman, was having his loyalty questioned. Nonetheless, Ronning remained untouched. Unlike Norman, who had studied at Cambridge, a putative fleshpot of intellectual Marxism, Ronning had not studied east of Minneapolis and was one of an almost unknown species – an Alberta social democrat. While Norman's sympathy for Asian Marxism was cerebral and expressed in his published works, Ronning's was less intellectual and based on practical experience. Each man had a great rapport with the common people of the land of his birth. While Norman could see why an Asian nationalist would become a Marxist, Ronning could see why Asians would use Marxism only as a cloak for nationalism. Ironically it was Norman, the expert on Japan, who was seared by McCarthyism; and it was Ronning, the China lover, who escaped unsinged. Norman, who had had tremendous influence on occupation policy in Japan, paid a terrible price; Ronning, who had had little influence on China policy, remained to wrestle on.[15]

Ronning was not alone in DEA in reaching different conclusions on China than those that prevailed in Washington, but it was Ronning – the late-harvested diplomat – who appeared to take the issue most personally. Undoubtedly this was because he tended to see the world almost exclusively in terms of the China question, and because DEA appeared to encourage him to do so. Ronning never missed a chance to discuss China and he never lost sight of what he termed 'the fallacious analysis' upon which American policy was based. Even his posting to Norway in 1954 provided opportunities because Norway had just recognized China. Moreover, it was from Oslo that he attended the Geneva conference on Korea. It was not an exile. Ronning's final posting to India in 1957 put him into the thick of Asian diplomacy. An engaging, loquacious man of optimism and good humour, Ronning was able to charm men like Mike Pearson, Paul Martin, Chou En-lai, Averell Harriman, John Kenneth Galbraith, and even John Diefenbaker. Ronning and Nehru admired each other, but he could not win over Dulles or Rusk, who saw him as an emotional preacher. To PRC recognition advocates in Canada, Ronning appeared to offer hope, while to its opponents, he was 'a Communist' and 'a China lover,' blind to the real threat. Nonetheless, while recognizing that his views were often unpopular, particularly in the United States, Ronning had an impact in a less obvious way. Through the marriage of his daughter Audrey to Seymour Topping, Ronning had an audience for his views with the *New York Times*. Topping was with Ronning when the People's Liberation Army took Nanking. Topping later covered the Geneva conference and the Laos conference, and, according to Topping, his visit as part of the family group on Ronning's return to China in 1971 provided an opportunity for Chou En-lai to quiz him about Kissinger who was, unknown to Ronning, shortly to visit Peking.[16]

By the time Ronning retired from DEA in 1964, the tide was clearly running in favour of recognition of the PRC. Public opinion, influenced no doubt by grain sales since 1960, by growing concern over American involvement in Vietnam, and by the realization that Peking was not going to go away, was perhaps reinforced by a sense of satisfaction Canadians feel when they become convinced that Americans are acting more foolishly than they themselves are. Even the sensational reporting of the sensational events of the Cultural Revolution in the last half of the 1960s did not seem to destroy the predominant view that Chiang Kai-shek was not, and was not likely ever again to be, the ruler of the mainland. The frustration for Ronning (and he was not alone) was that the step was not taken. Certainly to Ronning, the hold-up was the United States, whose 'fallacious analysis' of the China question was being repeated in Vietnam. Upon retirement, Ronning threw himself into the battle of the campus teach-ins, to add his weight to the general urge to point out to the American administration the error of its ways. The selection of Ronning by Paul Martin to undertake special peace missions to Vietnam in 1966 made him even more sought after, and he became the virtual darling of the late 1960s campus radicals. He spoke at universities and colleges on both sides of the border.

Although he had already made a few forays into the world of academic conferences, and had been active on the lecture circuit across Canada speaking about China, the Pacific, and the United Nations, it was his trips to Hanoi that suddenly made Ronning a household name. Whatever the original motives for the missions, and whatever the assessment of their impact upon the Vietnam morass, the missions to Hanoi gave him a lofty platform from which he could continue his education of the North American public on the China issue. From the obscurity of Camrose, Ronning strode forth, endorsed enthusiastically by Paul Martin and begrudgingly by Dean Rusk who suspected a hidden China agenda. The story of Ronning's career was told in a variety of forms in newspapers throughout North America, the reports in the United States emphasizing that Ronning was really of American origin. The fact that his missions failed only gave him greater credibility as a critic. He was approached by Senator Fulbright looking for angles of attack on the Vietnam issue, and he was embraced (figuratively) by John Diefenbaker who, judging from his words uttered in Parliament, looked upon Ronning as a dove of peace that might be dispatched from time to time, if only old Noah Pearson would see things more clearly. Thus, Ronning, a socialist, previously sheathed in the armour of the neutrality of a diplomatic career, was given a platform by the Liberal cabinet, and was applauded by the Conservative opposition. Ronning became the focus of Canadian anti-American feeling over the Vietnam War. He, in turn, used the opportunity to direct attention to the real issue behind it all, the correct perception of China.[17]

Ronning had made his views clear at Banff in the late summer of 1965. It was a message he repeated in the next half-dozen years, but to greatest effect in the period from the fall of 1966 to 1968: 'It disturbs me therefore to see that we continue year after year to support an Asian policy which was based on a fallacious analysis of developments, particularly in China. To deal effectively with the problems of the Far East we must have an understanding of the causes which produced the present situation in Asia, and our policies must be based on correct analyses of historical facts, not fantasies'.[18] In his post-Hanoi period, Ronning's message became more and more the highlight of teach-ins and special lectures, of convocation addresses, and of his talks to clubs. Whether he sat on a platform with Senator Edward Kennedy or stood before the Camrose Lions Club, he treated every listener as a possible convert. He felt that the issue of China was too important and had been left too long in the hands of an elite of policy makers. Already past his seventieth year, in the fall of 1966, Ronning set out on an exhausting speaking tour giving the Tory Lectures at the University of Alberta, addressing teach-ins at Toronto and McGill, speaking at the University of Calgary, and to United Nations Associations, foreign relations groups, and service clubs from Montreal to Victoria. Returning to some family roots in January 1968, he gave the convocation address at St Olaf College, Northfield, Minnesota, arguing for an independent Chinese policy for the United States, free of Vietnam. Ronning prefaced his remarks by the comment that he was 'speaking as a Canadian about a situation that is at least partially Canada's affair ... My hopes are for a new Western policy of co-existence with China.'[19] In July that year Ronning took his message to the Couchiching conference.

The majority of the thousands Ronning addressed in these years were students, but he had a wider audience as well through the press. Articles by

Ronning relating to Vietnam, but ultimately to China, appeared in newspapers from Montreal to Vancouver. Moreover, he was well received by reporters and columnists on both sides of the border. Charles Lynch was a fan. He had noted Ronning's retirement in 1964 from the post of high commissioner to India with the assessment that Ronning was the most remarkable man in DEA, and he remained a loyal supporter throughout the years. To John R. Walker, Ronning was the Canadian government's 'best old China Hand', and Frederick Nossal noted that Ronning was 'one of the few Canadian career diplomats who has come out openly in support of recognition of Peking.' David Kraslow in the *Washington Post* said that Ronning was 'considered one of the ablest Asia hands in the Western World.' Back in Alberta, the *Edmonton Journal* dubbed Ronning 'this quiet Albertan' and followed his progress with affection.[20]

In these years immediately prior to Canada-China recognition, Ronning's extraordinary activity generally brought favourable editorial comment and good press coverage. Ronning was a newsmaker, but it would be wrong to imply that he was universally liked and that his message was always accepted. John Kettle, who had earlier asked the question 'Is Canada helping Red China to conquer the world?' attacked Ronning and others in an article in *Canada Month* entitled 'The Great Canada–Red China Love-fest.'[21] Back in Camrose, Ronning received the odd letter denouncing him as a communist, but these were small voices compared with the general acclaim he received. Late in 1967 the *Montreal Star* endorsed Ronning's views as those of a man 'not driven by blind emotionalism.'[22]

The statements of Pierre Elliot Trudeau, the new prime minister of Canada, in the spring of 1968 regarding recognition of China indicated clearly that Ronning was in line with the thinking of the new leader. Audiences now asked Ronning to be more precise. What was to happen to Taiwan? The Ronning solution was for Canada to recognize only those parts of China over which the government in Peking had control. Taiwan, he said, was a question that would be settled in the fullness of time.[23]

With Prime Minister Trudeau pledged to a policy of recognition, one might have thought Ronning would have been content, but this would be failing to take into account his American dimension. A constant critic of American policy, Ronning had come up against it in Nanking and Geneva and again in Washington in 1966. The Hanoi missions had given him some favourable press in the United States, and although Dean Rusk was definitely not his fan, Harriman remained charmed and like Galbraith regarded Ronning as a wise head on Asian policy. Huang Hua, the first PRC ambassador to Canada, and shortly to go to the United Nations, was an old friend of Ronning's, and in 1971 Ronning was to become news once again in the United States, mostly courtesy of the *New York Times*.[24]

In May 1971 Ronning returned to China at the invitation of Premier Chou En-lai. It was a joyous homecoming, and his impressions and observations received wide publication in the Canadian and American press. In addition a film, *A Journey Forward*, was made of his trip for showing on Canadian television. The event was newsworthy in itself: Ronning, the old China hand – the pilgrim who had so made the recognition of China his own personal burden – was going home. Moreover, it was a chance to glimpse mainland China in what appeared to be a post–Cultural Revolution calm. But it was not just a Canadian story, for Ronning was accompanied by his daughter, Audrey Topping, who became one of the first American reporters to have access to Communist China. Ronning's interviews with Chou became an Audrey Topping exclusive, while, as an added bonus, Seymour Topping, an old China hand himself, was given a visa to Peking on behalf of the *New York Times*. In June 1971, the *New York Times* began the publication of the *Pentagon Papers* in which the Ronning missions to Hanoi received renewed attention. Then came the drama of the Kissinger visit to Peking in July. Critics of America's China policy were dangerously close to becoming the establishment.[25]

Ronning had already played a part in undermining the foundations of Cold War policy. In March 1969 the National Committee on United States–China Relations sponsored a first national convocation on 'The United States and China: The Next Decade.' Held in New York, it attracted some 2,500 people. Ronning was one of the three Canadian contributors. The conference took place at a time when the new Nixon administration was relaxing restrictions on trade and communications with China. After reminding the audience that the United States had never used troops to interfere in China's internal affairs, Ronning called for the U.S. to begin trade with the PRC in non-strategic goods and to welcome its correspondents.[26]

But as optimistic as he was, and as tired as he was becoming of public appearances, Ronning was constantly being called upon to comment on events in Indo-China. He condemned the bombing of Cambodia in May 1970 and could be counted on for comments on the progress of the war throughout that year. In February 1971 as he warmed up for his trip to China, he 'loosed another blast at United States policy toward Communist China,' as he testified before the Canadian Senate Committee on Foreign Affairs.[27] In June and July, amidst the publicity and flurry of stories about his impressions of the new China, Ronning was given space for two stories in the *New York Times*: 'China's 700 Million Are on the Way' and 'After

Mao What?' Following the release of the film of his trip in October 1971, Ronning appeared once again in the *New York Times*, this time with a picture – Ronning at the feet of a huge white statue of Chairman Mao. In January 1972, as Nixon prepared for his February trip to Peking, Ronning's article 'Understanding Chou En-lai' appeared in the *Boston Sunday Globe*.[28] The measure of Ronning's impact upon American thinking is very difficult – if not impossible – to assess, but for an outsider his views received considerable prominence. He was now being pressed to write his memoirs, a task he undertook with some reluctance, but with the hope that they would 'lead to better understanding of China.'[29] His old friend Alfred Knopf published them in 1974. The *Memoir* was the only book by a Canadian on China policy to be published in the United States during this period.

Following the Shanghai communiqué, Ronning had become less and less a critic of America's China policy and more and more the advocate of the new China. Made more compelling by his ability to compare the old China with the new, Ronning's lectures drew large crowds. His audiences were mainly sympathetic, but because the North American thirst for China was being slaked by others with differing perspectives the Ronning picture was becoming classified as too rosy. Among his harsher critics were his fellow Albertans. Late in November 1974 he spoke at the University of Alberta following a film on China. Wrote one local reporter: 'In the audience, the most conservative could not shake the uneasiness wrought by the made-in-China film. Not one of them would stand a chance in a hand-to-hand showdown with the terrible tykes, harbingers of a "yellow peril" if there ever was one.'[30]

The publication of his *A Memoir of China in Revolution* only brought more criticism. 'A hodge podge from Ronning' said Charles Taylor in the *Globe and Mail*, while Peter Worthington in the *Toronto Sun* called it 'a frivolous book ... of rather mundane anecdotes and trivia.' Dean Emeritus E.H. Soward of the University of British Columbia in the *Vancouver Sun* was kinder and John Kiely of the *Kitchner-Waterloo Record* was generally favourable but advised readers to skip the Korea sections. Christopher Young in the *Ottawa Citizen* called Ronning 'Canada's most eminent China-watcher and China-lover.' Young found little excuse for Ronning 'suggesting that freedom of religion exists in today's China; or for the implication that the typical worker's family has a flush toilet.' An anonymous reviewer in the *Meunster Prairie Messenger* made the perceptive observation that the book revealed two Chester Ronnings: the historian and the nostalgic grey-haired grandfather. Alberta reviewers were more demanding. Steve Hume of the *Edmonton Journal* set out the standard by which he judged Ronning: 'Diplomats as the instruments by which governments communicate, are at once a paradoxical union of elegant sham and nitty gritty reality; of the polished actor and the cool efficient analyst; of the elaborate ruse and the blunt ultimatum ... Far from being the impartial observer, [Ronning] has long been a participant in a love-affair.' Brian Brennan of the *Calgary Herald* wanted something more substantial. '[I]nstead of providing us with the literary equivalent of a 15 course feast at the Pan Hsi Restaurant, Kwangchow, Dr. Ronning has served us something akin to the luncheon special at Joe Wong's Fine Eats. An hour after reading the book one is left with a distinct feeling of unfulfillment.'[31]

Ronning's *Memoir* fared better abroad. Richard Harris gave it a serious review in the *China Quarterly*. In the United States, R.F. Swanson in the *New York Times* dismissed it in a three-book review as 'one of the those "contributions to a better understanding" volumes' after having told his readers, 'The fact is, Canada is not of overwhelming importance in the scheme of things, except to Canadians.' Another reviewer was put off by Ronning's anti-Americanism and his 'ideological blinders.' Others, however, from the *Washington Post* to the *Los Angeles Times*, to the *Fresno Bee*, were more sympathetic, characterizing Ronning as understanding rather than high-handed, and seeing in his career an American might-have-been. Several made the point that a Ronning could not have escaped the McCarthyite backlash in the United States.[32]

Ronning's *Memoir* had been put together while he was involved in a continuing round of lectures, travel, and interviews. As a speaker, he had the engaging habit of tantalizing his audiences with hints of secrets yet to be revealed. Many Canadians looked forward to the book, some in the hope that those ultimate revelations would provide some further evidence to advance a favourite argument either for or against the formulation, direction, and execution of Canadian foreign policy. For them, it was a disappointment. It raised more questions about the recollections of the author than it settled outstanding problems. The book made more sense, however, within the American context. Published in the United States, it carried Ronning's familiar message to the American public, where it did have an impact. Ronning had made it clear that his purpose was to further the understanding of China, and in his view, the U.S. had the greater need.

Through the Hanoi missions, the trips to China, *The Pentagon Papers*, his articles in newspapers, and his book, Ronning was before the North American public for nearly a decade – a rigorous retirement for someone who had only given up active diplomatic service at age seventy. It was the finale of a career that had become inextricably entwined with one issue: the recognition of China as an independent regime based in Peking. For him the issue went beyond the problem of Canadian acceptance of the view to the need for the United States, the home of so much of his family, to recognize the error of its ways. From his childhood days in China Ronning knew the virtue of harmony in human affairs. Since 1949 he had actively sought to bring harmony among his three homelands, China, the United States, and Canada. In his later years he pursued the China question with a singleness of purpose that at times appeared to be an obsession. Like Christian in *The Pilgrim's Progress*, a book he admired greatly, Ronning bore a burden – the recognition of China. It was with noticeable grief and joy in his voice that he greeted American recognition of China in 1979, and the burden was set down.[33]

Ronning the homesteader and teacher was an unlikely diplomat. He was brought into DEA to do a special job at a time when China was only beginning to loom a little larger on the distant western horizon of Canadian foreign policy. His views of Asia, however, were centred on Asia and perhaps China, and at first not likely to harmonize with policies that looked at Asian affairs as an extension of Western ones. His career in DEA coincided with the growth of a Canadian Asia policy as an expression of a Canadian commitment to internationalism. Although Ronning valued any display of an independent Canadian initiative on the question of China, he looked upon the question in its international context, not primarily as a Canada-China bilateral issue. Pearsonian internationalism and deep personal feelings for the land of his birth came together in Ronning without conflict. The cause of the United Nations and of international peace could only be achieved by the correct handling of the China question.

Vietnam was just a manifestation of the root problem, but it gave Ronning the extraordinary opportunity to pursue his issue – China and its proper place in the world – with greater effect than he could ever have dreamed of when he retired to Camrose in 1964. His trips to Hanoi in 1966 made him a martyr to President Johnson's policies in Asia. Canadian campus nationalists, inspired as they frequently were by anti-American Americans, listened in great numbers to Ronning's views on China and Vietnam with an attention previously unknown in the years of debate and argument over the recognition of the PRC and the seating of China in the United Nations. Once Canada had recognized the PRC, however, Ronning's own anti-Americanism on this particular issue became less appealing to Canadians. After his return to China in 1971 his enthusiastic descriptions of China caused him to run the risk of being dismissed as a Peking booster. He perhaps had a more sympathetic audience in the United States where the long years of nearly complete isolation from China had created a public eager to consume news of Mao's utopia. The different reception that

Ronning's book received in Canada and the United States can be partly explained by the fact that it contained little of Ronning the interested Canadian public had not already heard or read, while in the U.S. it was taken as the considered opinions of a senior diplomat who was highly honoured in his own country. It was published at a time when criticism of early American China policy was being welcomed as the debate over recognition gathered momentum.

James Endicott has recalled that in the early fifties Ronning commented to him, 'You work from the outside and I'll work from the inside.' Ironically, it was only when Ronning, too, began to work 'outside' that he appeared to get results. Ronning would not likely have been so successful, however, if his outside work had not had the stamp of approval from the inside – a stamp that was renewed in 1966. Although he would sometimes point out to this audience that 'unlike diplomats from other countries, [Canadian envoys] have complete freedom to express their opinions to their home Government regardless of whether it is in line with the political thought of the ruling party of the day,' it is unlikely that many among Ronning's listeners doubted his 'links' with official government thinking.[34]

Ronning was not an ideologue. He believed in harmony, fair play, and flexibility. He was also determined. These qualities and his particular understanding of China enabled him to have a unique impact on Canada-China relations and on United States–China relations. Ronning was once described as 'Born in China and spiritually living in Asia,' and there is probably more truth than jest in the story with which he used to tease Chinese children: 'I am Chinese you know. I was born in China, but I have lived so long in Canada that I am beginning to look like them!'

One might speculate on the course of Canada-China relations had recognition been accomplished in 1949 and on what contribution Chester Ronning would have made to those relations. But 'might have beens' need not detract from the achievement of Chester Ronning, whose frustrations over wrong-headed China policies led him into a indefatigable effort to correct them. Another, or others, might have undertaken the task, but none would have done it with such dedication and panache.

Notes

1 Much of the information in this paper comes from Chester Ronning, *A Memoir of China in Revolution* (New York: Random House 1974); taped interviews conducted by Tom Radford of the National Film Board of Canada (hereafter Ronning: NFB) on deposit at the University of Alberta Archives; taped interviews conducted by Brian L. Evans, May to August 1980

(hereafter Ronning: BLE); tape of a memorial radio broacast on Ronning by Mike Goetze, CFCW Camrose (hereafter Ronning: CFCW) first broadcast 31 Dec. 1984; Private Papers of Chester Ronning (hereafter Ronning Papers) loaned by Ronning to the author.
2 Ronning: BLE; Chester Ronning, 'Nanking: 1950,' *International Journal* 32.3 (1967), 441.
3 Ronning: BLE, Ronning Papers; Ronning, *Memoir*, 3-15.
4 Ronning, although he appreciated it intellectually, never fully understood the impact of China upon the outsider. He idolized his own mother, who had been revered by the people of Fancheng, and expected the same calm resourcefulness from his wife without taking into account that while he was going back home, she was heading into virtual isolation (Ronning: BLE).
5 Ronning: BLE; Ronning, *Memoir*, 17-19; Ronning: NFB.
6 See Stephen Endicott, *James G. Endicott: Rebel out of China* (Toronto: University of Toronto Press 1980), ch. 23.
7 Kim Richard Nossal, 'Chungking Prism,' *International Journal* 22 (1977), 457-83; Freda Utley, *Last Chance in China* (New York: Bobbs-Merrill 1947), 352.
8 Ronning Papers; Ronning: BLE. With the vision of hindsight, Ronning in later years heightened the differences between himself and Odlum over interpretation of the China scene. But these were the early years of Ronning's tour in China, when attempts were being made by the United States to reconcile the positions of the Kuomintang and the Communist Party of China. An interesting perspective on the Odlum-Ronning relationship is to be gained by reading their correspondence with each other in the early 1950s when Odlum was in Turkey and Ronning back in Ottawa (PAC, Odlum Papers, private correspondence with C.A. Ronning).
9 Ronning: BLE. Huang Hua has an equally clear recollection of Ronning on that occasion (private interview with Huang Hua, Peking, Nov. 1984).
10 My perspective is that of a prairie boy from a polyglot district in which a POW camp was located and into which Japanese Canadians had been evacuated.
11 Liao Dong, 'Chester A. Ronning and Canada-China Relations (1945-1954)' (unpublished MA thesis, University of Regina, 1983); Ronning: BLE; Ronning, *Memoir*.
12 Mackay, 'the Black Bearded Barbarian,' had been a missionary in Taiwan between 1870 and 1901. His Presbyterian mission succeeded in making the transition from Chinese to Japanese rule when Taiwan was ceded to Japan in 1895. He and his missionary style were remembered in Taiwan, where there is a hospital in his name and a mission that traces its roots to his pioneering efforts. (See Graeme McDonald, 'George Leslie Mackay: Missionary Success

in Nineteenth Century Taiwan,' *Papers on China* [Cambridge, Mass.: Harvard University, East Asian Research Center 1968], vol. 21, and John Geddes, 'Canada's Role in the Modernization of Taiwan: The Educational and Medical Work of Dr. George Leslie Mackay and Associates,' in Bernard T.K. Joei, ed., *Canada in the Evolving Pacific Community* [Taipei: Tamkang University 1988].) Bethune, of course, had Mao himself to thank for his immortality.

13 Ronning: CFCW. This tape contains interviews with Ronning's contemporaries in Camrose, with Paul Martin, with the late Grant Notley, then leader of the Alberta NDP, and with Ronning.

14 Ronning: BLE; Stephen Endicott, *Rebel Out of China*; Roger E. Bowen, *E.H. Norman: His Life and Scholarship* (Toronto: University of Toronto Press 1984).

15 See Roger Bowen, *E.H. Norman: His Life and Scholarship*.

16 See references to Ronning in John K. Galbraith, *A Life in Our Times* (Boston: Houghton Mifflin 1981) and *Ambassador's Journal* (Boston: Houghton Mifflin 1969); Peter Stursberg, *Lester Pearson and the American Dilemma* (Toronto: Doubleday 1980); George C. Herring, ed., *The Secret Diplomacy of the Vietnam War: The Negotiating Volumes of the Pentagon Papers* (Austin: University of Texas, Austin 1983); Ronning: CFCW (Martin interview); House of Commons, *Debates*, 15 June 1966. In Huang Hua's opinion, Chou En-lai was 'genuinely fond of Chester Ronning' (interview with author, Peking, Nov. 1984). Douglas A. Ross, *In the Interests of Peace: Canada and Vietnam 1954–1973* (Toronto: University of Toronto Press 1984), 157–8, implies a type of exile had been found for left-liberals in New Delhi, Wellington, and Oslo, 'inopportune locations for influencing policy in Ottawa on a crucial decision.' It is to be remembered that to Ronning Oslo was part of the deal for his staying in the DEA; it represented a family commitment as well (Ronning: BLE; Seymour Topping, *Journey between Two Chinas* [New York: Harper and Row 1972], 391).

17 Ronning: BLE; Herring, *Pentagon Papers*; Charles Taylor, *Snow Job: Canada, the United States and Vietnam* (Toronto: Anansi Press 1974); David Kraslow and Stuart H. Loory, *The Secret Search for Peace in Vietnam* (New York: Vintage 1968); House of Commons, *Debates*, 28 Oct. 1966, 27 Feb. 1967, 12 Nov. 1968, 1 May 1970. Diefenbaker's suggestions that Ronning be sent on further missions carried on into the Trudeau-Sharp era.

18 J. King Gordon, ed., *Canada's Role as a Middle Power* (Toronto: Canadian Institute of International Affairs 1966), 38.

19 *Manitou Messenger*, 19 Jan. 1968.

20 *Calgary Herald*, 8 July 1964; *Edmonton Journal*, 9 Mar. 1966; *Globe and Mail*, 12 Mar. 1966; *Washington Post*, 26 June 1966; *Edmonton Journal*, 12 Mar. 1966.

Evans: Ronning and Recognition 167

21 *Canada Month*, Dec. 1966.
22 Ronning Papers; *Montreal Star*, 18 Dec. 1967, editorial.
23 *Globe and Mail*, 30 July 1968; *Vancouver Province*, 28 May 1969.
24 The *Times* began publishing the Pentagon Papers on 13 June 1971; Seymour Topping was very much involved in the process (Topping, *Journey*, 376–80).
25 *Newsweek*, 17 May 1971; *Detroit Times*, 21 May 1971.
26 A. Doak Barnett and E.O. Reischauer, eds., *The United States and China: The Next Decade* (New York: Praeger 1970), 167–72. Alvin Hamilton and David Oancia were the other Canadian contributors.
27 *Montreal Gazette*, 6 May 1970; *Ottawa Journal*, 25 Feb. 1971.
28 *New York Times*, 7 June, 11 July, and 10 Oct. 1971; *Boston Sunday Globe*, 9 Jan. 1972.
29 *Montreal Gazette*, 6 May 1970; Ronning: BLE.
30 *St John's Edmonton Report (The Alberta Report)*, 2 Dec. 1974.
31 *Globe and Mail*, 13 July 1974; *Toronto Sun*, 27 Sept. 1974; *Vancouver Sun*, 6 Sept. 1974; *Ottawa Citizen*, 16 Nov. 1974; *Meunster Prairie Messenger*, 15 Sept. 1974; *Edmonton Journal*, 31 Aug. 1974; *Calgary Herald Magazine*, 6 Sept. 1974.
32 *China Quarterly*, Mar. 1976; *New York Times*, 22 Sept. 1974; *Bestsellers*, 15 June 1974; *Washington Post*, 23 July 1974; *Los Angeles Times*, 17 Sept. 1974; *Fresno Bee*, 1 Dec. 1974. Perhaps the most vivid was by R.M. Seaton who observed that 'Ronning remembers running barefoot during many happy days in the mountains with Chinese boys who herded cattle – "We enjoyed squishing fresh, green cow dung between our toes to flatten it out for quick drying" – 'I think a little of that stuff may have seeped into the pages of this book' (*Coffeyville Journal* [Kansas], 25 Apr. 1974).
33 Ronning: CFCW.
34 Endicott interview with Liao Dong reported in Liao Dong, 'Chester A. Ronning.' Ronning was not only seen to have the support of the Liberal cabinet in 1966, but when it was later rumoured that he had lost its support because he had been too outspoken, John Diefenbaker rushed to his rescue (House of Commons, *Debates*, 6 Feb. 1967). In January 1972 Ronning was made a Companion of the Order of Canada (*Red Deer Advocate*, 6 Oct. 1964; Indians of Canada publication, April 1969, Ronning Papers; Ronning: BLE).

CHAPTER SEVEN

Patrick Kyba

Alvin Hamilton and Sino-Canadian Relations

Alvin Hamilton's association with China began on 11 October 1960, when Prime Minister John Diefenbaker transferred him from Northern Affairs and National Resources to the Department of Agriculture. Despite the government's efforts to manage the manifold problems of Canadian agriculture during its first three years in office, the farm population, especially in western Canada, remained dissatisfied. The legislation introduced by the government had not met the expectations Diefenbaker had created during the 1957 and 1958 election campaigns. Douglas Harkness, then minister of agriculture, proved unable to mollify the farmers and Diefenbaker decided that a new minister was necessary to restore the government's fading popularity in rural Canada, especially on the prairies. Hamilton, after initial hesitation, agreed to take up the challenge. The one condition he placed on his move was that responsibility for the Wheat Board, Canada's sole grain marketing agency, be transferred to Agriculture from Trade and Commerce. If his principal task was to increase Canada's grain sales abroad, then he wanted to control as many aspects of the process as possible.

Diefenbaker agreed, and within hours of his appointment Hamilton asked the board for lists of countries to which Canada did and did not sell grain. Shortly thereafter he instructed diplomatic and trade representatives to start alphabetically at the top of both lists and make a sales pitch. Initially, he did not single out China for special attention. In fact, his early hopes were for increased sales to countries on the Mediterranean.[1] However, he knew that the PRC had bought forty-five tons of wheat from Canada in 1958 and that officials in Trade and Commerce had asked his predecessor for permission to approach the Chinese again. The PRC was a potential customer, and Hamilton asked Trade and Commerce, in conjunction with DEA, to send a two-person team to Peking to, in his own words, 'see if they would mix our own wheat with their wheat, which was the argument we used all over the world.'[2]

The two reported on their return that the food situation in China would be acute within six months as a result of poor harvests in 1959 and 1960. The Chinese badly needed substantial wheat imports.[3] Although the Chinese had been receptive, they had placed no orders. This state of affairs changed dramatically almost overnight. According to Hamilton:

Almost before I finished reading the report ... in late November 1960, I got this telephone call from the clerk at the Queen Elizabeth hotel in Montreal saying there were two Chinese gentlemen at the desk asking for me. Apparently they had flown on Canadian Pacific Airlines ... which took them to Montreal. They got to this hotel and asked for me and he had enough sense, bless his heart, to call me directly ... I said, well, if they are from China it must be in response to the wheat sales pitch. So, I told this chap on the phone to give them the best suite, put it on my account, look after them, and I had those fellows on a plane as fast as I could to Winnipeg where the Wheat Board was because only the Wheat Board could negotiate the deal.[4]

The Chinese had come to buy as much wheat and barley as they could for the amount of money they had available, approximately $60 million. Since the Wheat Board's charter permitted cash sales only, this would buy twenty-eight million bushels of wheat and twelve million bushels of barley. The agreement was signed in mid-December although Hamilton did not announce it to the House of Commons until 2 February 1961.

The circumstances of the sale intrigued Hamilton, for the Chinese negotiators apparently had shown more interest in the quantity of grain they were buying than its quality. This, together with reports coming out of Hong Kong, suggested that the PRC might be interested in further purchases and, just after Christmas, he sent the chief commissioner of the Wheat Board, W.C. McNamara, to Peking to investigate the possibility. Early in January he received word that the PRC indeed faced an acute food shortage, that it would soon enter the international grain market as a buyer in volume, and that it had already begun negotiations with Australia.[5] The Department of Trade and Commerce recommended that in order to compete with the Australians 'the Canadian Wheat Board should be authorized to continue their negotiations on the basis of a gift of a limited quantity of high grade wheat and the sale of a much larger quantity of wheat to China.'[6] Hamilton took this proposal to cabinet, but was turned down. DEA and Finance opposed the idea for fear that the Chinese would misconstrue Canada's charity as an insult, that it would disturb existing agreements with the United States and Australia with respect to the disposal of surpluses of grain, and that the government could not justify an outlay of almost seven million dollars which would benefit only the farm community at a time of high levels of urban and industrial unemployment.[7] Green at DEA and Fleming at Finance won the day. Cabinet decided that 'no gift of wheat be made to Red China, notwithstanding the fact that a gift might make possible a large sale of wheat to China.' At the same time, however, cabinet also agreed that 'the Minister of Agriculture should discuss further with the Canadian Wheat Board the availability of lower grades of wheat and the possibilities of mixing grades in order to make possible a large sale to China at prices consistent with the prices normally quoted for the various grades.'[8]

Although he lost the battle over the gift of grain, cabinet's approval of continued negotiations was all the encouragement Hamilton needed. By this time he had no doubts about the benefits of a sale of grain to mainland China. He instructed McNamara to persist in his discussions with the Chinese and by early March was able to report to cabinet that the China Resources Company, with the approval of the government of the People's Republic, would buy approximately 190 million bushels of wheat and 47 million bushels of barley from Canada over a two and a half year period 'if flexibility in payment arrangements could be negotiated.'[9]

These 'payment arrangements' proved to be an obstacle on which the deal nearly foundered. The Chinese wanted a large quantity of grain, but had very little cash to pay for it. They needed credit and, if the deal were to be struck, the Canadian government would have not only to guarantee any bank loans made to the Wheat Board in order to finance the sales but also to let the Chinese make their payments over time. Hamilton had no difficulty with these arrangements, but others in cabinet, especially the minister of finance, did not like them at all. The opposition was not ideological. There is no evidence that any minister objected to trade in non-strategic goods with 'Communist' China. Rather, the major reservations were financial and political. Some doubted that the Chinese could meet their obligations and believed they would default; others disliked the specific terms of the proposed agreement; and a final group feared the effect the sale might have on Canada's relations with the United States.[10] According to Hamilton the big obstacle turned out to be 'the city members of Cabinet who realized there were ethnic groups in these areas that were pretty worked up all the time about Russia's domination of their home countries and they didn't distinguish between communism in Russia and communism in any other country and they were terrified they would run into very strong opposition.'[11] Hamilton and his allies tackled each argument in turn, but with little initial success. Cabinet first instructed the Wheat Board to attempt 'to effect sales on a cash basis.'[12] The issue came to a head a month later when Hamilton reported back that 'The Mission fully explored the possibility of a sale of grain to China on a cash basis and is fully satisfied that the Chinese are not in a position to conclude an agreement on that basis.'[13] He also pointed out that a potential sale of over 230 million bushels of grain might be lost unless the credit management requested by the Chinese was approved.

By this time, opposition had abated somewhat. Reports from the cities indicated that most of the ethnic communities, with the exception of the Chinese Canadian, would not be antagonized by grain sales to China and even Fleming agreed that a large sale of grain would save Treasury the subsidies to farmers to store their surpluses. Yet sufficient opposition remained to force Hamilton to play his trump card. He wrote to Diefenbaker threatening to resign from cabinet and to publicize his reasons for leaving unless his colleagues accepted his recommendations. This spurred the prime minister to intervene decisively in the debate. In Hamilton's words: 'That ended the discussion very quickly. The Prime Minister said – "This man is willing to lay his portfolio on the line because he believes this is a sound proposal for Canada. Are you fellows equally prepared to lay your portfolios on the line?" Well, there was no more discussion. I got what I wanted.'[14] Cabinet authorized the minister of agriculture to instruct the chief commissioner of the Wheat Board to conclude an agreement with the China Resources Company on the basis of 25 per cent cash and the balance payable in a maximum of nine months. It also authorized the minister of finance to guarantee bank loans made to the Wheat Board to permit credit sales to China to a maximum of $50 million. This upper limit was raised two months later to $100 million despite Fleming's protests.[15]

Hamilton paid a short visit to Hong Kong at the end of April 1961, informing cabinet on his return that the PRC would purchase $362 million worth of Canadian wheat and barley over the next two and a half years.[16] The Liberals claimed later that this visit was no more than a political ploy to gain publicity, since the Chinese had approved the contract several days before he arrived. The larger issues had indeed been settled before the trip took place. Norman Robertson, under-secretary of state for External Affairs, had informed the secretary of state, Howard Green, that McNamara had signed a long-term agreement with Chinese authorities in Peking on 22 April.[17] Not all of the Canadian officials involved in the negotiations appreciated the minister's last-minute appearance. They feared that Hamilton's presence in Hong Kong would emphasize the importance the Canadian government placed on the deal and make future negotiations more difficult. As late as 28 April McNamara cautioned Hamilton that 'details have yet to be worked out.'[18] But Hamilton did not go to Hong Kong for the purpose of participating in the negotiations. Rather, because he had put his political career on the line for this agreement and believed he would have to resign if the Chinese did not meet their obligations under its terms, he wanted to find out for himself how the PRC planned to pay for its credit purchases.[19] The Chinese told him that they would be able to pay only if they could sell more of their own products abroad and, on hearing this, Hamilton took a larger risk and promised to help them expand their export markets. That commitment forged a lasting bond between Alvin Hamilton and the PRC.

On 2 May 1961, Hamilton rose in the House of Commons to proclaim the sale of approximately 187 million bushels of wheat and 47 million bushels of barley to be delivered by the end of December 1963. This was over and above the original contract announced in February. The benefits of the sale, as he saw them, extended far beyond farm incomes to include general invigoration of the economy and a significant increase in Canada's total export earnings.[20] The opposition parties welcomed the announcement, although not without the expected reservations which included fear of an adverse reaction from the United States.

Concern about Washington surfaced in cabinet as soon as it became apparent that the Chinese were serious about a large-scale, long-term purchase of grain. Diefenbaker and Eisenhower had agreed in 1957 that their countries would not undercut each other in the fiercely competitive international wheat market and had established a Joint Committee on Trade and Economic Matters which met quarterly to exchange information. The arrangement worked to the advantage of both countries. The United States undertook not to interfere with Canadian markets by gifts of grain or sales at cut-rate prices and Canada agreed not to protest American largesse if convinced it would strengthen the NATO alliance and the 'Free World.' No one in the government of Canada wanted to upset this quid pro quo. As early as January 1961, DEA officials warned Green of a possible adverse reaction and advised that Washington be informed of the impending sale. One argument used to support the proposed sale to China was that it 'would not displace an existing U.S. market,'[21] but at the same time it was recognized that: 'The strongest argument against the proposal was the fact that a communist country was involved ... Some Ministers said that the extension of credit to Communist China might cause serious concern in the U.S., and might lead to retaliation, e.g. in defence sharing or in the form of a reduction of U.S. investment in Canada.'[22] In these circumstances, the ministers involved took pains to keep their American counterparts informed of the progress of the negotiations. According to Hamilton, 'I phoned down to Kennedy's Agriculture Minister, Orville Freeman, every detail of the negotiations with the Chinese.'[23] In addition, in early March cabinet authorized him to communicate privately to Freeman that consideration was being given to further sales on a cash basis, 'but that, if cash sales proved impossible, the Canadian government was prepared to consider facilitating short-term credit.'[24]

The meetings of the Joint Committee took place on 13 and 14 March 1961, during which time the Canadians also met President Kennedy. Hamilton reminded Kennedy of the deal struck between Diefenbaker and Eisenhower and the new president agreed to honour it. As well, Hamilton tried to convince the Americans that the first step towards a lasting peace with the PRC was to begin to trade with it. In his words, 'in that 1961 series of meetings ... I offered the President half the sales of our grain to the Chinese ... because I could visualize even then there would be lots of markets for both our farmers.'[25] The idea attracted Kennedy and, although he did not accept Hamilton's offer, the Americans did not at that time object to the sales. As Fleming reported on his return to Ottawa, 'the Minister of Agriculture and the U.S. Secretary of Agriculture discussed, informally, the proposed sale of grain by Canada to Communist China. No objection or adverse comment had been made by the U.S. Minister.'[26] When Kennedy visited Ottawa two months later the matter was not even raised.[27]

The first indication that the United States might have changed its opinion with respect to the sales occurred in June when the Treasury Department halted the export of grain unloading pumps (vacuators) to Canada on the grounds that this violated American legislation forbidding trade with enemy nations. The crisis broke on 5 June when the general manager of the Shipping Federation of Canada warned Hamilton that the ships contracted to deliver the grain to China would not sail without the vacuators. DEA officials immediately lodged a protest with the State Department and the Americans responded favourably to the Canadian appeal. Within forty-eight hours Green was able to inform Diefenbaker that U.S. authorities were clearing a policy statement which would permit the Treasury Department to license exports of the necessary equipment to ships in Quebec.[28] Despite the fact that the statement would 'emphasize that this action is being taken as an accommodation to the Government of Canada and is not to be regarded as a precedent,' it did enable Canada to meet its commitments and also gave the government time to make alternative arrangements to avoid similar difficulties with Treasury in future. The United States also cautioned in early 1962 that Canadian grain would be used by the PRC to assist North Vietnamese aggression in South Vietnam, but never raised the issue to the level of a formal protest.[29] Shipments of grain to China proceeded apace, much to the relief of those who regarded the shipments as the salvation of prairie agriculture.

The sales to China transformed farm opinion in the west. Shortly after the sales were announced, Hamilton and other ministers began to receive an overwhelmingly positive response.[30] Even farm organizations such as the wheat pools and the National Farmers Union (NFU), which had led the protest march on Ottawa in 1959, expressed approval. The NFU was the first to congratulate the government. Its annual submission to cabinet in February, just after the first sale became public knowledge, expressed 'appreciation.' Then, after the announcement of the long-term agreement, the president of the union wrote to inform Hamilton that the farm unions were 'very pleased' by the sales. After Hamilton's stand during the debate in cabinet came to be known, various wheat pool associations passed resolutions praising his efforts.[31] The grain sales brought a much-needed influx of money to the economy of western Canada and helped restore the government's popularity with the prairie electorate.

Not everyone welcomed the deal. The Cold War had not yet thawed, memories of the Korean conflict remained, and some would not countenance any trade with a communist country. Within days of the announcement of the first contract Hamilton and his colleagues began to receive letters of protest. One, for example, pointed out 'that such a trade transgresses the treaty amongst Christian democratic nations ... for the specific purpose of countering Communist aggression.' Months later the criticism was just as pointed: 'In the name of reason, responsibility, and the 25 million urban Canadians [sic] who must ultimately face the awesome legacy of 800 million Chinese communist imperialists that we are leaving for them, let us have no more of such jingoistic junk as "Breaking the Embargo" or "feeding our enemies".'[32]

Merril Menzies, a long-time adviser to both Hamilton and the prime minister, dismissed such dissent as 'rather childish and need scarcely be dignified by serious rebuttal,'[33] but Hamilton did not treat it so lightly. He took pains to reply to each critic and invariably used the counterargument which formed the basis of his belief in seeking peace through international trade: 'We hold to the belief that world peace is only possible when you are talking and trading with potential enemy countries. Naturally, we do not trade in strategic or military goods. We feel that peace will be helped by building up trade and contact between nations.'[34] Nonetheless, he must have taken some comfort from the fact that a mere 5 per cent of letters to him opposed the sale, that most of these were from urban Canada east of Manitoba, and that his political contacts in the west were reporting a favourable reception for the sales and his part in them.[35]

He was so impressed with the response that he advised Diefenbaker to call an election in the fall of 1961 to 'take advantage of the China sales.'[36] Subsequent events may have proved him correct. An election in the fall of 1961 fought on the twin planks of the China sales and the second stage of the National Development Programme might have saved the government its majority. As it turned out, when the election was held in June 1962, the Conservatives were reduced from 208 to 116 seats despite the fact that only five of the ninety-two seats lost were in the west. Fleming's fears that the Chinese would renege on their commitments and that the government could be forced to make good the $100 million guarantee of bank loans were unfounded.[37] The Chinese met their obligations, and the untarnished success of the arrangement moved Hamilton to promise farmers that he would sell as much grain as they could grow. Such optimism had not been heard on the prairies for a generation. It seemed to restore farmers' faith in their future, and Hamilton's audiences were delighted, even though they were not prepared to gamble their future prosperity to the extent that he wished. They welcomed the sales, but did not want to share the financial risks if the Chinese should default.

Fleming continued to fret over the government's guarantee of credit despite the PRC's flawless record of payment. This finally led Hamilton to conclude that the farmers should place a small amount of their profits in a reserve fund to ensure credit sales. He believed they were accustomed to setting aside funds for various contingencies and Canadian businessmen took 15 per cent of the risk of any credit extended to foreign purchasers by the Export Credit Insurance Corporation. It seemed a good idea and Hamilton, on his own initiative, offered it to farm organizations in the fall of 1962. The response was swift and vocal. Farmers wanted nothing to do with it. The National Farmers Union, in its brief to a federal-provincial agricultural conference held in November, directly opposed the idea. Individual farmers were just as blunt in their opposition. According to one of them: 'I'm opposed to the pools financing your political ambitions. You took credit for the sales, you told us to grow all the grain we can and you would sell it. Now you want us to underwrite your sales and sink the earnings of our organization into promotional sales that other companies in the business do not want to risk. As far as I'm concerned, Mr. Hamilton, no deal.'[38]

The prime minister's formal response to his minister's trial balloon was to ask Hamilton to prepare a statement for the House outlining the proposal but not to deliver it until he himself had cleared it.[39] The *Montreal Star* reported a more colourful account of Diefenbaker's reaction, stating that Hamilton had been 'summoned in a hot fury and berated violently.' The prime minister then informed him that 'he had already arranged to have his estimates brought before the House of Commons on Wednesday so that the statements could be debated – in effect so that the Opposition parties could add their chastisement to the one Mr. Diefenbaker had just delivered.'[40]

Hamilton's unbridled enthusiasm also led to warnings from his closest advisers. Roy Faibish, Hamilton's private secretary, in particular, cautioned him against raising expectations about future sales, noting that he could be 'seriously and permanently harmed politically in the future if the breaks on sales don't come your way and grain piles up again.'[41] The caveat proved prophetic when in the fall of 1962 the PRC marched its troops into territory India regarded as its own, and the cabinet, in response to public outcry and pressure from the Indian government, considered stopping the shipments of grain to the PRC from Canadian ports. Most of the correspondence Hamilton received on the subject suggested that he was soft on communism and supported Chinese aggression.[42] At the same time Canada's high commissioner to India, Chester Ronning, informed Green that Nehru had asked him informally about Canada's wheat sales to China and had added that food being such an important factor in China's economy, 'Canadian wheat was giving strength to China during an aggressive invasion which threatened the very existence of India.' Green advised his colleagues that India's high commissioner had asked him whether Canada would cancel future grain sales to China under the circumstances.[43]

The debate in cabinet was protracted and there is reason to believe that the government came close to bowing to this pressure. As Hamilton wrote to Diefenbaker: 'I am still numbed by our conversation ... I gather that, because of the India–China situation, the national interest may best be served by slowing down efforts to sell in Communist countries ... My personal judgment is that, unless open war breaks out, we would lose far more support by weakening our efforts to sell abroad.'[44] Negotiations were then under way for a further sale of grain to the PRC and Hamilton feared that not only would Canada lose the contract but also the government would anger the farm population, the one solid base of Conservative support remaining after the 1962 election.

Cabinet eventually adopted a compromise position. Canada would meet its obligations under existing contracts and continue the discussions on further sales, but it would not grant permits for the export to the PRC of products other than grains because they might be used to support 'continued aggression against India.'[45] In addition, Canada would assist its fellow member of the Commonwealth in other ways. Cabinet agreed in November to give India six Dakota aircraft and in December reversed its decision to cut its contributions to the Colombo Plan on the grounds that 'the suggested assistance to India would be an effective reply to the criticism that the government of Canada was selling wheat to Communist China and reducing its aid to India.'[46] By the new year Hamilton was sufficiently confident to be able to defend the government's position in forceful terms:

> we have never refused to sell non-strategic materials such as grain to any country because of its political persuasions. This has also been the case with other Commonwealth countries, including Great Britain, Australia and India itself, all of whom have been trading with China in foodstuffs or other products. It might be noted in this connection that the more of its foreign exchange resources that China is required to use for imported foodstuffs, the less is available for manufactured goods which may have a more direct bearing on its military strength.[47]

Finally, despite its sympathy for India, Cabinet did not regard the conflict as sufficient reason to sacrifice either the long-term agreement with the PRC or the prospect of additional sales.

There were some costs, however, that cabinet was not prepared to pay to ensure further sales, and this led Hamilton into another lengthy conflict with some of his colleagues. During 1961 Canadian exports to the PRC totalled $122.8 million – $120.2 million of which were cereal grains – while Canada imported a mere $3.2 million worth of PRC goods.[48] The Chinese wanted to reduce this deficit as much as possible and throughout 1962 pressed the government to grant their products easier access to the Canadian market. The future of the grain sales soon became a bargaining lever and the Chinese used it as best they could. After meeting with Chinese officials, Canada's new trade commissioner in Hong Kong reported in July that 'the inference was clear that if the Chinese continue to be thwarted in marketing their textiles in Canada by what they regard as discriminatory and unfair tactics then they would be forced to reconsider the extent of their future wheat purchases in Canada.'[49] Peking recalled its trade mission to Canada earlier than scheduled because of Ottawa's 'intransigence,' and in December one of the commissioners of the Wheat Board, in Hong Kong to sign another contract under the long-term agreement, warned Hamilton that the Chinese were insisting on more favourable access to the Canadian market.[50] The contract signed in December covered the first six months of 1963 only. The Chinese refused to negotiate deliveries for the latter half of the year without some sign that Canada would accommodate them.

Peking wanted to sell more textiles in Canada to reduce the huge disparity in trade between the two countries and asked Ottawa repeatedly for help. It understood that increased sales of textiles alone would not correct the imbalance and, further, that Ottawa could not grant free and open access to the Canadian market. But the PRC did want as a gesture of goodwill a change in the tariff which would enable it to compete on more favourable terms with domestic and other foreign suppliers. An increase in sales from one to four million dollars would have been considered satisfactory.[51] The Chinese position met with some sympathy in Ottawa, and Hamilton, as might be expected, led the fight to oblige. As he explained to Diefenbaker, 'there is no question in my mind that we have no choice but to allow three or four million dollars' worth of Chinese textiles in each year. As Westerners, we both understand that to be able to sell 50 million bushels of wheat to these new markets of China and Eastern Europe means that we can probably hold the west politically for years to come.'[52] No political or economic argument, however, could convince the prime minister and cabinet to provide the accommodation the Chinese sought. Canadian textile companies, fearful of increased competition, urged the government to refuse the request, and officials in Trade and Commerce and DEA warned that any favour granted to Peking would be resented by Canada's other trading partners, especially Japan and the Republic of China on commercial grounds, and the United States and possibly India on political grounds. They also predicted that China could not afford to go without Canadian grain in light of her shortage of food and advised the government to call Peking's bluff.[53] Cabinet referred the issue to the Interdepartmental Committee on Low-Cost Imports which recommended nothing more than an extension of the list of goods China could export to Canada. But the government was defeated before even this small concession could be granted.

The history of the early grain sales was not a series of easy triumphs for Hamilton and his supporters. On balance, however, the sales did more to enhance his reputation than any other accomplishment of his years in office. During the 1961-2 crop year Canada's exports of wheat were the third highest on record and the Wheat Board made the highest average final payment to farmers in its history. Cartoonists portrayed Hamilton as a modern-day Marco Polo, and he acquired a status on a par with Diefenbaker in the eyes of the farm community. The sales also left a lasting and positive political legacy to the Progressive Conservative party on the prairies, a legacy which bore considerable electoral success in the coming years.

The grain sales were also the first act in an ongoing relationship between Hamilton and the PRC. Peking did not forget the pledge he made in April 1961 to help it sell its exports abroad or the efforts he made while in office to keep that promise. While in Hong Kong he invited the Chinese to send a trade mission to Canada as soon as possible and, on his return to Ottawa, helped arrange the tour which took place in October. During that visit he advised his guests to send more specialized missions the following year and again did everything he could to ensure their success. In addition, he contacted companies across Canada and urged them to take advantage of the opportunities created by the grain sales. Then, when the business community failed to respond, he turned to Canada's friends in Asia and South America and asked them to welcome Chinese trade as a favour to this country. They did, and China's exports increased dramatically, although not to the extent desired in Peking.

Early in 1964 when the Chinese wanted advice on international trading operations, they turned to Hamilton, despite the fact that he no longer held a cabinet post. He arrived in China in March and spent several weeks in various parts of the country. In Peking he discussed international trade with Chinese officials, including communications channels, credit arrangements, and the difficulties of a state-trading nation doing business with private enterprise economies. Later, he and his wife Beulah travelled the country enjoying the exotic fare of Chinese tourism. The lavish reception gave Hamilton more than a moment's pause because he regarded the sales, however important, as a business transaction unworthy of such fervent expressions of gratitude. He has recalled that his Chinese hosts told him that their pride had been shattered between 1959 and 1961 by bad weather. The expenditure of vast amounts of energy and enthusiasm during the Great Leap Forward produced very few results. 'Just at the moment when we were in the midst of this tremendous national effort thinking we had no friends, you came selling wheat.'[54] This not only explained Peking's gratitude, it also suggested to him that perhaps the PRC was beginning to regret its isolation from the rest of the world.

These suspicions were confirmed during a conversation with Chou En-lai before Hamilton left Peking. They touched briefly on Hamilton's discussions with the Chinese trade officials and then Chou turned to his country's current economic and political difficulties. He admitted that the PRC could not reach its economic objectives without foreign trade and agreed that it would have to restore links with former trading partners regardless of the differences in their economic and political philosophies. Furthermore, he declared that China's national security required a return to the world political stage. He made it clear that Peking feared the Soviet presence on its northern border more than any threat posed by the Americans, that it regarded Taiwan as the only major difference with the United States, and that he was prepared to wait fifty years if necessary to settle the question. In Hamilton's words, 'After ninety minutes I realized that he was trying desperately to tell me that the one thing he wanted to do before he finished his political life was to bring the United States and China back into some form of harmony.' Hamilton was convinced that the PRC wanted to end its isolation and achieve a rapprochement with Washington. In his opinion, Chou would welcome discussions to that end with American politicians and businessmen.[55]

Hamilton tried to convey this message to America's politicians. In the summer and fall of 1964 he approached several senators, congressmen, and members of the campaign committees of both President Johnson and Barry Goldwater, but they would not talk to him until after the elections in November. Then, in January 1965, Senator William Fulbright, chairman of the Senate Foreign Relations Committee, arranged for him to meet unofficially with some members of both the Senate and House and an official from the White House staff. Hamilton informed them of Chou's wishes and urged them to accept the invitation to visit the PRC. The Americans split on the question – some wanted to go, others did not because, in accordance with prevailing sentiment at the time, 'they thought that dealing with a Communist was like a dealing with the devil.' Nothing of immediate significance came of that meeting, leading Hamilton to turn to another audience. He approached several boards of trade in cities on the west coast in an attempt to convince American businessmen of the advantages of restoring trade. This led to an invitation from church groups in the Midwest to participate in a series of debates on the issue of Sino-American relations, culminating in a conference in March 1965, sponsored by the Kansas Institute of International Relations. During the final debate Hamilton put forward the argument that would be his lodestar in future years. This was 'peace through trade,' the belief that 'the quickest way to achieve peace with your enemies is to start trading with them.'

> The Chinese are willing to trade. They are willing to talk. In time
> our political differences can be resolved if basic interests are
> accepted, but first let us get on with the task of raising the
> standards of living by bringing the newly developed nations into the

orbit of world trade. If we have faith in the ability of our economic institutions to prevail, then there should be no doubt that we can arrive at political solutions.[56]

The argument was appealing to many. Even former Governor Alf Landon, 'Mr Republican' in conservative Kansas and one-time candidate for the presidency, admitted to Hamilton that 'we should trade with the bastards.'[57]

The demands of Hamilton's own political career and the outbreak of the Cultural Revolution intervened to interrupt his proselytizing efforts in the United States. In 1969 he wrote Chou that several high-ranking senators and members of Congress were interested in visiting the PRC and that the United States had recently relaxed travel restrictions making travel possible if visas could be obtained.[58] 'Ping-pong' diplomacy superseded Hamilton's efforts and led eventually to Richard Nixon's visit to Peking. Nevertheless, these early efforts at encouraging a dialogue planted the idea of rapprochement in the minds of several powerful American politicians, and perhaps helped soften the extreme anti-Chinese attitudes of some of the American public.

Hamilton's position was that the PRC's problems in increasing exports could not be solved by any one approach alone, and so he tackled them on several different fronts simultaneously. Throughout the 1960s he continued to persuade Canadian businessmen of the profits to be made from trade with the PRC, and he returned to China in 1966 in an attempt to smooth the way for Canadian firms, albeit with little success because of the Cultural Revolution's suspicion of anything foreign. He also kept a close watch on Canada's continued grain sales to China and urged the Pearson government to do more to help Peking balance its large trade deficit with Canada. In May 1965, for example, he stated in the House of Commons that grain sales were 'not a windfall type of arrangement but will be here permanently.' He added the recommendation that Canada permit the PRC to establish an unofficial trade office in Canada to increase business contacts. He concluded that Canadian policy should be 'to help the Chinese in every way to establish legitimate trade relations with us.' This included pressuring Washington to allow American business to trade with the PRC.[59]

Another of his approaches was global in scope. He advised the government not to forget the less-developed nations of the world when formulating its trade policy and not to join other industrialized countries in erecting barriers against trade with the emerging economies of Asia, Africa, and Latin America. He feared that the GATT negotiations under way in the mid-1960s would perpetuate the poverty of the Third World. His most comprehensive set of recommendations came in a speech to the House in the fall of 1964 in which he urged government to accept a six-point proposal for altering commodity pricing, creating a new agency to assist Third World exporters wishing to do business in Canada, establishing new purchasing boards, encouraging Canadian companies to work co-operatively, establishing a new world trading bank, and reducing tariffs.[60] Three years later he added an expanded 'export credits programme' to encourage sales abroad. The objectives and philosophy were straightforward: if developed countries such as Canada helped nations such as China to prosper, then Canada would benefit in return.[61]

The opportunities open to Alvin Hamilton, MP, to influence Canadian attitudes toward China ended abruptly with the loss of his seat in the House in the election of June 1968. His defeat also left him without a regular source of income. Here his connection with China proved useful. Initially he wrote articles for the press and toured the United States, lecturing audiences on the enormous potential of trade with the PRC. In 1971 he accepted an invitation from Peking to return once again to advise them on methods of increasing exports and reducing the trade deficit. He discovered that he could be of most assistance in developing the PRC's oil and gas reserves.[62]

Hamilton's role as a consultant to the Chinese government and his involvement with a private oil supply company were the main elements of his contact with China for the next decade. Although he returned to the House of Commons in 1972, he spoke only occasionally on the subject of Sino-Canadian affairs. In part this was because there was less need for him to do so. Sales of grain continued unimpeded, Canada began to buy more from China, and the Trudeau government had extended formal recognition to the PRC in October 1970. Excluded from cabinet under later Conservative prime ministers, he had much less opportunity to contribute to debates on foreign relations. He has, however, remained active advising China on its development strategy and promoting trade relations.[63]

At one time Hamilton predicted that history would judge his role in shaping the National Development Programme of the Diefenbaker government to be the most important contribution of his political career. More recently he has changed his mind and now believes that the benefits at home and abroad which have derived from his long association with the PRC will receive pride of place. He acknowledges freely the political advantages which the sales brought his party in the early 1960s, but cautions that their significance should not be over-emphasized. Of far greater importance was the opportunity those sales gave him to accomplish much more of value on the international stage than he could have foreseen at the time. Today, he sees the grain sales, for which he is most often remembered, in the larger perspective of mainland China's emergence from its isolation and his efforts to increase trade between the PRC and other nations as part of a positive approach to world peace.

The last image should be reserved for the cartoonists who found Hamilton such an irresistible subject. One depicted him as the captain of a sailboat laden with wheat for China under the caption 'Red Sales in the Sunset.' Another simply had him grinning broadly over the Great Wall of China on which he had scrawled 'Alvin Was Here.'[64]

Notes

1 Hamilton interview, 26 Oct. 1982.
2 Ibid.
3 Memorandum, C.J. Small (DEA representative with Canada's Trade Commission in Hong Kong) to DEA, 7 Nov. 1960 (DEA file 9030-40, vol. 6).
4 Hamilton interview, 26 Oct. 1982.
5 See, for example, a Draft Memorandum to Cabinet, R.M. Esdale, Trade and Commerce, to Hamilton, 13 Jan. 1961 (Hamilton Papers, PAC, Box 269150).
6 Ibid.
7 See, for example, memorandum from N.A. Robertson to H. Green, SSEA, 14 Jan. 1961 (DEA file 9030-40, vol. 6).
8 Record of Cabinet Decisions, 16 Jan. 1961 (PCO file A-1-7(a)-C2).
9 Cabinet Conclusions, PCO vol. 84, 1940, 9 Mar. 1961.
10 Ibid.
11 Hamilton interview, 26 Oct. 1982.
12 Cabinet Conclusions, PCO vol. 84, 1940, 9 Mar. 1961.
13 Hamilton, Memorandum to Cabinet, 10 Apr. 1961 (Cabinet Document 151/61, PCO file A-1-7(a)-C2).
14 Hamilton interview, 26 Oct. 1982.
15 Cabinet Conclusions, PCO vol. 85, 1951, 11 Apr. 1961. Cabinet approved the change on 16 June 1961.
16 Cabinet Conclusions, PCO vol. 86, 1960, 2 May 1961.
17 Memorandum, N.A. Robertson to H. Green, 28 Apr. 1961 (DEA file 9030-40, vol. 6).
18 Memorandum, McNamara to Hamilton, 28 Apr. 1961 (Hamilton Papers, PAC, Box 268694.18.6).
19 Hamilton interview, 26 Oct. 1982.
20 House of Commons, *Debates*, 2 May 1961, p. 4205.
21 Undated *Aide-mémoire*, 'Wheat for China: Arguments for the Proposal' (Hamilton Papers, Box 269150).
22 Cabinet Conclusions, PCO vol. 84, 1940, Mar. 9, 1961.

23 Hamilton interview, 26 Oct. 1982. This is confirmed by a DEA message to Canadian embassies on 2 May which read in part: 'At eleven o'clock this morning Mr Hamilton spoke to Mr Freeman and informed him of the announcement he was about to make in the House' (DEA file 9030-40, vol. 6).
24 Cabinet Conclusions, PCO, vol. 84, 1940, 9 Mar. 1961.
25 Hamilton interview, 26 Oct. 1982.
26 Cabinet Conclusion, PCO vol. 84, 1944, 16 Mar. 1961.
27 Memorandum, O.G. Stoner (DEA Economic Division) to A.E. Ritchie, 11 May 1962 (DEA file 9030-40, vol. 8). The memorandum read in part: 'We have also received the file on President Kennedy's visit to Ottawa on May 17, 1961, and we find that while there was some discussion of the question of Chinese representation in the United Nations there was apparently no mention of Canadian grain sales to China.'
28 Memorandum, H. Green, SSEA, to P.M., 7 June 1961 (Hamilton Papers, Box 199).
29 See DEA file 9030-40, vol. 8.
30 See, for example, J.H. Wilson to Hamilton, 13 June 1961, and H. Zondervan to Hamilton, 3 July 1961 (Hamilton Papers, Box 119).
31 Submission of the NFU to the Government of Canada, 15 Feb. 1961 (Hamilton Papers, Box 269150); A.P. Gleave to Hamilton, 4 May 1961 (Hamilton Papers, PAC, Box 268712); see, for example, Resolution, District 10 of the Saskatchewan Wheat Pool, 8 Mar. 1962 (Hamilton Papers, Box 268662).
32 F.L. Williams to Hamilton, 4 Feb. 1961 (Hamilton Papers, Box 268656); F.C. Quelenton to Hamilton, 16 June 1961 (Hamilton Papers, Box 199).
33 Memorandum, Menzies to Hamilton, 1 June 1961 (Hamilton Papers, Box 199).
34 Hamilton to G. McLean, 14 Sept. 1961 (Hamilton Papers, Box 269118);
35 Hamilton to J. Kelly, 9 June 1961 (Hamilton Papers, Box 219);
36 Hamilton to J.G. Diefenbaker, 15 Nov. 1961 (Hamilton Papers, Box 225).
37 On 11 July 1961, Fleming wrote to Hamilton (Hamilton Papers, Box 268644) as follows: 'I am entertaining increasing concern over the credit which has been established to China through the Wheat Board to finance purchases of wheat. In particular, I am concerned over the enlargement from $50 million to $100 million in the authorized credit at any one time ... In view of the size and nature of our wheat contracts and "intents" with China, I think we should instruct the Wheat Board to keep us fully and very promptly informed on payments or defaults. If she defaults in excess of 10 or 15 (or at the most 30 days) we should seriously consider suspending shipments until payments are up-to-date.'

38 Submission, NFU, 19 Nov. 1962 (Hamilton Papers, Box 268265); H.C. Kreutzwieser to Hamilton, 3 Jan. 1963 (Hamilton Papers, Box 269126).
39 Cabinet Conclusions, PCO vol. 96, 2152, 13 Nov. 1962.39.6.
40 W.A. Wilson, 'Hamilton's Humiliation,' *Montreal Star*, 17 Nov. 1962.
41 R. Faibish to Hamilton, 8 Nov. 1962 (Hamilton Papers, Box 268695).
42 See, for example, R.M. Bond to Hamilton, 23 Oct. 1962 (Hamilton Papers, Box 199); and Hoseng to Hamilton, 10 Dec. 1962 (Hamilton Papers, Box 268644).
43 Telegram, C. Ronning to DEA, 23 Nov. 1962 (Cabinet Documents, PCO file A-1-7(a)-C2); Cabinet Conclusions, PCO, vol. 96, 2160, 27 Nov. 1962.
44 Hamilton to Diefenbaker, 19 Dec. 1962 (Hamilton Papers, Box 225).
45 Cabinet Conclusions, PCO, vol. 95, 2145, 23 Oct. 1962.
46 Cabinet Conclusions, PCO, vol. 96, 2169, 20 Dec. 1962.
47 Hamilton letter drafted in response to those received concerning the Sino-Indian dispute, 3 Jan. 1963 (Hamilton Papers, Box 268644).
48 Figures taken from Cabinet Document 362/62, 5 Nov. 1962 (PCO file A-1-7(a)-C2).
49 R.K. Thomson to Trade and Commerce, 12 July 1962 (DEA file 9030-40, vol. 8).
50 W. Riddell to Hamilton, 14 Dec. 1962 (DEA file 9030-40, vol. 9).
51 A more complete explanation of the Chinese position can be found in Hamilton's memorandum to the cabinet, 'Trade with Mainland China – Duty Valuation of Textile Imports,' 5 Nov. 1962 (Cabinet Documents, PCO file A-1-7(a)-C2).
52 Hamilton to Diefenbaker, 23 Oct. 1962 (Hamilton Papers, Box 199).
53 See, for example, memoranda from the Far Eastern Division to the Economic Division of DEA, 10 Jan. 1963, and N.A. Robertson to H. Green, SSEA, 5 Mar. 1963 (DEA file 9030-40, vol. 9).
54 Hamilton, Speech to the Thirtieth Annual Kansas Institute of International Relations Conference, 29 Mar. 1965 (Hamilton Papers, Box 199).
55 Ibid.; Hamilton interview.
56 Speech to the Thirtieth Annual Kansas Institute of International Relations Conference, 29 Mar. 1965 (Hamilton Papers, Box 199). Chester Ronning also spoke at the conference; see chapter by Brian Evans in this volume.
57 Hamilton interview, 17 Nov. 1982.
58 Hamilton to Chou En-lai, 10 Dec. 1969 (Hamilton Private Papers, Manotick).
59 House of Commons, *Debates*, 25 May 1965, p. 1604.
60 House of Commons, *Debates*, 18 Oct. 1964, pp. 8876–9.60.6.
61 See House of Commons, *Debates*, 30 June 1967, p. 2159.

62 Hamilton interview, 26 June 1981.
63 Hamilton interviews, 21 Jan. 1981, 26 June 1981 and 30 Apr. 1984; see also his 'Report from Parliament Hill,' 22 Feb. 1984, and R. Sheppard, 'Back Door Opens on Friendship,' *Globe and Mail*, 8 May 1984.
64 *Montreal Gazette*, 6 May 1961, and *Winnipeg Tribune*, 20 Dec. 1962.

SECTION IV

Recognizing the People's Republic of China

CHAPTER EIGHT

B. Michael Frolic

The Trudeau Initiative

In 1968, a new Canadian prime minister set out to put his imprint on Canada's foreign policy. Armed with a view of Canadian external relations that would later be defined as 'activist' and 'realist,'[1] Pierre Elliot Trudeau sought to distance himself from the strong commitment to multilateralism and close partnership with the United States which had characterised the Pearsonian period.

Trudeau was no stranger to China. He had been there twice, and after his second trip in 1960, he had co-authored a popular book with Jacques Hébert, *Two Innocents in Red China*.[2] A decade earlier Trudeau spent several weeks travelling in China, then in the throes of civil war. This first trip, in 1949, made a great impression on the thirty-year-old Trudeau. He recalls that the journey from Hong Kong to Canton took three days instead of the customary few hours because soldiers stopped the train to loot and to steal the animals carried on board.[3] In 1950, after his return to Canada, he committed himself on the pages of *Cité Libre* to supporting the recognition of

---

This essay is part of a larger monograph on Canadian-Chinese relations, 1968–70, currently being completed. It is based on files made available by the Department of External Affairs, and also on documentary materials and interviews. The relevant DEA files are: 20-China-14; The China Policy Review, 1968, file 20-265-C3; and 20-1-2-PRC. The author wishes to thank the Historical Division of DEA for its co-operation in making files available and providing other assistance. For earlier works on this general topic, see John D. Harbron, 'Canada Recognizes China: The Trudeau Round 1968–1973,' *Behind the Headlines*, 33.5, October (1975), and Maureen Appel Molot, 'Canada's Relations with China since 1968,' in N. Hillmer and G. Stevenson, eds., *Foremost Nation* (Toronto: McClelland and Stewart 1976), 230–67.

the new Communist government, even if its policies at the time were unpalatable to much of the Western world. In 1960, he and Hébert wrote that 'the two-China policy is based on ignorance of the Chinese mentality' while American policy supporting Taiwan was 'based only on a question of prestige.' China could afford to wait: 'Time is on its side and China is in no hurry,' although it was in the world's interest to bring China out of its isolation.[4]

Trudeau's decision to move toward recognition of the PRC stemmed from more than his personal experiences there. In the spring of 1968 he was establishing himself first as the new leader of the Liberal party and then as Canada's prime minister. In contrast to most of his peers and especially his predecessor, Lester Pearson, Trudeau cultivated an image of positive change signalling a departure from policies of the past. Foreign relations was one of his main targets. Canadian foreign policy had been too closely identified with American interests and Trudeau and his advisers sought to alter that perception. Canada's relationship with the PRC was one of the focal points for a symbolic, if not real, emancipation from American influence.

In 1966 Trudeau had served in the Canadian delegation which sought to gain admittance for the PRC to the United Nations. The lessons of the failure of this initiative were not lost on Trudeau. Canada had been embarrassed by the Americans who took advantage of Pearson's indecisiveness. Not only was it clear that Canada needed strong leadership and a reassessment of its relationship with the United States, but its foreign policy professionals, the Department of External Affairs, had to be reminded that a new prime minister was in charge of foreign policy. No friend of DEA at the outset, Trudeau felt that Canadian foreign policy no longer coincided with Canadian national interests. DEA through its close ties with Pearson and its traditional role as foreign policy adviser, if not its actual maker, was in good part to blame. Trudeau's decision to recognize the PRC was seen as a first step in changing the relationship of DEA to the prime minister. The installation of Ivan Head, Trudeau's foreign policy adviser, as the key link between the prime minister and DEA, put the latter on notice that both the content of foreign policy and the decision-making process itself were up for review.[5] In addition, the new secretary of state for External Affairs, Mitchell Sharp, a former public servant *par excellence*, could be counted on loyally to follow the wishes of his new leader and his prime minister's office. With the support of these men, Trudeau was thus well-positioned to carry out his plans.

Within a month Trudeau asked for a major review of Canadian foreign policy. He argued that it was time to recast Canadian foreign policy in new directions.[6] Change was his order of the day. The subsequent report, *Foreign Policy for Canadians*, issued in 1970, stands as a benchmark in this transition from Canada as 'the helpful fixer' to a nation that aspired to more than middle power status, at least in the early years of the Trudeau period.[7]

In this transition Canadian relations with China represented an opportunity for Trudeau to seize the initiative in dramatic fashion. China policy had been trapped in the bogs of U.N. admission, mired in inconclusive debates over 'two-Chinas' or 'one-China,' or 'one-China, 'one-Taiwan' policies. Canadian initiatives in 1964 and 1966 at the United Nations had failed. Despite the fact that Canada had developed a major trading relationship with the PRC, and that the Canadian public image of China was not unfavourable,[8] Canada had been unable to make any apparent progress in restructuring its political relationship with China.

In early May 1968 Trudeau tested the waters by suggesting that recognition was feasible, although 'The PRC would probably say no unless we agreed to break relations with Taiwan. We wouldn't do that.' A few days later, on 10 May, he again returned to China in Vancouver when he noted, 'The present situation in which a government which represents a quarter of the world's population is diplomatically isolated even from countries with which it is actively trading is obviously unsatisfactory. I would be in favour of any measures including recognition on suitable terms which can intensify the contacts between our two countries and thus normalize our relations and contribute to international order and stability.' On 20 May in a CTV interview he stated, 'The China which the U.N.. Charter speaks of is the PRC. That is the China – this did not work in the U.N. – I am saying now it is time not to continue doing it through the back door and instead try the front door.' On 25 May in a CBC interview, Trudeau observed: 'I feel our hands are free. I feel that there are two facts of life in international politics in this particular area – the fact there is a government in Peking which represents 700 or 800 million people, and the government of Taipei represents – what is it – 10, 12, or 14 million people. These are two facts. Now what will happen, what Peking will answer me, how Taiwan will react, we will see.'[9]

On 29 May the prime minister made a major policy statement in which he referred to China as 'both a colossus and a conundrum,' a country about which we have 'incomplete information – which opens an area of unpredictability.' China must become a member of the world community because many of the major world issues 'will not be resolved completely or in any lasting way unless and until an accommodation has been reached with the Chinese nation.'

Trudeau went on:

We shall be looking at our policy in relation to China in the context of a new interest in Pacific affairs generally. Because of past preoccupations with Atlantic and European affairs we have tended to overlook the reality that Canada is a Pacific country too. Canada has long advocated a positive approach to mainland China and its inclusion in the world community. We have an economic interest in trade with China – no doubt shared by others – and a political interest in preventing tension between China and its neighbours, but especially between China and the United States. *Our aim will be to recognize the People's Republic of China government as soon as possible and to enable that government to occupy the seat of China in the U.N., taking into account that there is a separate government in Taiwan.* (my emphasis)

The Move toward Implementation

Recognition was to take place 'as soon as possible.' The prime minister had enunciated his policy objectives, and it was now the job of others to carry out his instructions. Trudeau's simple pronouncement masked a host of complex issues that might not be waved away by Canada's sudden willingness to consider recognition. First, did the PRC want to be recognized? For the past one and a half years, Mao's China had withdrawn in inner turmoil from the rest of the world. It had ignored diplomatic conventions and immunities by humiliating foreign diplomats in Peking. Indulging in acts of anti-foreignism and isolating itself from the rest of the world in a revolutionary posture, the PRC in mid-1968 did not appear to be a candidate for normalization of relations with anyone. It was conceivable that Peking might not respond at all to the Trudeau initiative and that Canada would then be in the embarrassing situation of unilaterally recognizing an unwilling China. Second, since past Canadian attempts at normalizing relations had invariably come to grief, why should Canada assume that this latest venture would succeed? The government had considered recognition at least four times and failed. It had sought to establish trade offices, and had been rebuffed at the United Nations over the admission issue. Would this latest attempt turn out to be a hastily conceived solution to what seemed to be an insoluble problem? Third, while the past record and China's current behaviour might give Trudeau pause, of more immediate concern was American reaction to his decision. Was the time ripe for Canada to embark on a China policy that differed sharply from its neighbour's? Would there be political and/or economic consequences? Canada's abstention on, rather than rejection of, the Albanian resolution (which would have admitted the PRC to the United Nations by a simple majority vote) caused considerable American resentment in 1966. Would this attempt at accommodation with China in the midst of the Vietnam War provoke angry American reactions, for example, through the imposition of economic sanctions against Canada? Fourth, a number of Canadians were concerned that negotiations for recognition might adversely affect existing trading relations with the PRC. Canada already was doing a booming business with the PRC without recognition. Trade was not likely to increase noticeably after the normalization of relations, so why proceed in this direction? At the present time Canada had the best of both possible worlds, trade with both the PRC and Taiwan. Why jeopardize this situation? Fifth, what about the security implications of a Chinese embassy located in Ottawa? For many Canadians, the establishment of diplomatic relations was like issuing a licence for spying and subversion. The Chinese were communists, and, like their communist Soviet 'elder brothers,' would likely use their diplomatic representatives to promote world revolution abroad. More important, the Chinese would have a golden opportunity to infiltrate the Canadian Chinese community. At the present time this community was pro-Kuomintang and generally apolitical, but with the establishment of a Chinese embassy in Ottawa this situation might easily change. The formerly peaceful Chinese community in Canada might become a 'fifth column' for the Chinese revolution in North America.[10]

All these concerns had to be taken into consideration when proceeding to implement the new policy, but the most important was Trudeau's instruction, 'to take into account the fact that there is a separate government in Taiwan.' What did this mean? Was Canada formulating a 'two-Chinas policy' or a 'one-China, one-Taiwan policy,' despite the PRC's adamant rejection of such positions? If so, prospects for Chinese agreement seemed gloomy at best. If not, the phrase 'taking into account the fact that there is a separate government in Taiwan' was vague enough to permit possible slippage from a 'one-China, one-Taiwan policy.' But to what? The Chinese soon made it clear that this was the key sentence in Trudeau's speech, noting that China would watch closely how Canada intended to interpret this phrase.[11]

In a subsequent analysis DEA observed that it never received any detailed direction from above on how to interpret this qualification. Indeed, had DEA been consulted by Trudeau before he gave his foreign policy statement of 29 May 1968, it would have advised against seeking diplomatic relations at that time. Still, Trudeau had provided the policy and it was now up to the professionals to make it workable. DEA was entrusted with the difficult task of taking what initially appeared to be a 'one-China, one-Taiwan policy' and repackaging it into a 'one-China policy' without losing Canadian credibility in the process. That they managed to do this is a testimony to their skill at developing the political formula and negotiating plan which eventually made it possible for Canada to 'derecognize' the ROC (Taiwan) without losing too much Canadian face.[12] Trudeau was the catalyst, the one person able to make the dramatic act that changed our China policy, but it was DEA which he had initially criticized that in the end provided the resources and expertise to realize this policy. Well before Trudeau's 29 May speech, DEA had begun collecting material for a general review of China policy. Earlier reviews on the recognition question, done in 1963, 1965, and 1966, were available in the files. DEA contained a number of officials with special knowledge of China, who could again be asked to search for the elusive recognition formula. On 6 June 1968, a memorandum was prepared for Mitchell Sharp, the secretary of state for External Affairs, which examined the various options open to Canada, assessing the legal and practical implications of each option, and the likely international repercussions involved. DEA noted in this memo that, based on the experience of other countries, it was reasonable to assume that it would not be possible to enter into diplomatic relations with Peking while maintaining relations with Taipei.[13]

The Taiwan issue quickly became the main topic at the minister's press conference following Trudeau's 29 May speech. Sharp was asked whether the government intended to follow the course taken by General DeGaulle when France recognized Red China at the price of breaking off relations with Taiwan. He replied that in the French case in 1964 it had been the government of Taiwan which had withdrawn its representation, thus ultimately making the French task an easy one. When asked if this would also be Canada's strategy, the minister replied, 'I hope we can bring about a situation in which the existence of a separate government in Taiwan is recognized and that we can, at the same time, recognize that the PRC government is effectively in control of the mainland area.'[14]

Sharp was asked whether he had 'any hints of some kind of opposition from the American authorities,' or whether 'he had any contact and had let the Americans know about these developments.' He replied that, shortly after his appointment as secretary of state for External Affairs, he had met Dean Rusk in Washington 'to acquaint Secretary Rusk with our plans to review these patterns and, quite explicitly, so there would be no misunderstanding.' Mr Sharp also noted the American position on China was becoming more flexible, for example, in a discernible shift from a rigid 'one-China policy' to a possible 'one-China, one-Taiwan policy.' Nevertheless, on 7 June Assistant Secretary of State William Bundy called in the Canadian ambassador and stated that while Canada's policy was for Canada to decide, the Americans wanted to make Canada aware of problems that could exist if Canada moved towards recognition. He discussed the French experience and implied that Canada would have to force the Nationalists out of Ottawa if the government decided to establish relations with Peking. Bundy emphasized the importance of the Republic of China for Americans. He spoke of the unfortunate effects that recognition by Canada would have for the Vietnam negotiations in Paris. Recognition of the PRC would increase Peking's influence in Hanoi and Paris and could strengthen Hanoi's intransigence. Bundy also expressed concern that recognition would upset the political-strategic balance in the Asia-Pacific region, not only because it would undermine the security of the ROC, but because it would have an unsettling effect on China's neighbours, especially Japan.[15]

If there was to be any change in American relations with the PRC, it could not come at the expense of Taiwan. That was the official American position and, by and large, represented American public opinion on the issue. Doak Barnett, author of the phrase 'containment without isolation,' had suggested Canada might make a reasonable offer to Peking while holding the line on Taiwan. DEA's 'America watchers' in the Washington embassy and in Ottawa cautioned the drafters of the department's China policy review not to underestimate the American administration's response to the Canadian recognition initiative. While an increasing number of Americans in 1968 were prepared to accept relations with China as a 'necessary evil,' they were not prepared to sacrifice Taiwan. One could expect, therefore, that following Bundy's example, American official reaction would be vigorous in the months to come.

In the first week of July 1968 a draft of the China policy review was submitted to Sharp and to senior officials in External Affairs, Finance, and Industry, Trade and Commerce. By August the final version was sent to the prime minister and to all members of the cabinet. The document assumed that Canada's relationship with Taiwan would alter but made no specific recommendations regarding the nature of this change. It was expected that cabinet would consider the document in September, although, in fact, cabinet did not deal with the matter until December. One can suggest several reasons for this three-month delay. First, Finance had raised objections to the China policy because it gave insufficient emphasis to economic factors, in particular to the threat of American economic retaliation. More time was needed to study the economic repercussions of closer relations with the PRC. Second, the Far Eastern Division of DEA was still searching for a political formula that could solve the PRC-Taiwan recognition problem. It was continuing to explore various options in consultation with the Legal Division of DEA. If the department could present a workable formula to cabinet, then the thorny matter of Taiwan might be resolved. Third, behind the scenes Canadian diplomats were trying to gauge Chinese reaction to the Canadian initiative. This was not easy, given the internal confusion in China due to the Cultural Revolution. Finally, Canadian authorities could benefit by waiting until after the fall vote in the United Nations on Chinese representation, to get a better assessment of how the new recognition policy could be linked to the question of U.N. representation.[16]

The reservations of the Department of Finance helped focus attention on the economic and trade implications of Canadian recognition. A section of the China policy review had been devoted to the possible establishment of a non-official resident trade office, in case recognition was not achieved. The PRC had already concluded such arrangements with Japan, Italy, and Austria. Finance and DEA were hesitant to recommend this possibility because resident trade offices would have to be staffed from non-governmental organizations and as such could not provide for diplomatic immunities from civil or criminal actions. In any case, the establishment of resident trade offices was viewed by the department as a poor alternative to full diplomatic relations. The prospect of recognition, however, raised other concerns. The Wheat Board felt that recognition would protect the high levels of Canadian wheat sales in the China market and improve the potential for additional Canadian exports to China. Yet, the Wheat Board made it clear that if Canada pursued a 'two-Chinas' or 'one-China, one-Taiwan' policy Canada could seriously jeopardize its share of the wheat market in China. This position was endorsed by both Finance and Industry, Trade and Commerce. The general consensus was that recognition would protect and possibly expand Canada's strong trade with China. If Taiwan had to be sacrificed to appease the PRC, so be it.[17]

The Wheat Board's views on recognition were vital since it was responsible for the sale of over $100 million of wheat on an annual basis to the PRC. The Wheat Board was in frequent contact with its Chinese counterparts and had earlier arranged for a Chinese trade delegation to visit Canada. Yet the board also preferred to keep its delicate trading operations separate from the equally sensitive political operation co-ordinated by the department. One would have imagined that the two would have co-ordinated their activities as closely as possible. If there was such co-ordination, however, it was at the cabinet level because there is little evidence elsewhere to support the argument that there was close consultation. Indeed, in the fall of 1968 the files show that the department sought by letter to be more closely involved in the briefing program for the Wheat Board representatives before the board left for China. The department observed that it would be helpful if the board were kept informed of 'the state of play' regarding the China policy review in case Wheat Board representatives were asked leading questions by their Chinese counterparts when visiting Peking. Despite these suggestions, the board's China activities, by and large, proceeded independently from the government's China policy review, and from that of DEA, at least on the operational level.[18]

With respect to the economic repercussions for Canadian-American relations arising from Canadian recognition of China, Finance and Industry, Trade and Commerce pointed to overland oil imports, balance of payment guidelines, and the interest equalization tax. All were areas in which Canada enjoyed preferred treatment from the United States, and these arrangements could be at risk. In addition, Congress could pass legislation limiting Canadian imports and the Americans could well reduce defence purchasing contracts in Canada. These were real concerns, although to be sure, they were more muted than when they had been voiced a few years previously. Also, Canadian relations with Cuba served in part to counterbalance the fear of American economic sanctions. Had not the initial American reaction to continued Canadian trade with Cuba been hostile, yet in the end, had not American anger subsided? While China was not Cuba, the Cuban example suggested that Canada need not fear American economic sanctions.

By the fall of 1968 these considerations had been incorporated into a formula which was presented to the minister. Canada would recognize the Peking government as the only government of China, without necessarily accepting China's territorial claims over areas in which it did not exercise jurisdiction. At the same time the Canadian government was prepared to say that Canada considered it desirable and necessary to deal with the government which was in effective control of Taiwan for matters concerning that island. Canada would take the position that such relations were not intended to constitute recognition of Taiwan as an independent state, or to imply any other position as to the status of that territory. The formula also envisaged the possibility that Canada might permit representatives of the Taiwan government to have a trade mission in Canada if they chose to do so, to facilitate Canadian dealings with Taiwan in matters of mutual interest. This constituted de facto recognition of Taiwan, but not de jure recognition.[19]

This proposal was submitted to the cabinet Committee on External Affairs and Defence in December, and following the meeting a memorandum to cabinet was prepared making fourteen specific recommendations. This was discussed in cabinet committee on 27 January 1969, and the recommendation on Taiwan was amended to make it clear that Canada would not accept any commitment that precluded Canadian recognition of an independent state of Taiwan were this at all feasible. The ambassador of the Republic of China, Hsueh Yu-chi, called on the secretary of state for External Affairs on the same day. Sharp outlined the basic aspects of the government's thinking, and, when Hsueh expressed the view that this step would represent the failure of his mission in Ottawa, Sharp commented that the Canadian decision in no way reflected upon the ambassador's distinguished service in Canada.[20]

When the decision of cabinet to proceed with negotiations as soon as possible was taken, the first stage in the process of implementing the prime minister's statement of 29 May 1968 was over. The China policy review had focused on a wide range of economic and political issues. It was clear that there was strong public and cabinet support for the proposed initiative. As well, all three major political parties were in favour of recognition, although a portion of the Conservative party led by John Diefenbaker was extremely suspicious, especially of any formula that might sacrifice Taiwan.[21] A strategy had been produced which somewhat clarified the Canadian position on Taiwan and gave ground for cautious optimism that Canada might be able to recognize the PRC without sacrificing Taiwan or alienating its American neighbour. Now it would be up to the Canadians to persuade the Chinese to meet with them in some location, to discuss the issues, and to ascertain the likely prospects for success.

Agreement to Negotiate in Stockholm

On 30 January 1969 cabinet instructed the Canadian ambassador in Stockholm, Arthur Andrew, to call upon his Chinese counterpart and propose talks on recognition and the establishment of diplomatic relations. The Canadian embassy in Washington was instructed to inform the State Department of these developments. Specifically, Canada wanted to reassure the anxious Americans that even if Canada might ultimately break diplomatic relations with the ROC as a price of recognition, Canada planned to continue good relations with Taiwan. Ottawa would break off discussions with Peking rather than being forced to sever all relations with Taiwan. Ottawa would also break off negotiations if Peking insisted that Canada endorse the PRC's claim to Taiwan. The intention was to refrain from expressing any position on Taiwan, arguing that this was an internal Chinese matter, and therefore not a condition for recognition.

The State Department was not surprised at the Canadian decision to proceed with formal negotiations. It was, however, concerned about the political implications of Canadian 'abandonment' of Taiwan. The Americans were disappointed that Canada had not attempted to pursue a modified 'two-Chinas' policy further into the negotiations, and hoped that the Canadian willingness to break diplomatic relations, if necessary, with Taiwan would not be made public before the upcoming Sino-American talks which were scheduled to resume in Warsaw in February.[22]

In the House of Commons on 3 February, Diefenbaker asked the government 'whether it intended to carry out the undertaking the Prime Minister gave in May of 1968.' He noted that the prime minister had at that time said that Canada would not break relations with Taiwan as a price for recognition: 'What I am asking the Government is, are they going to keep the undertaking that was given by both the Prime Minister and the Secretary of State for External Affairs, that there would be no breaking of relations with Taiwan as a condition of the recognition of Communist China?' Sharp replied, 'the question which is in issue, of course, is who speaks for the Government of China? The question is, which government of China do we recognize?' Pressed by Diefenbaker to be more specific, Sharp admitted that, 'Relations between Taipei and Canada will, of course, be affected since the Government of Taiwan does claim jurisdiction over the whole of China and we cannot have two conflicting authorities.'

A few days later, on 12 February, in a reply to another question, Sharp commented, 'I doubt very much that the Canadian Government would recognize or challenge the sovereignty of Peking over Formosa. That is a matter of dispute. When we recognize other countries we do not necessarily recognize all their territorial claims or challenge them.' In a reply to yet another question from Diefenbaker concerning Taiwan, Sharp observed: 'The Government's policy with respect to the recognition of China has been expressed by the Prime Minister and myself in recent days. *That is our policy and if it varies in any respect from what has been said previously it varies*' (my emphasis).[23]

Canadian shift from a 'two-Chinas,' or a 'one-China, one-Taiwan' policy had now become part of the public record. Eight months after the prime minister's 29 May 1968 statement the Canadian position had been clarified by Sharp at the expense, although not the complete sacrifice, of Taiwan. Whether this would be enough to persuade the PRC to enter into serious negotiations still remained to be seen.

On 4 February the Canadian ambassador in Stockholm was instructed to call the Chinese chargé d'affaires on 6 February for an appointment on 8 February. The Chinese chargé, however, turned out to be unexpectedly elusive. The Canadian embassy sought several times to establish contact without a reply. Apparently, the Chinese were waiting for guidance from Peking. After several days of waiting the Canadian government chose not to wait any longer for a formal Chinese reply and unilaterally announced that Canada was proposing that the two countries enter into discussions with a view to establishing diplomatic relations. On 19 February the PRC chargé called to arrange a meeting with the Canadian ambassador. Significantly, the meeting took place the day after the date when the Americans and the Chinese had been scheduled to meet in Warsaw to resume their talks. That meeting had just been abruptly cancelled by Peking.

The first session with the Chinese lasted forty-five minutes and was extremely cordial. After some talk about the weather, and after tea was poured, Arthur Andrew informed the chargé, Liu Chi-tsai, that the Canadian government wished to have its representatives meet with representatives of the PRC, at a convenient time and place, to discuss mutual recognition and an exchange of ambassadors; and that concurrently with discussions on diplomatic relations, the respective representatives might explore possibilities of concluding consular and trade agreements, as well as considering all other areas in which Sino-Canadian relations might be developed. The Chinese chargé replied that he had listened to the Canadian proposals with utmost seriousness and would report them at once to his government. For his part, the chargé wished to inform the Canadian side of the 'three constant principles' on which the Chinese could agree to establish diplomatic relations with foreign countries. These were:

1 A government seeking relations with China must recognize the central People's Government as the sole and lawful government of the Chinese people;
2 A government which wishes to have relations with China must recognize that Taiwan is an inalienable part of Chinese territory and in accordance with this principle must sever all kinds of relationships with the 'Chiang Kai-shek gang';
3 A government seeking relations with China must give support to the restoration of the rightful place and legitimate rights in the United Nations of the PRC and no longer give any backing to so-called representatives of Chiang Kai-shek in any organ of this international body.

The Canadian negotiating team's reaction was to treat the 'three constant principles' as an expression of the Chinese view, rather than a precondition for further discussion. The Canadian side assumed it would take three to four weeks for the Chinese to receive instructions from Peking.

As an initial impression, it was generally felt that agreement on the first and third principles was in the realm of possibility, but that the second principle, which required Canada 'to recognize that Taiwan is an inalienable part of Chinese territory,' was unacceptable.

The long delay between the first meeting (21 February) and the second (3 April) gave rise to considerable press speculation that the Canadian effort was encountering Chinese indifference. The *Washington Post* reported on 7 March that 'the Peking Government has shown itself cold to Canadian overtures looking to recognition of Communist China. After a first meeting here between Canadian Julian [sic] Andrew and Chinese Embassy officials, Robert Edmonds, Counsellor of the Canadian Embassy remarked, "We were not talking on the same wavelength." This stumbling block is understood to be Canada's relationship with Taiwan ... there can be no compromise on this issue.'[24] In the House, the minister was asked to comment on the negotiations and could only report that 'there have been meetings in the last few weeks and I expect that there will be others held soon.'

Several explanations were put forward to account for the slow Chinese response. It was known that foreign policy decisions of this magnitude had to be referred to Chou En-lai personally.[25] With Peking absorbed in preparations for the critical Ninth Party Congress, and with the intensification of the Sino-Soviet border dispute, Canadian recognition could not have been an immediate priority. Furthermore, the Chinese Ministry of Foreign Affairs was still rebuilding itself after the first chaos of the Cultural Revolution and could not respond as swiftly as anticipated. Other explanations were of a tactical nature: for example, the Chinese did not wish to be too eager, or they felt Canada had now committed itself and it was in China's interest to delay as long as possible to gain a better bargaining position. There was speculation that the Chinese thought that Canada was acting as an American surrogate.[26] Other countries were also interested in establishing diplomatic relations with Peking, for example, the Italians and Belgians. Perhaps the Chinese were waiting to see what the other countries had to offer before entering into substantive discussions with Canada.[27]

Yet the prevailing view in Ottawa was that the Chinese would respond in a positive fashion. It would cost the Chinese very little to enter into the next phase of negotiations. They only had to listen to what Canada had to offer without making any commitments. Failure to respond would remove the possibility of Canadian recognition in the foreseeable future and would affect the likelihood of recognition by other countries as well. There had been indications that the PRC might wish to begin repairing the damage wrought by the Cultural Revolution. If so, the Canadian initiative could refurbish the PRC's tarnished image in international affairs. Finally, if

Peking was indeed interested in better relations with the rest of the world, especially the Americans, Canadian recognition would be a major step in that direction, given Canada's special relationship with the United States.

On 3 April the Chinese called at the Canadian embassy and proposed that the negotiations take place in Stockholm. Both sides agreed that English would be the official language of these discussions. The head of the Chinese mission in Stockholm would serve as head of the Chinese negotiating delegation. The Chinese suggested that talks begin as soon as possible. The Canadian side reacted positively. Arthur Andrew, the ambassador, was a skilful diplomat and the counsellor, Bob Edmonds, had been born in China and had a working knowledge of Chinese. The Swedes were cooperative, had relatively good relations with the Chinese, and could be counted on to provide a favourable environment for the talks. Stockholm was a better choice than Paris or Peking: Paris was too exposed to public view, Peking too isolated. The choice of Stockholm was ideal from a variety of perspectives.

At the third meeting on 10 April the Canadian side formally accepted the Chinese proposal that Stockholm serve as the locale for the negotiations. The Canadians asked that the next meeting be held in May, at which time the Canadian side privately hoped that discussion could begin on practical matters, rather than dwelling on the explosive political issues contained in the 'three constant principles.' The Chinese agreed to refer to Peking 'practical' questions raised by the Canadian side about trade and/or consular agreements; administrative details of the operation of a Canadian embassy in Peking; telecommunications arrangements; travel arrangements, travel restrictions; diplomatic immunities; and the sending of a survey team to Peking in advance of embassy staff. The Chinese noted that the Canadians had not responded to their statement of 'constant principles' made at the first meeting, but they did not insist that Canadian acceptance of these three principles was a precondition to negotiations. The Chinese side apparently accepted the explanation that their three principles would be discussed during substantive negotiations.

After this third meeting the Canadian side took stock of its position. Both parties had agreed to sit down and discuss substantive issues with the stated objective of mutual recognition and the establishment of diplomatic relations. The Canadian side had made a thorough inventory of its needs, had consulted closely with its friends, and was reluctantly prepared to deal with the issue of Taiwan. In the course of a year, Canada had moved steadily from a 'one-China, one-Taiwan' position to a formula that would essentially 'de-recognize' the ROC without accepting the PRC's territorial or political claim to Taiwan. What Ottawa clearly hoped was that this would be enough to secure Chinese agreement on terms favourable for Canada. At the next meeting, when the substantive negotiations were to begin, the Canadian side, led by Arthur Andrew, the head of the negotiating team, intended to steer the discussion in the direction of practical matters, such as the administrative details of opening and running an embassy in Peking. Canada did not want to end up debating first principles. Based on these initial encounters with the Chinese, there was guarded optimism that an agreement could be secured, without prolonged negotiations, centred on the Taiwan issue, and on questions of principle.

Formula for Recognition

The optimists were wrong and seventeen long months elapsed before agreement was finally reached. The ensuing talks consumed a total of eighteen meetings. At one point it was thought that the thread had broken: there was a gap of nearly five months in 1970 when no meetings were held. Finally, in a joint Sino-Canadian communiqué of 13 October 1970, the two countries announced the establishment of diplomatic relations. Canada recognized the government of the PRC as the 'sole legal government of China' and 'took note' of China's territorial claim to Taiwan 'without either challenging or endorsing' it. The diplomatic log-jam was broken and the 'Canadian formula' became the model for most of the Western nations which subsequently established diplomatic relations with the PRC in the 1970s.

At the fourth meeting on 20 May 1969, however, the Canadian side was more concerned with the practicalities of recognition. Invoking both the spirit of Norman Bethune, the Canadian communist doctor whom Mao had made into a hero, and the prime minister's desire to develop closer relations with mainland China, the Canadian side indicated it had no intention of pursuing a 'two-Chinas' policy and quickly moved to discuss the conduct of diplomatic relations between the two countries. This occupied a large part of the Canadian presentation and was accompanied by an *aide-mémoire* outlining rules and principles of diplomatic relations in detail. The Canadians raised the matter of compensation for the former Canadian embassy premises requisitioned by the Nanking city government in 1959. Canada also wanted China to repay an outstanding loan for six ships belonging to the Ming Sung Company and presumed to have been seized by the PRC after 1949. In addition, there was an assortment of smaller claims against the PRC made by individual Canadian citizens. The Canadian shopping list also included a consular agreement to cover such matters as dual citizenship, reunification of families, and access of consular officials to nationals who might be detained or arrested. The Canadian side referred to trading arrangements currently in existence between the two countries and stated that it was Canada's intention to negotiate a more permanent agreement, including the establishment of a civil aviation link between the two countries.

The Chinese insisted that before these 'practical' matters could be discussed there must first be agreement on the establishment of diplomatic relations, and this meant that Ottawa must first accept the 'three constant principles.' It was true that the Canadians had partially dealt with some of these principles, but not adequately. Ottawa had not indicated that it was willing to break off relations with Taiwan. Some Canadian leaders were saying in public that Canada was prepared to have de facto relations with Taiwan after de jure relations had ended. What did this mean? Canada's position in the United Nations was also unclear. Was Canada still giving support to the 'Chiang Clique' which was 'propped up by the bayonets of American imperialism'? It was apparent that the initial Chinese and Canadian negotiating agendas were not the same and the first real encounter between the two sides had pointed out significant differences in assumptions and tactics.

At the next meeting, the Chinese did not linger over administrative details, diplomatic immunities and privileges, trade, or civil aviation. Nor did they wish to discuss a consular agreement or compensation for claims. The fact that Canada had asked for an explicit statement of diplomatic privileges and immunities for Canadians was seen by the Chinese as an expression of unfriendliness. This attitude carried over into the sixth meeting. This meeting, held on 10 July, was the toughest to date. The Chinese negotiating team was now headed by Ambassador Wang Tung (later to become ambassador to Canada) fresh from Peking. He repeated the three principles, together with the first quotation from Chairman Mao. During this difficult sixth session the Chinese demanded that Canada recognize Taiwan as an integral part of Chinese territory, and indicated that the statement that Canada 'neither challenged nor endorsed' the Chinese position on Taiwan was inadequate. The Chinese pressed the Canadians hard on this point throughout the meeting although, at the end, they appeared ready for another session.

In the House on 21 July Mitchell Sharp made the following statement to clarify the Canadian position on Taiwan:

> We are not promoting either a 'two-China' or a 'one-China, one-Taiwan' policy. Our policy is to recognize one government of China. We have not asked and do not ask the Government of the PRC to endorse the position of the Government of Canada on our

territorial limits as a condition to agreement to establish diplomatic relations. To do so might cast doubts on the extent of our sovereignty. We do not think it would be appropriate, nor would it be in accordance with international usage, that Canada should be asked to endorse the position of the Government of the PRC on the extent of its territorial sovereignty. To challenge that position would, of course, also be inappropriate.[28]

In the ensuing nine-week interval between sessions, the Canadians also changed the head of their negotiating team. Margaret Meagher, an experienced career diplomat and skilled negotiator, replaced Arthur Andrew as ambassador in Stockholm. The Canadian Wheat Board left for a major negotiating session in Peking. Ottawa was uncertain if the Chinese would raise the matter of the Stockholm negotiations during the board's visit, but if this were to happen, the board was instructed by the government to say that its only mandate was wheat sales and nothing else. If the Chinese were to bring up the question of Canadian trade with Taiwan, the board, while avoiding any controversial opinion, might express its hope that trade could continue with Taiwan even though there would be no diplomatic relations with authorities there once Canada had recognized Peking.[29]

With the annual U.N. debate over the representation of China drawing near, the focus shifted. The Chinese side, at the sixth session, had questioned the Canadian voting position at the United Nations. How could Canada seek to recognize China and claim it had a 'one-China' policy, yet abstain on the Albanian resolution and continue to vote in favour of the 'important question' resolution? Was this not a contradiction? The Canadian side had replied that the Canadian position was consistent: until bilateral relations with China changed, Canada's position at the United Nations would remain the same. When Canada agreed to recognize Peking, its U.N. vote on the admission of China would reflect this changed status. The Canadian position also reassured Canada's close friends that there would be no abrupt switch in the Canadian U.N. vote in 1969. This was gratifying to the Americans who, although they were inching towards a more favourable view of the PRC, were anxious that it remain outside the United Nations for yet another year.

With the seventh meeting the focus shifted to discussion of the form and content of a possible announcement of agreement. The minister's 21 July statement had been noted with satisfaction by the Chinese representatives. The Canadians declared their preference for a simple communiqué announcing the establishment of diplomatic relations. The Chinese agreed to prepare a draft communiqué, which was submitted at the next meeting, on

18 October. The Chinese draft communiqué was longer than anticipated. It contained three paragraphs and, of course, one of them outlined the position that the PRC expected Canada to take on Taiwan: 'The government of the PRC reaffirms that Taiwan is an inalienable part of the territory of the PRC, the government of Canada expresses respect for the above stand of the government of the PRC, and will not pursue the policy of so-called "two-Chinas" or "one-China, one-Taiwan" and, therefore, decides to sever all relations with the Chiang Kai-shek clique.'

To the Canadians this statement implied far more agreement than was, in fact, the case. While the Chinese had moved closer to the Canadian position of 'neither challenge nor endorse,' the Chinese statement was unacceptable to the Canadians. This message was quickly conveyed to the Chinese at the ninth meeting on 24 October. As an alternative the Canadian delegation proposed a draft modelled on the Sino-French communiqué of 1964, accompanied by a document setting forth the position of both sides on questions of principle. The Sino-French communiqué had simply announced mutual recognition and the decision to establish diplomatic relations at the level of embassies headed by ambassadors without specifying any further details. In the discussions, among those representing the Canadian side prior to this session, a document was prepared outlining the Canadian position on a number of key issues. In this document the Canadian government 'noted' the position of the PRC that Taiwan was an inalienable part of Chinese territory.

At the tenth session the Chinese reiterated their insistence that any communiqué could not follow the Sino-French model but must contain statements of principle regarding Taiwan. The 'three constant principles' had now really become one: acceptance of the Chinese position regarding Taiwan. A long delay now ensued because the Chinese did not indicate their readiness to continue discussions for nearly two months. Why had the negotiating process apparently come to a halt just as it seemed there was some progress toward agreement? One likely factor was the overload of work on the shoulders of a few top Chinese officials. It was suggested that the highest organs in the Chinese party were involved in an astonishing number of relatively trivial day-to-day decisions. One recalls the anecdote related by one foreign visitor to China who, in the midst of an early morning meeting with Chou En-lai, was astonished to see the prime minister personally read and approve the front page of the next day's *People's Daily*. If decisions such as the daily news required Chou's approval, then any key developments in the Stockholm negotiations also had to receive his personal attention.[30] Given Peking's many urgent concerns at the end of 1969 (restoring internal order, the Sino-Soviet conflict, the upcoming Warsaw talks with the Americans), it was conceivable that the Sino-Canadian talks could not have received the undivided attention of the Chinese leaders.

It was also possible that the Chinese wanted to show their irritation with the Canadians for not having accepted the Chinese draft communiqué. The Chinese may also have been miffed at Canada's stubborn insistence not to change its U.N. vote until it had reached agreement on recognition. The Canadian ambassador sat next to the PRC's ambassador at the opening of the Swedish Parliament in early January 1970, but all that the Chinese ambassador said to her was 'Happy New Year.'[31]

Was the Canadian side getting anxious and eager to make concessions after ten months of negotiations? There is no tangible evidence to support this view. DEA cautioned the minister to put the present delay in proper context. The latest proposals had introduced complexities which could not quickly be assessed by the Chinese. There were no grounds for pessimism. If anything, one had to remain optimistic. There was no public pressure to make a decision. Canadians seemed inured to the possibility that the negotiations might go on forever. The government had shifted from a 'one-China, one-Taiwan' position to what was, essentially, the imminent abandonment of Canada's relationship with Taiwan. By and large, there was support in Parliament, cabinet, and among the public for this position. Trade was continuing on an even keel and did not pose a problem. Canada's American neighbour appeared resigned to the inevitability of recognition and apparently would not place any major obstacles in Canada's path.[32]

What about the prime minister whose sense of history, and perhaps his impatience with it, had thrust the recognition of the PRC into the centre stage of our international relations? Was he becoming weary of the tedious, blunted encounters in Stockholm? Having already distanced himself from Taiwan, was he ready for further compromises? In a fairly realistic appraisal of the Canadian position during a press conference in December, the prime minister noted: 'I am optimistic in the sense that nothing until now has shown to us that we should break off the talks or give them up as hopeless ... It is taking a lot of time, more than I would hope for, but there is nothing in the talks which gives us cause to be discouraged or to say that the whole thing is finished and we shouldn't continue them.'[33]

Mitchell Sharp commented on New Year's Day 1970 that, from the beginning, he had expected that 'the negotiations would be prolonged and deliberate. This is the way the Chinese negotiate ... Of course, we won't let them go on indefinitely. If they look as if they are bogging down we will suspend them.' In reply to the inevitable questions about Taiwan, the minister reiterated that Canada neither challenged nor accepted the sovereignty of Peking over Taiwan, and concluded with the phrase: 'We don't ask the Chinese to accept our sovereignty over the Arctic.'[34] Nevertheless, the question of sovereignty remained the central issue during the next sessions. The Chinese returned after a two-month hiatus to insist on their claim that Taiwan was an inalienable part of Chinese territory. In their view, the Canadian phrase 'do not challenge or accept' China's sovereignty over Taiwan was 'vague and self-contradictory,' notwithstanding Sharp's clever equation of Taiwan with the Canadian Arctic.

In formulating a response the Canadian side came up with the phrase 'taking due note' ('the Canadian government, while taking note of this position of the PRC government nevertheless considers it inappropriate ...'). The discovery of this phrase did not appear especially momentous at the time; indeed the Canadian side thought that the phrase could be inserted in the communiqué if it were likely to make a difference between success and failure, which, they concluded, was doubtful. Later, however, it became the key to breaking the log-jam over Taiwan, because 'taking note' did not imply agreement with the Chinese position. The Chinese could thus proclaim their sovereignty over Taiwan while the Canadians could avoid commenting on the Chinese position. With such a compromise both sides could maintain their respective positions on the status of Taiwan without losing face.

Between March and August 1970 there were no formal meetings, but there was considerable activity behind the scenes as both sides tried to locate the final formula that could bring forth recognition. It seemed that recognition was close at hand, yet once again there ensued a long delay. In the House on 18 June the minister was asked about the state of the negotiations. Sharp replied: 'We are waiting for the Chinese representatives to make another appointment with our Ambassador in Stockholm ... the Chinese are very patient and I think we have to be the same way.' Sharp was asked if Canada would be withdrawing recognition from Taiwan:

Mr. Sharp: Yes, Mr. Speaker. I have made it quite clear on a number of occasions that we have a one-China policy now. We will have a one-China policy in the future.

Mr. Lambert (Edmonton West): You used to have a two-China policy.

Mr. Paul Yewchuk (Athabaska): Does this mean that Canada will be asking the Taiwan Ambassador to withdraw from Canada and has he been informed of this clearly?

Mr. Sharp: Since we have a one-China policy we will recognize one government of China and will not recognize two.

At the fifteenth session on 1 August 1970 the first and last paragraphs of the communiqué were agreed to by the negotiators. That left only the second paragraph dealing with Taiwan. Canada put forth a new proposed text for paragraph two which was rejected by the Chinese. The PRC opposed any reference to Ottawa's reluctance to express views on China's territorial limits, a proviso which Canada was unwilling to drop. At the next meeting, on 18 September, two Canadian alternative proposals for paragraph two were communicated to the Chinese side. Further suggestions were made by both sides for the solution of the difficulty over Taiwan. On 3 October, at the seventeenth meeting, the Chinese finally accepted a Canadian proposal for the elusive second paragraph. Both parties now agreed on the text of a four-paragraph communiqué, the second paragraph having been separated into two parts at the suggestion of the Canadian side. The four-paragraph communiqué was released in the House, on 10 October, by the secretary of state for External Affairs, in a speech which announced mutual recognition and the establishment of diplomatic relations. The key second and third paragraphs read as follows:

2 The Chinese Government reaffirms that Taiwan is an inalienable part of the territory of the People's Republic of China. The Canadian Government takes note of this position of the Chinese Government.
3 The Canadian Government recognizes the Government of the People's Republic of China as the sole legal Government of China.

The minister noted that officials from the Departments of External Affairs and Industry, Trade and Commerce would be leaving shortly for China to begin administrative preparations for the opening of a Canadian embassy in Peking by early 1971. He observed that there were many issues that still required discussion: for example, cultural and educational exchanges, expansion of trade, a consular agreement, and 'settling a small number of problems left over from an earlier period.' The journey toward recognition of Communist China, begun in 1949, had thus come to an end. It had been long and arduous. The weary negotiators in Stockholm drank sherry and ate dinner with their Chinese counterparts. The Canadian ambassador was personally congratulated by the minister for her successful efforts on Canada's behalf. The ambassador of the Republic of China was asked to close his embassy in Ottawa and consulate in Vancouver and to arrange for the immediate departure of all Taiwanese diplomats, staff, and their families. The world press generally applauded the Canadian-Chinese agreement as an important step toward accepting the reality of the existence of a country with a quarter of the world's population.

For Canada the conclusion of these negotiations appeared to be a substantial diplomatic coup. The government had pursued a difficult policy without alienating Canada's American neighbour, even though the American administration was officially opposed. Canada had occupied the centre stage of world diplomacy for almost two years, showing off a newly independent foreign policy, excellent diplomatic skills, and the potential to be more than just a middle power. The recognition of the PRC was good for Canada and for Trudeau, who was its catalyst. At the time it stood out as a Canadian success story by any standard, and it deserves to be recorded in history in those terms.

Conclusion

The recognition process, formally initiated by Trudeau's May 1968 statement, was complicated, involving politicians, statesmen, public servants, the media, and a variety of interested groups and individuals. The bilateral negotiations lasted nearly two years, requiring skill, determination, and patience on both sides. The Stockholm discussions, although they were secret, were monitored by a host of major countries, especially the United States, whose views had to be taken into account, though not necessarily followed.

The first question to ask is, 'Is this the real story?' What has been left out, either by accident or by design? How close to the real record can we get, a generation after the fact? We need more information on the internal debates regarding the security implications for Canada of Chinese recognition; on the vital role of the Wheat Board which was conducting its independent negotiations to sell more wheat in Peking, even as talks were going on in Stockholm. We lack details about the decision-making process at the highest levels. Conversations with Trudeau, Sharp, and Head can fill many gaps but also make us aware of the dangers of relying too heavily on the written record.[35] Still, at this juncture, given that we have been able to draw on sources beyond the written files, it is possible to conclude that we have the main elements of the 'real story,' if not all its subtleties.

The second question concerns the importance of the decision itself. Were the negotiations really that successful? What do we mean by 'success'? One can argue that Ottawa was so obsessed with its determination to fulfil its predestined role as China 'legitimizer' that Canada failed to see the limitations of the Stockholm agreement. Should Canada have bowed to Chinese pressure and sacrificed Taiwan so swiftly? In retrospect, Canada abandoned its stated principles concerning the support of Taiwan abruptly and with little public discussion. Did Canada do the right thing? As it turned out, the Americans and Japanese eventually found better solutions, managing to maintain a level of official ties with Taiwan, while recognizing the PRC. Could it be said that Canada was 'out-negotiated' by the Chinese? Ottawa took pride in its tough bargaining stance, yet our diplomats soon were debating first principles with their Chinese counterparts, even though this was not the Canadian strategy. The Canadian side wanted to avoid discussion of 'principles' (which really meant Taiwan) by focusing on 'practicalities,' that is, the concern Canada had over the maintenance of diplomatic immunities and privileges, consular agreements, and trade. All these so-called practical matters were pushed aside in the discussions at Stockholm. What about the hundreds of millions of dollars worth of claims which Canada had against China? Only later, after diplomatic relations had been established, were these claims settled and, in the estimation of many, Canada came away disappointed with the results. To be sure, it may have been unrealistic to expect Chinese settlement of claims or discussion of the practicalities of diplomatic relations until the political questions had been settled. That clearly is the view held by those who participated in the negotiations. From their perspective, Canada got the best 'deal' it could have obtained.[36]

Third, what does the recognition decision tell us about Canadian politics and the Canadian decision-making process at that time? To begin with, recognition was no longer the contentious political issue that it appeared to have been a decade earlier. The major political parties supported closer relations with the PRC, as did a majority of Canadians. The prime minister used the China decision to distance himself from his predecessor and to stake out a popular claim for Canada's increased independence in foreign affairs. By combining the China initiative with a major review of foreign policy, Trudeau and his advisers sought to take firm control of the foreign-policy-making process and to reduce the influence of DEA in this process. In the short run, the department's power may have been diminished, yet in the day-to-day discussions with the Chinese which took nearly two years, the prime minister and his advisers came to rely heavily upon the very bureaucracy they had criticized. DEA's professionalism and discretion were vital elements in the successful completion of the negotiations. Once the talks were under way, Trudeau 'let the professionals do their job.' Trudeau wanted to make the big foreign policy decisions, but he had no patience for the day-to-day administration of foreign relations. He had confidence in Mitchell Sharp, whom he describes as a 'loyal soldier.' Only occasionally in the following months did Trudeau become personally involved in the negotiations.[37]

212 Reluctant Adversaries

Recognition was not a significant electoral issue in Canadian domestic politics. Quebec's traditional objection to dealing with the Communist regime in Peking had dissipated with the coming of the Quiet Revolution. The Chinese communities in Canada, while profoundly interested in the outcome, remained essentially apolitical.[38] No federal members of Parliament had seats which might have been in jeopardy over the recognition issue. One can say that for Canadians, by and large, the recognition of the PRC was only a significant issue insofar as the decision was perceived to affect Canadian-American relations. The Canadian recognition of China could be seen as an act of emancipation from the suffocating embrace of bad American policy. While American influence undoubtedly had been a factor preventing Canadian efforts to improve relations with China in the 1950s and again in the early 1960s, by 1968 enough influential Americans were no longer disposed to prevent Canada from establishing diplomatic relations with the PRC. American protests in the late sixties had a hollow ring; the Vietnam War had diminished American credibility; American policy towards China was itself beginning to change. The bogeyman of American sanctions had been dispelled by changing circumstances and by the fact that Canadians could no longer blame the Americans for Canadian failure to establish relations with the PRC.

Finally, did Canadians have a 'special relationship' with China and did the negotiations in Stockholm reinforce this view? Reflecting on their experience, the heads of Canada's negotiating team both concluded that the Stockholm discussions had not been noticeably different from other diplomatic encounters they had experienced. In its instructions and during the negotiations, the department chose to minimize China's uniqueness. The official language of the talks was English, and the reference points were universally held principles of international diplomacy. The impression given by the department, its negotiators, and the relevant ministers and politicians was that Canada was negotiating with a large, stubborn power with an authoritarian government, not especially unique, or having any particularly close relationship to Canadians. Yet, many Canadians, at that time and afterwards, continued to refer to Canada's special relationship with China, a relationship that was, in their minds, confirmed by expanding wheat sales, the existence of Norman Bethune, the legacy of Canada's missionary experience, and, perhaps most important, by the fact that the Canadian image of China appeared to be different from the one held by the Americans. Were not Canadians more flexible and open to China and less burdened by history? Canadians were thus well positioned to break down the barriers between China and the outside world. A variety of Canadian public figures, from Trudeau to Chester Ronning and Alvin Hamilton, contributed to this idealization of Canada's special role. In their view, Canada had been given a mission to bring China out of isolation.

The myth of a unique Canadian relationship with China may have led to exaggerated assumptions by Canadians as to the significance of the establishment of diplomatic relations with the PRC in 1970. Then Canada basked in the glow of friendship and, not incidentally, increased trade prospects. A decade later, however, while still paying homage to Norman Bethune, Canada had become but one of a large number of favoured foreign petitioners in the newly opened Chinese court. By then, Canada's moment in history had already passed and, with it, the myth of Canada's special relationship with China. In the end, this is undoubtedly what Trudeau and others had in mind when they advocated recognition. Trudeau's goal had been to help bring China into the world community of nations where the mystique of its uniqueness, born in good part from its isolation, would be tempered by the conventions and practices of the modern state system. This is indeed what happened, and if Canada's special relationship with China has faded today, Canadians can nevertheless point to a brief moment in time, in 1968–70, when their relationship was unique and on the cusp of history.

Notes

1 See K. Nossal, *The Politics of Canadian Foreign Policy* (Englewood Cliffs, NJ: Prentice Hall 1985).
2 Jacques Hébert and Pierre Elliot Trudeau, *Two Innocents in Red China*, translated by T.M. Owen (Toronto: Oxford University Press 1968).
3 From a conversation with Pierre Trudeau, 27 Jan. 1987.
4 Hébert and Trudeau, 150–1.
5 All major decisions made by DEA had to be communicated to Ivan Head. In the case of China policy this did not cause any special conflict, since all parties involved were, by and large, in agreement with policy goals and methods. This was not the case, however, in some other areas, such as NATO policy, where there were substantial disagreements between DEA and the Prime Minister's office. (From interviews with Ivan Head, Ralph Collins and Arthur Andrew.)
6 See Nossal, *Politics*; B. Thordarson, *Trudeau and Foreign Policy, a Study in Decision-Making* (Toronto: Oxford University Press 1972), ch. 4; and J.L. Granatstein and Robert Bothwell, *Pirouette, Pierre Trudeau and Canadian Foreign Policy* (Toronto: University of Toronto Press 1990), ch. 1.
7 Cf. P. Lyon and B. Tomlin, *Canada as an International Actor* (Toronto: Macmillan 1979); J.K. Gordon, ed., *Canada's Role as a Middle Power* (Toronto:

214 Reluctant Adversaries

Canadian Institute of International Affairs 1966); and D. Dewitt and J. Kirton, *Canada as a Principal Power* (Toronto: Wiley 1983).

8 The best analysis of the Canadian public image of China is found in P. Evans and D. Taras, 'Canadian Public Opinion of Relations with China: An Analysis of Existing Survey Research' (Toronto: Joint Centre on Modern East Asia 1985, Working Paper No. 33, March 1985); and idem., 'Looking (Far) East: Parliament and Canada–China Relations, 1949–1982,' in David Taras, ed., *Parliament and Canadian Foreign Policy* (Toronto: Canadian Institute of International Affairs 1988), 66–100.
9 DEA, Canadian Public Statements on China Recognition, 1968.
10 For more on this point see ch. 9 by J. Lum in this volume.
11 *Ta Kung Bao*, 'New Tendencies in the Canadian Political Situation,' 11 July 1968.
12 From interviews with Ralph Collins, Arthur Andrew, and Blair Seaborn. For more on Taiwan 'de-recognition' see ch. 10 by A. Andrew in this volume.
13 See DEA, file 20-China-14.
14 DEA, Prime Minister's policy statement of 29 May 1968 and the secretary of state for External Affairs' Press Conference of 29 May 1968.
15 The Japanese and Australian positions, as well as those of other Asian-Pacific nations, were also of considerable importance to Canadian policy makers. The Canadian government consulted regularly with a handful of key foreign governments, providing up-to-date information on the state of the negotiations on a 'need to know' basis (see DEA, file 20-China-14).
16 Key participants in the negotiation could not agree on any one reason for the delay. Trudeau claimed there was no hurry. Sharp thought that all the reasons were valid ones. They both insisted, along with Ivan Head, that Ottawa never resorted to any sort of secret diplomacy to ascertain the Chinese position. According to all three, no emissaries were utilized by the Canadian government to contact Peking.
17 From interviews with DEA and with Industry, Trade and Commerce officials, and from DEA files; see also 'China Policy Review,' 1968, file 20-265-63.
18 From interviews with Mitchell Sharp, Ralph Collins, and Arthur Andrew.
19 DEA, file 20-China-14.
20 Ibid., and interview with Mitchell Sharp, 1987.
21 See Evans and Taras, 'Canadian Public Opinion' and selected interviews.
22 DEA, file 20-China-14.
23 Ibid., 13 Feb. 1969.
24 The embassy quickly repudiated the alleged statement. In a 1986 interview, Edmonds notes that he was quoted out of context (interview with Edmonds, Ottawa, 1986).
25 Confirmed by Yao Guang, adviser to the Chinese ministry of foreign affairs

and former Chinese ambassador to Ottawa, in an interview in Peking, 25 May 1987.
26 The Chinese at the outset did indeed harbour these suspicions (from an interview with Yao Guang; see n. 25).
27 The Italian case is of particular interest. For a while Canada found itself in competition with the Italians in the 'recognition race.' This created problems for the Canadian negotiators who were initially concerned that the PRC would play off the Italians and the Canadians to the PRC's advantage (see DEA, 20-China-14 and also interviews with Arthur Andrew, Ralph Collins, and Margaret Meagher).
28 This was deliberately done to provide the Chinese with an official policy statement on Canada's position; the Chinese in Stockholm had asked for such a statement, and Ottawa felt that the best forum would be Parliament (from interviews and DEA, file 20-China-14).
29 DEA, file 20-China-14. This is the only documented evidence in the files of any communication between the Wheat Board and the Stockholm negotiations and there is no evidence of the board's response, if there was one.
30 Confirmed by Yao Guang (see n. 25).
31 The ambassador's reply may have had little to do with politics. Margaret Meagher, his Canadian counterpart, observes that the Chinese ambassador could simply have been trying to be friendly, uttering the only English words he knew; what can be interpreted as a snub may actually have been a brief moment of friendliness (from an interview with Margaret Meagher, 1987).
32 We should bear in mind that, in 1970, the Americans began their own effort to change their relations with China. This secret enterprise, under the complete control of President Nixon and Henry Kissinger, was unknown even to the American State Department which was busy trying to dissuade Canada from normalizing relations, even as the American president was exploring this possibility. Trudeau claims that the Americans never informed him of their secret initiative, but that, at their March 1969 meeting, Nixon said, more in sorrow than in anger, that the timing and tactics of the Canadian approach were unwise (from a conversation with Trudeau, 27 Jan. 1987).
33 DEA, file 20-China-14.
34 Ibid.
35 A number of officials whom I interviewed remarked on this point, suggesting that what in hindsight appeared to be a logical sequence of events sometimes seemed less and less so, the longer one thought about it. They also noted that even as the good public servant is writing his daily dispatches or numbered letters, he is aware he is writing for the record. He already may, consciously

or otherwise, be omitting facts that later may be deemed to have been pertinent parts of the historical record.

36 Canadian participants in the negotiations were unanimous that Canada was not 'out-negotiated.' In their view, the Canadian focus on practicalities was a tactic designed to deflect the Chinese from their relentless focus on principles (e.g., Taiwan). They argue that the final agreement did not sacrifice Taiwan, and that Canada's subsequent claims settlement with China was a good one. Officials of the Chinese Ministry of Foreign Affairs concluded that the negotiations were 'hard and fair,' and 'each side made numerous compromises' (from interviews, 1986–7, in Ottawa, Montreal, Halifax, and Peking).

37 Conversation with Pierre Trudeau, 1987, and interviews with Ivan Head, 1986.

38 See ch. 9 by Lum in this volume.

CHAPTER NINE

Janet Lum

Recognition and the Toronto Chinese Community

Until recently, little attention has been focused on the response of the Chinese community to the recognition of the PRC.[1] This paper takes a step toward filling this gap by asking the following questions: What were the fears of those Chinese in Toronto who opposed recognition? What strategies did Chinese community organizations use to sway public opinion? Did these tactics have any effect in shaping the Canadian government's position? How widespread were the sympathies at either extreme? While it is virtually impossible to find out exactly who stood on which side of the recognition issue at the time, it is possible to provide reasonable assumptions about the ability of key organizations to state their views based on their status within the Chinese community, their legitimacy, and their use of the local Chinese-language media. We must not only consider the saliency of recognition as an issue, but also the local power configuration in Toronto's Chinatown, a community that in the mid-sixties was in the midst of significant political and social change.

The study focuses on Toronto because it was the centre of anti-recognition activity. Nationalist Chinese (Kuomintang, or KMT) influence

This study utilizes DEA archives, press accounts, and detailed interviews with 28 Chinese informants. Some of the respondents hold or have held prominent positions in Chinese community organizations. Subjects were interviewed twice, and in some cases, as many as six times. The follow-up interviews were designed to test respondents' ability to recall events that happened more than 20 years earlier. Interview responses have been correlated with newspaper accounts and government files where possible. Sources have been protected to maintain respondents' confidentiality. The research is part of a larger study of the political attitudes, values, and structure of the Toronto Chinese community.

was strong, but pro-PRC elements were also present. The Toronto Chinese community had been largely apolitical, choosing to stay out of national and local politics. The recognition issue served to draw members of the community into the political process and can be viewed as a benchmark in the political maturation of the Chinese in Canada. From the perspective of the Canadian government under Trudeau, neither the apparent pro-KMT sympathies of the Chinese community, nor the potential threat of PRC subversion, was seen as a major impediment in the recognition process.

Recognition and the Chinese Community Centre (CCC) in Toronto: An Overview[1]

Beginning in the late 1950s, the Chinese Community Centre (CCC) spearheaded a persistent drive to oppose recognition of the PRC. Although at the height of its strength, the CCC claimed only 500 members, this was substantial relative to the total Chinese population of about 8,000 in Toronto at the beginning of the 1960s. Furthermore, the CCC put forward the only organized response in Toronto to the recognition issue. Its leaders were prominent Chinese Canadians who had earned considerable admiration for their participation in the war effort and for their leadership in immigration matters. Thus, there were good reasons to believe that the CCC reflected the opinions of a large number of Chinese Canadians, not just in Toronto, but also nationally.

The centre resorted to a wide range of strategies to publicize its views. There were, of course, the predictable banquets. The centre sponsored at least one dinner celebration a year to mark the founding of the Republic of China on the tenth day of October. Invitations were extended to municipal, provincial, and federal politicians who represented Chinese areas, and to members of Parliament whom the centre felt were particularly sympathetic to the Chinese community.[2] One of these occasions received considerable media coverage because the centre entertained Prime Minister Diefenbaker, Ian Wahn, the Liberal member from St Paul's, and Douglas Jung, the former Conservative MP from Vancouver. It was at this nine-course luncheon that Diefenbaker clutched a copy of the pro-Nationalist *Shing Wah Daily News* and thundered, 'Now there is a paper with which I can agree.'[3]

Leaders of the CCC often extended invitations to members of Parliament to speak at their public meetings. The presence of politicians served to lend legitimacy to the CCC and to give these politicians a sense that they had strong Chinese constituency support. Such meetings also provided a forum to merge local Chinese and national Canadian politics. For example, the Toronto *Globe and Mail* reported that, in an 18 March 1963 CCC meeting,

Perry Ryan, Liberal member for Spadina, and Joel Aldred, PC candidate for St Paul's, shared the platform with Hsu Hsu hsi, ambassador from Nationalist China. During the course of the meeting, the ambassador delivered an ominous warning for the 1,000 Chinese in the audience that 'should the Communists be left unchecked, both Chinese and Western civilizations will die a slow death because the Communists despise human rights and humanity.'[4]

Those familiar with Chinese communities will recognize that the wining and dining of politicians is consistent with the cultivation of personal ties in Chinese culture. *Guanxi*, or personal connections, are utilized to develop an extensive interpersonal network with those who hold key positions in the political structure. One exerts political influence by working through such a network.[5] The unwritten understanding was that the CCC could deliver Chinese votes in exchange for political policies sympathetic to the CCC's views. It was then up to the CCC to prove that it did represent the Chinese community.

Within this context, one can better understand the political trade-offs implied in Diefenbaker's attendance at that nine-course luncheon in 1962. From the CCC's point of view, the prime minister's joviality and his unabashed support for the *Shing Wah Daily News* were comforting. The key politician of the country was reassuring the CCC of Canada's continued recognition of Nationalist China. In addition, the CCC looked upon Diefenbaker's amplification of the recently announced termination of the federal investigation into illegal Chinese immigration as another personal victory, since the CCC had been prominent in opposing the investigation. For Diefenbaker, attending the banquet was his way of maintaining personal popularity while dissociating himself from the unpopular policies of his immigration minister. A federal election was imminent and, since the margin of victory was in doubt, Diefenbaker could use the support.

The CCC actively nurtured good feelings with prominent political figures, but it also employed other strategies. One of the earliest CCC antirecognition activities was triggered in 1960 with the announcement of a Canadian tour by the Peking Opera, and a *Globe and Mail* editorial which criticized the Chinese community for its negative reaction to the upcoming tour. The paper suggested that the Peking Opera was primarily a cultural, not a political, organization. Instead of boycotting the performance, members of the Chinese community were urged to welcome the opportunity to offer themselves as 'living proofs of freedom,' as a sort of counterpropaganda device.[6] In an angry retort, Chong Ying, editor of the *Shing Wah* and a prominent member of the CCC, declared that there was no such thing as 'art for art's sake' for communists. Rather than being an innocent cultural organization, the Peking Opera would 'foment intrigue and spread propaganda in Canada.'[7]

In a separate interview with the *Globe and Mail*, Chong Ying outlined the CCC's plan of action.[8] He revealed that the CCC had co-ordinated with Chinese communities 'from Vancouver to Montreal,' to prepare a statement which would be printed in both the Chinese and English press. The statement was to appear as a paid advertisement and would be released as the Peking Opera reached each step of its itinerary. The advertisement appeared in the *Globe and Mail* on 6 September 1960, and featured a sympathy-arousing 25 by 20 cm photograph of five Canadian nuns with bowed heads and shackled hands. The caption, 'Canadian Nuns Shackled by Chinese Communists,' was intended to lay bare the realities of communist 'culture.' The tightly worded accompanying statement touched a nerve that was to remain sensitive for those in charge of Canada's national security for a decade to come. There was considerable speculation that the CCC was deliberately fuelling RCMP concerns that recognition would open the doors to communist subversion in Chinatowns across Canada.[9] The warning that 'a penny spent today for attending the Peking Opera is a penny invested in the Communist war chest which will one day be used against us all' played on the fear that communist friendship would pose threats to freedom and democracy. The advertisement was signed by leaders of twelve Chinese community centres and benevolent associations in Montreal, Toronto, Winnipeg, Ottawa, Halifax, Victoria, Edmonton, Calgary, Vancouver, and Saskatoon.[10]

In a final push to publicize its opposition to the Canadian tour of the Peking Opera, the CCC organized one hundred Chinese Canadians to picket in front of the Royal Alexandra Theatre. The picketers carried signs which read: 'To the Memory of Our Fallen in Korea,' 'Mao Tse-tung the Killer,' 'People's Commune = Hell on Earth,' 'This Show Is a Camouflage for Genocide in Tibet,' 'There Are Already a Billion Slaves Who also Thought Communism Was a Joke.'[11]

The activities of the CCC culminated in 1968 with the formation of the Chinese Community Centre of Canada, an ad hoc organization including community centres and benevolent associations across Canada. Although the rationale of the CCC of Canada was to act as a lobbying force to give Chinese Canadians a stronger voice in presenting their views to the federal government on a number of issues, its immediate goal was to devise a hasty response to Prime Minister Trudeau's announcement in 1968 that Canada intended to establish formal ties with the People's Republic of China. The organization decided to send a twenty-four-member delegation to Ottawa to present External Affairs Minister Mitchell Sharp with a four-page brief.[12]

On 9 August 1968, the CCC sent a letter to the prime minister. It expressed congratulations on his recent election victory and politely requested that, with respect to a change in recognition policy, the government not embark 'upon such a program, which in our view is fraught with danger.'

The letter gave four reasons for reconsidering any change in policy toward the PRC:

> First, we abhor the policies of war, aggression and subversion relentlessly pursued for almost 20 years by the Communist regime on the mainland of China. It is now clear that these policies are formulated and carried out with the purpose of communizing first Asia and then the whole world. They have not been and can not be changed or modified by a policy of accommodation or compromise on the part of other countries and, in particular, Western countries. The results would obviously be detrimental to the cause of peace in general and to the peace and security of countries in Asia and the Pacific in particular.
>
> Secondly, the communization of North America is the ultimate objective in the global strategy of the Chinese Communists ... Even now, Chinese Communist Asians are known to have infiltrated in North American communities to pave the ground for this final stage of the Communist strategy. The exchange of Embassies between Canada and the Chinese Communist regime would fling the door wide open to a flood of Communist Asians to this continent ... The Chinese communities in Canada would be the first to be infiltrated, divided and subverted.
>
> Thirdly – we know for certain that the overwhelming majority of the Chinese people are opposed to the Communist regime. They resent the inhuman and oppressive Communist rule under which they have suffered miserably. From our own information, we know that the stage is being reached when the Chinese people will no longer tolerate the ever worsening situation but will rise up to overthrow the Communist regime. For Canada to grant diplomatic recognition to the Communist regime in these circumstances would be acting against the Chinese people and giving support to the regime which they oppose.
>
> Fourthly – the Chinese Government in Taiwan is the best Government China has ever had in recent 100 years. It has, therefore, become the center of attraction and the hope for a brighter future for Chinese people on the mainland as well as

elsewhere in the world. The recognition of the Chinese Communist regime by Canada would mean the abandonment of the Chinese Government supported by the Chinese people and disregard for the reality of Chinese life ...'[13]

On 13 August 1968, Sharp held a public hearing to listen to these arguments. The CCC's brief focused on the Cultural Revolution in the PRC. The turmoil inside China was portrayed as a 'clear indication' that the 'overwhelming majority of Mainland China' was ready to 'overthrow the Communist regime.' Dr Y.C. Ma, professor of economics at the University of Manitoba, counselled that since 'widespread unrest in Mainland China' might cause 'anything to happen,' it would be imprudent to change diplomatic ties before the outcome of the struggle was known. The brief reiterated most of the arguments contained in the letter of 9 August.

The CCC's focus on communist subversion struck a responsive chord with a number of Canadians. The RCMP had steadfastly lobbied the government about 'the potential infiltration of the Canadian Chinese community by Communist agents.' The American State Department made known its concern that Communist espionage would accelerate, once the PRC had acquired an operation base in Ottawa. At a press conference a year later, in the fall of 1969, Commissioner W.L. Higgitt reiterated the RCMP's concern that after recognition there would be increased activity by PRC agents in Canada. According to DEA officials, the Canadian government took the 'subversion factor' into account in its decision to negotiate with the PRC to establish diplomatic relations. The government never felt that the establishment of a PRC embassy posed a threat, either as a centre of espionage, or as a means for penetrating and disrupting local Chinese communities.[14] The outcome of the meeting was not favourable to the delegation. Given that Sharp basically reaffirmed the government's commitment to recognition, the hearing concluded with polite political formalities. After the meeting, the secretary of state for external affairs wrote a memorandum to the prime minister. Sharp observed that,

> the discussion following the reading of their presentation was cordial even though, as you might expect, we did not find a meeting of minds. I said that while the Canadian Government was very much aware of the difficulties and risks involved, it wanted to bring about mutual recognition of mainland China as a means of better communication between China and the rest of the world. This was not related to direct material Canadian interests such as the promotion of trade. When I asked the delegation under what

circumstances, in their view, it would be possible to, and desirable to recognize Peking, their spokesman said only when the regime in Peking was fully supported by its own people, but this was probably not possible under Communism. I made the usual comments about recognition not indicating approval or otherwise of the policies of the country being recognized. I also mentioned the practical desirability of being in a position to communicate officially with China when we had business to do with it. There might be some question as to whether Peking had full and effective control over the mainland but it was an obvious fact that Taipei did not have that control.

I thanked the delegation for making their representations and told them this was the first group to respond to the Government's expressed desire to engage in a dialogue on foreign policy with the Canadian people ... their views would certainly be taken in account but ... the Government had not changed its objective with respect to China as given in its foreign policy statement May 29. Press reports indicate that the members of the delegation were happy with their reception even though they did not get much satisfaction on matters of substance.[15]

The final phase of the CCC's efforts occurred during the twenty months of negotiations between Canada and the People's Republic in Stockholm. It was reported that 'thousands of Chinese Canadians had signed petitions opposing the talks and that more than 100 Chinese intellectuals – most of whom were on university faculties – had sent protests to Trudeau and Mitchell Sharp.' As the talks droned into their ninth month, however, correspondence related to the Canada-China question fell to a trickle. The relatively quiet months of negotiations in 1970 reinforced the government's view that 'opposition was not strong enough to influence the Stockholm talks.' In fact, one spokesman for the prime minister's office made this point by drawing a contrast between the fairly subdued reaction against recognizing the PRC and the flood of opposition aroused when Canada proposed to recognize the Vatican. The heavy flow of correspondence and the heightened emotionalism either supporting or decrying the proposed diplomatic exchange with the Vatican, even without any formal negotiations, prompted the government to postpone action in this area and to avoid controversy.[16]

As the negotiations moved into their later stages, the PRC press, which until then had been silent on the activities of the Canadian Chinese community, printed several articles about the pro-PRC sympathies of some

Chinese Canadians. On 16 February 1970, the *New China News Agency* (*NCNA*) observed that in front of a large portrait of Mao Tse-Tung, 'over two hundred patriotic Chinese residents in Toronto, Canada, warmly praised the invincible Mao Tse-tung Thought at a soiree they held recently – The soiree reflected that the Chinese residents in Toronto have drawn great inspiration from the great victory of the great proletarian cultural revolution in the motherland.' Later *NCNA* articles described the friendly reception of the newly built Chinese freighter, the *Dongfeng*, which visited Vancouver 'and received a rousing welcome from over 1,000 patriotic overseas Chinese and Canadian friends there.' These were among the few instances where the PRC appeared to comment on the affairs of Canada's Chinese community. By and large, throughout the negotiations, and indeed since the start of the Cultural Revolution in 1966, the PRC had shown little inclination, publicly, to comment on either Canadian politics or on any KMT-PRC conflict within the local Chinese communities.[17]

At the conclusion of the Stockholm talks, when recognition of the PRC was proclaimed, the CCC quickly dashed off an angry letter to Trudeau, and then immediately turned its attention to blocking the admission of the PRC into the United Nations. The CCC placed an advertisement in the *New York Times* on 10 November 1970,[18] ostensibly sponsored by 385 organizations in 52 countries, including Canada, and representing 17.5 million overseas Chinese. The advertisement entreated the U.N. General Assembly 'to keep mainland China out' because 'it is legally and morally not qualified to represent our 700,000,000 brethren under enslavement.'

Although the CCC continued its 'anti-propaganda compaign,' after recognition the English press was less interested in reporting the CCC's activities. Recognition was no longer a debatable issue, and the threat of world communism seemed remote. The more the CCC railed on about 'centres of subversion,' the more it discredited itself, especially as increasing numbers of overseas Chinese and non-Chinese were beginning a love affair with China and things Chinese. A year later, when Diefenbaker called for probes into the claims of harassment by Chinese Canadians who had expressed and continued to express anti-Communist sentiments after recognition, Trudeau and his government brushed off the request with a curt, 'We are looking into the matter.'[19]

Throughout most of the 1950s and 1960s, the CCC had used both personal and impersonal means. Once recognition became more of a concrete threat, the centre relied primarily on petitions, letters to editors, briefs, delegations, and rational arguments. This shift toward using impersonal, formal strategies can be explained in a number of ways. Although the CCC believed that it had cultivated fairly strong personal connections with prominent members of Parliament over the years, most of those ties were with Conservatives who, after Diefenbaker's defeat in 1963, no longer held the reins of power. The CCC's informal network of *guanxi* had suffered a significant blow.

Another reason for the shift to formal techniques may have been related to the manner in which the CCC wanted to present the issue of recognition. The centre had been careful to demonstrate its strong commitment to Western democratic tradition in contrast to the authoritarian policies of the Peking government. For example, letters to editors and newspaper advertisements were often prefaced by statements that Chinese Canadians were loyal citizens who were defending 'free people and free institutions' against 'totalitarian regimentation.' In this way, the centre defined its interests as part of the democratic agenda of Canadian society as a whole.[20] Using the language, tools, and procedural channels of a Western democratic system was one method of publicizing the CCC's faith in the ability of that system to be responsive to the concerns of particular interest groups, and it was a way of playing on residual Cold War fears regarding the spread of communism.

Finally, the CCC wanted to generate as much publicity as possible for its cause. Taking the route of personal connections would have relegated recognition of the PRC to an 'unpublic realm.' The matter would have remained an issue for political elites to discuss behind closed doors. In contrast, impersonal strategies ensured media coverage and opened the possibility that the issue could gather a broader basis of support.

As the Stockholm talks drew to a close, and recognition was in the air, the centre reverted to using personal channels in a last-ditch attempt to influence the Government's stand. During the negotiations, the centre tried to persuade key MPs to take all-expenses paid 'cultural exchange' trips to Taiwan, to 'reaffirm Canadian-Taiwan friendship' and to permit Canadians to witness Taiwan's economic miracle. A total of fifteen MPs were contacted by telephone. According to one informant who was responsible for extending these invitations, the attempts were not successful. Each politician politely declined the offer, saying that such a trip would counter the spirit of recognition and would jeopardize the ongoing negotiations between Canada and the PRC.

Since recognition, the *cause célèbre* of the CCC appears historically outdated. The fear expressed in the 1960s that Chinatowns across Canada would become centres of subversion in North America has not materialized. The relatively quiet presence of the PRC embassy and consulates general has persuaded Chinese Canadians and the general public that diplomatic recognition can be separated from ideological approval. Tourists, student exchanges, ballets, operas, symphonies, and trade delegations have further cemented relations between the two nations. Today, when one listens to the strident anti-PRC message of the CCC, it is difficult to depict it as anything but an alarmist, anachronistic organization. Yet, it would be a mistake to dismiss the CCC and its ideas. There was a time when the CCC did indeed voice the fears and values of the majority of ordinary Chinese Canadians living in Toronto.

The CCC's Pro-Nationalist (ROC) Views in the 1950s and 1960s

The general consensus among respondents is that, in the 1950s and 1960s, the CCC did strike a responsive chord. Like the CCC, individual Chinese Canadians were afraid that, under the PRC, Toronto Chinese would be forced to send money back to China on a regular basis to their relatives. They dreaded the possibility that a Chinese embassy would somehow force them back to China. They worried that if they chose not to do the biddings of communist representatives, their relatives in China would suffer. Some said that they were haunted by a 'Manchurian Candidate' paranoia which credited the Communists with all sorts of brainwashing tactics unknown to the West. Many loathed communism because their relatives had lost their land or lives during the revolution or in the subsequent land reforms. As Edgar Wickberg notes, when the Kuomintang in Canada launched an 'Overseas Chinese Anti-Communist National Salvation Convenant Movement' in 1952, many Chinese Canadians, including some who were otherwise apolitical, supported these campaigns.[21]

A newspaper clipping with the heading 'Angry with Reds; B.C. Chinese Bury Dead in Canada' sums up the mood of the early 1950s.[22] According to Foon Sien, head of the Chinese Benevolent Society in Vancouver, the Chinese were so incensed at the communist regime that they no longer wanted to be buried in China. Further exposés in the English-language press concerning RCMP investigations into 'communist-led extortion rackets' in Vancouver augmented fears that the communists were 'capable of anything.' Reports claimed that 'some Chinese have had to withdraw $10,000 to rescue families from Red threats.'[23] By the mid-1960s, letters from relatives depicting the political and economic chaos during the Cultural Revolution confirmed that prospects for immediate stability, peace, and prosperity under communism were poor.

It would be somewhat of an overstatement to say that Chinese Canadians held these apprehensive sentiments solely as a result of the ideological work of the CCC. One can, however, suggest that the CCC held enough power and prestige within the Toronto Chinese community in the 1950s and early 1960s to enable it to reinforce and to play upon residual anti-communist sentiments. The good reputation of the CCC in the Chinese community can be traced to its association with the Kuomintang (KMT) and its wartime activities. During the war and in the immediate post-war years, the CCC and its precursor, the Chinese Protection Federation (CPF), derived legitimacy from the KMT's stature as China's ruling party until 1949, and as the officially recognized representative of China in Canada until 1970. Members of the KMT gave to a socially and politically downtrodden Chinese community much of its energy, expertise, and leadership.[24] By the same token, both the CPF and the CCC enabled the KMT to mesh the causes of the Nationalist government with social, cultural, educational, and political concerns which were close to the hearts of Chinese Canadians.

Although the CPF drew its leadership from the Chinese Christian Association, the Freemasons, and other organizations, KMT members provided the most unified and coherent leadership. A relatively small group of strong KMT adherents like Chong Ying and E.C. Mark occupied leading positions in the CPF year after year.[25] In the 1940s, a Chinese War Relief Association grew out of a CPF subcommittee. In November 1945, a KMT-dominated CCC replaced the CPF in Toronto. In the following years, the KMT worked to organize a series of crusades to rescue China from communism.

But the CCC did not ignore issues closer to home. On 27 October 1943, Madame Chiang Kai-shek made what was to become in the eyes of Chinese Canadians a celebrated visit to the Canadian House of Commons. There she emphasized to Prime Minister King that the Chinese expected to be looked upon and to be dealt with 'as equals, not as inferiors.[26] The favourable publicity which her speech evoked in the English-language press may have reflected the changing mood of the nation. For Chinese Canadians, however, Mme Chiang's words, coupled with the subsequent tough exchanges between the Chinese embassy and the Canadian government, did much to impress upon them that the KMT would speak up on their behalf. Mme Chiang, in effect, laid the groundwork for the CCC to take the national lead in agitating for the repeal of the 1923 Exclusion Act. The KMT, in fact, gave the 'Committee for the Repeal of the Chinese Immigration Act' its initial funds.[27] The CCC's proximity to Ottawa and the contacts which it had cultivated with non-Chinese community leaders and politicians during its fund-raising drive and war relief program caused it to stand out among other Chinese organizations across Canada.

After the 1923 Immigration Act was repealed in 1947, the CCC immediately turned to opposing order-in-council P.C. 2115. This order-in-council restricted Asian family immigration to a citizen's wife and unmarried children under eighteen years of age. Because of the policy of exclusion prior to 1947, many Chinese Canadians had been unable to establish families in Canada. Instead, they married in China and periodically visited their wives and children. For these pre-1923 immigrants, adult children and other categories of close relatives, such as siblings and aged parents, were excluded from Canada. Such rules did not apply to European groups.[28]

During its fight against the Exclusion Act and the order-in-council, the CCC received support from labour congresses and leaders of all religious denominations. A deputation from the Committee for the Repeal of the Chinese Immigration Act, which appeared before the Senate Committee on Immigration and Labour in March 1948, included A.R. Mosher, president of the Canadian Congress of Labour, Rabbi Abraham Feinberg of the Canadian Jewish Congress, and representatives from the major churches.[29] Again, while the willingness of other sectors to join forces with the Chinese may have reflected changes in popular attitudes, many respondents believed that this show of solidarity was very much the result of active lobbying on the part of CCC leaders. One respondent credited widespread church support to the persuasive energy of several elders of the Chinese Presbyterian Church who were Christians and prominent CCC members. A few years later, a convention of Chinese community centres in Toronto in May 1952 once more highlighted the CCC's organizational skills. Among the resolutions passed during the meetings of the elite from thirty Chinatowns across Canada was the decision to send to immigration minister Walter Harris the demand that Chinese be given equal rights on immigration matters.[30]

Shortly after the order-in-council was finally abandoned in 1956, Chinese communities faced another crisis which again gave the CCC the opportunity to take the lead in Toronto. In the mid-fifties American authorities in Hong Kong uncovered a major conspiracy to evade immigration laws of the United States. The organized sale and purchase of false identities enabled almost any Chinese to bypass the regulation barriers and to enter the United States illegally. The Canadian government became convinced that a large number of Chinese immigrants were also gaining admission to Canada illegally, and Canada launched its own investigation by the RCMP in 1959.[31]

The intensity of the investigations, the massive violation of civil liberties, and the implication that all Chinese were somehow involved in a huge immigration 'racket' incensed the Toronto community. Embittered by the seizure of typewriters, adding machines, account books, and other documents from business premises and private residences, members of the CCC promptly drafted a telegram to Roland Michener, Conservative member for St Paul's, to ask him to arrange a meeting with Prime Minister Diefenbaker.[32]

In June, William C. Wong, former editor of *Shing Wah*, chairman of the CCC, and executive member of the KMT, led a twenty-three-member delegation to Ottawa to protest to Diefenbaker the 'unfair, unwarranted and malicious allegations' implied by the RCMP raids on major Chinese communities across Canada, and charged the Hong Kong police with 'Gestapo' techniques.[33] In July, Wong announced to the *Globe and Mail* that the centre would 'take any charges of improper conduct by the police to Prime Minister Diefenbaker.'[34] Within the same period, an advertisement appeared in the *Toronto Telegram* carrying the caption 'The Chinese Community Centre Asks Fair Play for Minority Group.' In essence, the advertisement argued that Chinese Canadians were being slandered and treated as criminals when they had proved to be loyal, responsible, law-abiding citizens.[35]

In examining the participation of CCC members in community concerns, it is obvious that immigration matters directly affected their interests as well. The added bonus was that each leadership experience broadened the centre's contacts and heightened its visibility among non-Chinese. At the same time, it legitimized itself as a broad, overall benevolent association. Although no organization had ever been able to speak with unquestioned authority on behalf of the Toronto community in the 1920s and 1930s, in the immediate post-war years and for two decades thereafter, the CCC was able to operate as the prototypical, community-wide association.[36] By portraying itself as the guardian of the entire community, intent on protecting the rights and image of Chinese Canadians, it was able to create opportunities to mesh Canadian concerns with Chinese politics. For example, the CCC had recently emerged from its struggle with Ottawa over the order-in-council P.C. 2115 when Y.C. Seetow, editor of *Shing Wah*, announced the following to the *Globe and Mail*: 'Recognition of Communist China and Canada's immigration restrictions are the two questions uppermost in the minds of the Chinese Community in Toronto.'[37] He went on to estimate that 'ninety-nine percent of the Chinese in Toronto are anti-Communist.' Similarly, the CCC organized the boycott of the Peking Opera at about the same time as it organized protests against the RCMP raids. After the twenty-three-member delegation returned from visiting Diefenbaker in Ottawa, it reported to a Toronto audience. On stage was the Nationalist Chinese flag, the Canadian ensign, and a picture of Sun Yat-sen.[38]

The impression conveyed by the respondents in this study is that prior to recognition, the pro-KMT stand of the CCC was non-controversial. It was accepted not only because it represented the status quo, but also because it reflected political leanings with which the majority of Chinese Canadians were most comfortable. Furthermore, the Nationalist position was associated with an organization, the CCC, which had done much for the Chinese community in the past.

Opposition to the CCC Before Recognition

The CCC, by and large, created a sympathetic context for its political ideas throughout its years of community work. The legitimacy and prestige of the CCC was, however, as much the result of its active leadership as a reflection of the relative weakness of other Chinese organizations which represented different views of both the KMT and China.

The Freemasons provide the most notable example of an association which had historically rivalled the KMT since the 1920s and had continuously voiced ideals contrary to the KMT, but had lost much of its vitality by the mid-1950s.[39] The Freemasons had initially rallied around the objective of overthrowing the Ching dynasty. Once a republican government was nominally established in China, it surfaced as a more active political and welfare organization and jockeyed with the KMT for membership and non-Chinese support and co-operation. As might be expected, the tensions between the KMT and the Freemasons went deeper than vying for territorial supremacy. There were ideological disagreements as well. Although the Freemasons attempted to direct attention to Canadian society and to maintain an ostensibly neutral mediating position as far as post-1949 politics in China were concerned, neutrality was a suspicion-arousing position in the Cold War years. By the 1950s, a KMT-dominated CCC could hurl incriminating 'leftist' labels at the Freemasons whenever the latter tried to criticize CCC activities or ideology. In fact, allegations that the Freemasons' newspaper, the *Hung Chung She Bo* (*Chinese Times*), held communist sympathies persuaded the organization's board of directors to discontinue the paper for fear of broader accusations of disloyalty. The demise of the *Hung Chung She Bo*, in 1959, left the *Shing Wah* as the unchallenged Chinese newspaper until the appearance of the *Toronto Shang Bao* (*Chinatown Commercial News*) in June 1966. Whereas the Freemasons never recovered their pre-war prominence in the community, the CCC was strengthened by the Cold War and Canada's involvement in the Korean War.

As for family clans, one could trace overlapping memberships between the CCC and some of the larger clans. But it would be inaccurate to claim that the CCC exercised control over clans through such overlapping members. Rather, respondents gave the impression that if a clan chose to be associated with the CCC, this support could be attributed more to the CCC's community prestige than to its politics. Events after recognition reinforce the argument that the CCC's ideological influence was fragile. After recognition, two of the larger family associations publicly questioned the CCC's legitimacy and soon severed themselves from the centre and its Taiwan-oriented politics. Until 1970, however, when recognition of the PRC appeared imminent, there was little indication that family associations provided an institutional basis for the expression of political views in opposition to the CCC. In any case, regardless of the political leanings of the clans and locality associations, by the 1960s they had reached a period of decline.[40]

The role of the church in Toronto's Chinese community is more difficult to assess. Official church policy is to 'stay out of politics' and to concentrate on providing education, recreation, fellowship, and other social services. When the Rev Y.S. Lee, minister of the Chinese United Church, was asked his opinion on the recognition issue, he declined to comment on the grounds that ministers should 'steer clear' of politics.[41] Nevertheless, an unofficial, unspoken alliance between the church and anti-communist forces existed in the past, given the well-publicized intolerance of communism toward religious freedom.

This was especially true of the Chinese Presbyterian Church which had as church elders such eminent CCC members as E.C. Mark, Harry Hung, B.F. Wong, and William Wong. Their presence helped shape at least one important aspect of the church's policy: the direction of its Chinese school.[42] In 1948, the administration of the Chinese school was transferred to the CCC by the school's board of directors on the advice of Chong Ying. Although Chong Ying belonged to the Chinese United Church, he was a member of the Toronto Chinese Young Men's Christian Institute (YMCI) which housed the Presbyterian church prior to 1956. He also headed the church's school-board. The CCC's control of the school-board enabled it to hire teachers who supported the KMT, to define the course curriculum largely favourable to Nationalist China, and to inspire in students a loyalty to the symbols of Taiwan. In so doing, the CCC was hoping to mould the opinions of the next generation of Chinese Canadians. In return, the church was to be relieved of the financial burden of running the school.

The relationship between the church and the school has never been smooth. Recurrent disputes have largely revolved around finances and not politics. It seems that the church was more than willing to leave the educational content of the school to the CCC and to turn a deaf ear to the complaints voiced by parents, after 1970, of the 'overly political' nature of the lessons. In contrast, the church became angry when the CCC reneged on its financial agreements and worse when the CCC began to make claims to part of the church's property. It was not until financial disputes escalated into a court battle in July 1984 that politics was dredged up as an issue. Among the numerous submissions which the church presented in its case against the CCC was the accusation that it was more interested in promoting its brand of Nationalist politics than in teaching the educational aspects of Chinese heritage and culture.

One could argue that, in comparison with clans and other regional associations, the churches had more compelling reasons to lean toward the CCC. The appearance of the Chinese Presbyterian Church, the Chinese United Church, and the Chinese Catholic Centre on the letterhead of the CCC provides evidence of their political sympathies. Even so, the unwillingness of the various churches to enter the ideological fray (at least overtly) makes it difficult to determine whether or not churches exercised any influence over their congregation on the recognition issue. At the very least, one could assume that their unofficial position would be against recognition.

Generally speaking, there were no outstanding social groups to challenge the CCC. The most telling indication was revealed in interviews with several pro-PRC respondents who held communist sympathies since the revolution. These respondents confided that they recognized the social good embodied in communist philosophy even though their houses and land back in China had been confiscated. They mentioned also that since 'very few' Chinese Canadians held similar ideas, they didn't dare make their views known outside their homes. Besides, they knew of no organization within the Chinese community which brought together individuals who shared their beliefs. A *Globe and Mail* article on 10 August 1960 noted that a 'pro-Peking' Chinese Canadian Welfare Society received a 'cold shoulder' when it asked Chinese merchants to come out and welcome the Peking Opera when it arrived in Toronto.

The *Shang Bao* (*Chinatown Commercial News*) was the first organization sympathetic to the PRC. Since its inception in June 1966, *Shang Bao* proceeded discreetly, taking care never to portray itself as a pro-communist newspaper. Instead, it claimed to serve the Chinese Canadian community by providing primarily Canadian news and, occasionally, some news about China. If, initially, *Shang Bao*'s low profile was no match for the aggressive tactics of the CCC, its caution later turned to boldness with the announcement of Canada's impending recognition of the PRC.

The *Shang Bao*'s first editorial on Canada-China relations followed the CCC's announcement that it was sending a delegation to Ottawa to meet with Mitchell Sharp. The editorial's purpose was to challenge the representatives of the delegation and the CCC's insistence that its posture accurately reflected the stand of the majority of Chinese Canadians.[43] The next editorial appeared in December 1969 after Canada had publicized the beginning of the Stockholm talks. The *Shang Bao* reported the changing international mood toward the PRC and the tough bargaining terms imposed by China. It went on to admonish the die-hard 'Chiang gang' for attempting to disrupt the negotiations and for trying to block the PRC's entry into the United Nations. In an inadvertent admission of the weakness of the pro-PRC forces at the time of recognition, the editorial condemned the CCC for building up its dominance in Chinese communities on the basis of false rumours, fear, and intimidation.[44]

The late appearance of these editorials suggests that they could not have played any significant role in shaping the opinions of the Chinese community, prior to recognition, let alone those of the Liberal government. The newspaper did, however, attempt to reinforce the government's decision once it was a foregone conclusion. In a series of articles appearing between October 1970 and the arrival of the Chinese ambassador in Ottawa in 1971, *Shang Bao* repeatedly praised the diplomacy of Trudeau and assured the Canadian government that the CCC and other 'Chiang people' were 'in the minority.' In all cases, the articles stressed the patriotism of the overseas Chinese and carefully separated recognition, friendship, and 'internal politics.' Curiously enough, none of these articles were ever passed along to the English press.[45]

To return to the question as to who was on which side of the recognition issue, it seems that the activities of the CCC and the editorials of the *Shang Bao* represented the two sides of the issue. Within the Toronto community, at the time, the pro-KMT position had considerably more support than the pro-PRC position. Part of the reason lies in the skilful organization and activities of the CCC, but the CCC in the end drew its support, tacit or otherwise, from the Chinese community. Up to 1970, this community remained wary of the PRC, and it was 'natural' for Toronto Chinese to support the status quo in a mood of quiet sympathy.

The Mood of Quiet Sympathy and the Eclipse of the CCC

One must distinguish between attitudes and actions. While many Chinese Canadians were willing to discuss the implications of recognition and exchange anxieties and fears with family and friends, far fewer were willing to take overt public action. Interviews with key informants of the Chinese community show that recognition was not salient enough as an issue to mobilize the Chinese population to action. In fact, except for the two representatives from the CCC, the other twenty-six respondents placed recognition fairly low on their list of issues of importance to them. Although members of the Chinese community had shown that they were capable of concerted action in the past, calculated reasons weighed against active participation on this particular issue in the 1960s. Identification with the anti-recognition message of the CCC could best be described as one of 'quiet sympathy.' This was the most intense response which the CCC could inspire despite its prestige inside the Toronto community.

One spokesman of the Chinese Canadian Welfare Association echoed the sentiments of other respondents when he stated that the overriding concern of almost all Chinese Canadians in the 1950s and 1960s related to immigration rather than recognition. Not only were the Toronto Chinese attempting to free Canada's immigration laws of discriminatory elements, they were working diligently to find ways to bring their relatives to Canada. They worried about cultural adaptation, social isolation, education, welfare, and mutual aid. All such concerns occupied their minds much more than did Canada's recognition of the PRC. The truth of the matter was that most Chinese Canadians had adopted Canada as their home, and as they turned their thoughts toward improving their life-style in Canada, China was becoming remote, and home country politics appeared increasingly irrelevant.[46]

By 1968, it became evident that the Liberal government under Trudeau was intent on negotiating diplomatic ties with the PRC. After the recent experience of the RCMP immigration probes, Chinese Canadians were not about to demonstrate their disloyalty by opposing the government's public stand. Besides, many Chinese felt this was a matter between governments and, no matter how strongly one opposed recognition, one would be wasting one's time by interfering with international affairs. If, as our respondents indicated, Chinese Canadians worried about the somewhat remote consequences of recognition, they worried more about those issues which immediately affected their daily lives, such as immigration.

It has been argued that the CCC's wartime activities and its post-war leadership in immigration matters placed it in a prominent position in the 1950s and early 1960s. It could, to a degree, define its own interests as the community's interests. This initially engendered sympathetic approval for its ideological position. By the late 1960s the influx of new Chinese immigrants had changed the size and composition of the community. Substantial revisions of immigration regulations in 1962, and again in 1967, removed the emphasis on country of origin as a major criterion for admission to Canada, and permitted immigrants to enter on the basis of a points system.[47] As a result, the Chinese population in central Toronto more than doubled between 1961 and 1971 to 18,000. In addition, the Chinese population began to spread rapidly beyond the traditional confines of

Toronto's Chinatown. As the numbers grew and dispersed, the community became more varied, stratified and fragmented along the lines of education, occupation, generation, period of immigration, place of origin, and class background. The political structure of Chinatown was changing quickly. In contrast to the earlier immigrants, members of this new community no longer shared roots in southern China. They had no strong memory of the Toronto Chinese community's struggle with discriminatory immigration laws. They no longer had close sentimental attachments to the KMT.

The emphasis of the amended immigration laws on skill opened the doors to an urban, educated, English-speaking, and professional elite.[48] Members of this new stratum spawned a variety of organizations which increasingly pushed the CCC to the periphery. The proliferation of new groups included youth clubs, political associations, university student associations, kung-fu clubs, community service groups, workers' associations, professional organizations, cultural organizations, and independence organizations, to name only a few.[49] Such organizations focused directly on Canadian life and distinctly ignored Chinese politics in general and the recognition issue in particular.

The Chinese newspaper 'war' provides another sign of the increasingly diverse needs of the community. *Shing Wah*, the KMT paper, had held a virtual monopoly over the Chinese readership in Toronto since the demise of the *Chinese Times* in 1959. As well, *Shing Wah* never treated the *Shang Bao* as a serious challenge. By 1972, however, two former *Shing Wah* editors who became tired of the paper's polemics left to organize a new local newspaper called the *Chinese Express*, which soon began to outpace the *Shing Wah*, selling approximately three times as many newspapers. After 1975, the competition intensified when the *Sing Tao Ribao*, part of a Hong Kong publishing empire, and the *World Journal*, with headquarters in Taiwan, also cut into the Toronto market.[50]

Although most of these organizations did not arise until after recognition, the growing size and heterogeneity of the Chinese population in Toronto had begun to affect the political configuration of the community much earlier. By the mid-sixties, the CCC found it increasingly difficult to ride on its past distinctions. No single organization, let alone the CCC, could claim to speak for Chinese Canadians as a whole, and no one could legitimately be called the unofficial 'mayor' of Chinatown (a title once reserved for Chong Ying). A larger, more complex community served to diffuse and to muffle much of the CCC's message. If the old immigrants ranked issue of recognition low on a list of personal and community priorities, the new immigrants found the issue to be largely irrelevant.

Postscript to Recognition

The CCC and *Shing Wah* have not abated their efforts to discredit the PRC and, from time to time, have found occasions to vent their political temper.[51] The most curious issue to emerge involved a six-month dispute in 1981 in Toronto over a statue of Sun Yat-sen. At face value, the wrangling concerned whether Sun Yat-sen or a railway builder would more appropriately represent Chinese Canadians. The squabble had its roots in the conflict between pro-Taiwan and pro-Peking forces. For the pro-Peking forces, permitting a statue of Sun in Toronto would be a concession to the strongest symbol of Nationalist China, a country with which Canada had no official relationship.[52]

If Chinese Canadians in the main treated recognition as an issue of secondary importance and exerted minimal influence on the Canadian government's position, the fact of recognition itself has had a major impact on Chinese Canadians, in their attitudes both to China and to themselves. One formerly staunch supporter of the KMT and active CCC member explained and defended her 'change of heart' in a *Shang Bao* interview.[53] She confided that, as a Canadian citizen, she felt that she had the responsibility to support her country's decision. She watched as her former colleagues increasingly isolated themselves from the rest of the Chinese and non-Chinese community. She sensed that there was something wrong when children had to plead and to argue with absolutely unyielding parents for permission to travel to China. Given that the passing of time has dispelled many of the myths and fears associated with recognizing a communist country, the recalcitrance of this older generation appeared irrational, more a matter of face and past vested interests than of reason. In a similar vein, a chief writer for *Shing Wah* for eighteen years, who has since left the newspaper, dismissed his old friends as narrow extremists who were as guilty as their ideological opponents of one-sided propaganda.

These examples may or may not represent 'typical patterns,' but they suggest that a positive attitude to the People's Republic of China gained momentum after the establishment of formal relations. In the end, Chinese Canadians were willing to display an active interest in the PRC when it became officially acceptable to be proud of China's social and cultural achievements without worrying about political repercussions.

Respondents noted another important consequence of recognition. On the whole, they felt that recognition gave Chinese Canadians a basis for renewed self-worth and international regard. Overseas Chinese had always felt that restrictive immigration legislation, discriminatory employment laws, racist rules regarding citizenship rights, and political participation were extensions of the humiliating way in which foreign powers had historically treated China and persons of Chinese descent. In contrast to Japan, until the communists took power in China, no world nation looked upon China as a major power. Weak, fragmented, and internally torn, China was in no position to defend itself or its people. Recognition marked a political 'coming of age.' The PRC had entered the international arena as a superpower. As nations, leaders, and ordinary citizens joined together to praise China's progress, its self-reliance, and its ability to deal with foreign powers from a position of strength, increasing numbers of Chinese Canadians began to take pride in their language, culture, and heritage. In the process, they developed a more positive self-concept, a more assured sense of ethnic consciousness. Recognition has promoted greater respect for China and this heightened respect has had a halo effect by improving the image of the Chinese among non-Chinese and Chinese alike. As one respondent declared, 'Now I can hold my head up.' Dignity, respondents concur, is the lasting effect of the recognition of the PRC for Chinese people all over the world.

Notes

1 See Edgar Wickberg et al., eds., *From China to Canada: A History of the Chinese Communities in Canada* (Toronto: McClelland and Stewart 1982), 248; Anthony B. Chan, *Gold Mountain* (Vancouver: New Star Books 1983), 150; Peter S. Li, *The Chinese in Canada* (Toronto: Oxford University Press 1988), 102–4.
2 For example, until his defeat in 1980, Peter Stollery, Liberal MP for Spadina, attended regularly.
3 *Globe and Mail*, Nov. 1962. The *Shing Wah Daily News* was Toronto's most established Chinese-language newspaper. The editors and staff, more often than not, were active members of the Chinese Community Centre. The paper strongly supported Taiwan and its ruling party, the Kuomintang.
4 From informants who attended the meeting.
5 Lucian Pye, *The Dynamics of Chinese Politics* (Cambridge: Oelgeschlager, Gunn and Hain 1981), 6, 20.
6 *Globe and Mail*, 11 Aug. 1960
7 *Globe and Mail*, 17 Aug. 1960
8 *Globe and Mail*, 10 Aug. 1960
9 Interview material; see also *Globe and Mail*, 20 May 1969.
10 *Globe and Mail*, 6 Sept. 1960.
11 Ibid.
12 One informant recalls that the majority of the twenty-four delegates came from the Toronto contingent. Toronto's proximity to Ottawa was cited as one

reason for Toronto's over-representation. The willingness of other major Chinese centres to defer to Toronto's leadership was cited as another reason.
13 From DEA file 20-China-14, 1968–70 and personal interviews.
14 Ibid.
15 Ibid.
16 *Globe and Mail*, 8 Oct. 1969.
17 *NCNA*, 17 Feb. 1970, 15 Aug. 1970, 17 Aug. 1970, 8 Sept. 1970; and DEA, 20-China-14, 1970; see also Roger Dial, 'The Several and Competing Chinese Perceptions of Canada: A Content Analysis of *Hsinhua*, 1950–1972' (Halifax: Dalhousie University, Centre for Foreign Policy Studies 1974).
18 *Globe and Mail*, 11 Nov. 1970.
19 *Globe and Mail*, 12 Aug. 1971 and 10 Sept. 1971.
20 According to Glickman, an important factor in the political accomplishments of the Jewish community was its capacity to 'universalize its political action so as to make it palatable to groups otherwise indifferent or hostile to Jewish concerns' (Yaacov Glickman, 'Political Socialization and the Social Protest of Canadian Jewry' in *Ethnicity, Power and Politics in Canada*, ed. Jorgen Dahlie and Tissa Fernando [Toronto: Methuen 1981], 123–50).
21 Wickberg, *From China to Canada*, 228.
22 *Globe and Mail*, 23 Nov. 1951. One of the functions of benevolent societies across Canada was to gather the bones of deceased Chinese and ship them back to relatives in China.
23 *Globe and Mail*, 9 Dec. 1951, 12 Dec. 1951, and 26 July 1956.
24 According to Paul Levine, by the mid-1930s the Chinese Protection Federation (whose legitimacy had been conferred by Chiang Kai-shek) had achieved the position as sole mediator between the Chinese and the Canadian government (Paul S. Levine, 'Historical Documentation Pertaining to Overseas Chinese Organizations,' unpublished MPhil thesis, University of Toronto, 1975, 106–7).
25 Wickberg, *From China to Canada*, 197.
26 F.J. McEvoy, 'A Symbol of Racial Discrimination: The Chinese Immigration Act and Canada's Relations with China, 1942–1947,' *Canada Ethnic Studies* 14 (1982), 28, 29.
27 Wickberg, *From China to Canada*, 222.
28 Ibid., 204–18.
29 Ibid., 211–12.
30 *Globe and Mail*, 17 May 1952.
31 Wickberg, *From China to Canada*, 214; see also Freda Hawkins, *Canada and Immigration: Public Policy and Public Concern* (Montreal and London: McGill-Queen's University Press 1972), 131–4.
32 *Globe and Mail*, 27 May 1960.

33 *Globe and Mail*, 24 June 1960.
34 *Globe and Mail*, 7 July 1960.
35 *Toronto Telegram*, 6 June 1960.
36 Wickberg, *From China to Canada*, 221–2.
37 *Globe and Mail*, 30 Jan. 1959.
38 *Globe and Mail*, 24 June 1960.
39 Interview material; see also Wickberg, *From China to Canada*, 164–5 and 226–7.
40 According to Thompson, the mutual aid, recreation, and other social welfare functions which were the raison d'être of the traditional family and regional associations have been increasingly taken over by government-subsidized social service agencies (Richard N. Thompson, 'Ethnicity versus Class: An Analysis of Conflict in a North American Chinese Community,' *Ethnicity* 6 [1979], 314. A similar phenomenon has occurred in San Francisco and New York. See V.G. Nee and B. Nee, *Longtime Californ': A Documentary Study of an American Chinatown* (Boston: Houghton-Mifflin 1972) and Bernard Wong, 'Elites and Ethnic Boundary Maintenance: A Study of the Roles of Elites in Chinatown, New York City,' *Urban Anthropology* 6 (1977), 1–22.
41 *Globe and Mail*, 30 June 1959.
42 Interview material.
43 Interview material.
44 *Shang Bao*, 31 Dec. 1969.
45 *Shang Bao*, 2 Aug. 1970, 14 Oct. 1970, 25 Oct. 1970, 8 July 1971.
46 As well, there were issues which were important to specific sectors of the Chinese community but were not broad enough to unite the entire community. For example, the 'Save Chinatown Campaign' arose in the late 1960s and demanded the energy of those who lived and worked in the vicinity of Toronto's old city hall. The 'Save Chinatown Committee' fought for reassurances from city council that the existing Chinatown would not be wiped out by unilateral government actions (*Globe and Mail*, 17 June 1969, 8 Apr. 1969).
47 Louis Parai, ('Canada's Immigration Policy, 1962–74' *International Migration Review* 9 (1975), 449–77.
48 Thompson argues that the immigration amendments permitted the emergence of new entrepreneurial and social service elites. Members of these two groups effectively challenged the leadership of the traditional elites (see 'Ethnicity versus Class,' 308).
49 Ibid., 311.
50 *Globe and Mail*, 18 May 1978.
51 In 1972, when Yao Guang, ambassador of the PRC, made a courtesy call to Toronto's city hall, the CCC delivered a letter of protest which accused Mao

240 Reluctant Adversaries

of being responsible for the deaths of 50 million Chinese. During the visit, a group of 40 Chinese children staged a demonstration in Nathan Phillips Square (*Globe and Mail*, 12 Aug. 1972). Over a decade later, when Premier Zhao Ziyang arrived in Canada, the CCC organized a similar demonstrastion to protest his presence (*Globe and Mail*, 12 Jan. 1984). In the late 1970s conflict over plans to expand Chinatown had as much to do with the clash between new money and the life-style and livelihood of working-class Chinese residents as it did with the efforts of the traditional leaders to reassert their dominance in face of challenges posed by an emergent social service elite (see Thompson, 'Ethnicity versus Class,' 306–26).
52 *Globe and Mail*, 17 July 1981.
53 *Shang Bao*, 9 Feb. 1985.

CHAPTER TEN

Arthur Andrew

'A Reasonable Period of Time'
Canada's De-recognition of Nationalist China

In the course of the month of August 1970, the Canadians negotiating mutual recognition with the People's Republic of China came to believe for the first time that there was a clear desire in Peking to reach an agreement. In Ottawa this led to thinking about the legal forms and the consequential actions that would be required to give practical effect to the emerging new policy.

The main responsibility for seeing that plans were made and, later, that the necessary action was taken fell to the Far Eastern Division of the Department of External Affairs. It was vital that this successful negotiation should not be jeopardized by any inadvertence or lack of forethought that might follow the actual reaching of an agreement. Questions then had to be addressed which, up to that point, had really never been asked. How should the agreement be announced? What should be said by way of explanation to Canadians and to our allies? What should be the Canadian attitude toward the regime on Taiwan? What was implied in a withdrawal of recognition? What sorts of contacts could be maintained without jeopardizing the entire process? What was the accepted procedure for changing recognition? And later, how would Canada go about implementing the agreement to exchange ambassadors within six months, and provide all necessary assistance for the establishment of diplomatic missions, as the agreement required?

There were obviously more questions than there were answers. Moreover, there seemed to be a very large number of things that could not be started until an agreement was secured but which had to be done between the reaching of an agreement and the time it was to become effective. A rough scenario was prepared in Far Eastern Division and people went to work preparing draft documents for tentative approval, subject to amendment in the light of anything that might happen later.

As the wording of the agreement began to emerge, it also became obvious that the Canadian government's acceptance of the emerging formula would have to depend on its being able to explain publicly what we considered the words to mean. The phrase that presented the problem appeared in the communiqué after the Chinese reaffirmation that Taiwan was an integral part of China and it read: 'The Canadian Government takes note of this position of the Chinese Government.'

As is now well known, the Canadian government considered it essential to record its long-standing position that it was not appropriate or relevant to the process of recognition either to 'endorse or challenge' the territorial claims of the state being recognized. Thus, 'taking note' in the agreement meant that Canada was aware of the Chinese view on Taiwan 'and we realize the importance they attach to it, but we have no comment to make one way or the other.'

All concerned were aware that it was advisable not to present the Chinese with any surprises, particularly in the very early stages of the new relationship, and yet the government was determined that its position should be understood at home and abroad. Accordingly, it was decided that the Chinese should see a draft, in advance, of what the secretary of state for External Affairs intended to say when announcing the agreement. This was done. A 'piece of paper' (*bout de papier*) containing the minister's statement was given to the Chinese in Stockholm. They were not asked to approve or even to comment on it, as it was regarded as the unilateral Canadian view of how the words of the agreement should be interpreted so far as Canada was concerned.

After an appropriate interval – something under two weeks – had elapsed, the Canadian side felt justified in assuming that there would be no reaction to our clarifying statement. It was also decided that so far as Canada was concerned, the agreement would always be published within the context of the minister's, Mitchell Sharp's clarifying statement, which we regarded as the authentic Canadian interpretation of the meaning of the formula we had accepted.

In fulfilment of 'Murphy's Law,' there were two last-minute hitches that could not easily have been anticipated. The first was a very firm Chinese insistence that the text of the communiqué that would embody the agreement had to be signed by the two representatives in Stockholm, Margaret Meagher and Wang Tung. Our assumption had been that, when agreed, the communiqué would simply be released in the two capitals. When this

Chinese requirement came to the attention of DEA legal experts, there was an immediate objection. The draft communiqué was just that, and at no time had there been any thought that a formal legal instrument was being negotiated. To have it signed as if it were a formal international instrument would in the lawyers' view require a complete recasting of the language. In short, we would have to start all over again and renegotiate a document from the beginning. One can imagine the feelings of those who had been involved in the negotiation over the previous year and a half. The intradepartmental contretemps quickly found its way upward and eventually it was presented to the minister, who decided what the communiqué represented was an understanding which both parties had worked to reach and intended to implement. If either of them did not want to honour it, no amount of signing would make any difference and it would fall by the wayside. In any case, they could do so, with or without signatures. Mitchell Sharp could not foresee the day when either party would take the other to court over the terms of the agreement; they would honour it or they would not. Its form and language was only to make sure we understood each other.

Margaret Meagher was instructed to sign, and a date was set for the ceremony. She was asked to phone and let Far Eastern Division know when the act was done. About the time the phone call was due, one arrived, but with the second unanticipated hitch. Wang Tung, who had taken a liking to Margaret Meagher, the Canadian ambassador, did not approve of the Chinese character that had been used by the Canadian interpreter to render Miss Meagher's name into Chinese. There would be a slight delay while he found a better one. Later that same day, however, the communiqué was finally signed and the then head of Far Eastern Division placed the following on file:

NOTE FOR HISTORY

China: Canadian Recognition

At 11:00 a.m. Ottawa time, Miss B.M. Meagher, Ambassador of Canada to Sweden, informed the Head of Far Eastern Division by telephone that she had signed the Joint Communique of the Government of Canada and the Government of the People's Republic of China concerning the establishment of diplomatic relations between Canada and China, as representative of the Government of Canada, Stockholm, October 10, 1970.

A copy of this pretentious note was sent to Ralph Collins, who was to be Canada's first ambassador to Peking. Other interested parties in Ottawa were, no doubt, informed by telephone.

At this point, the contingency plans and the draft documents prepared over the previous six weeks or so came into their own. The agreement was to come into effect in three days' time and there was much to be done. The signing had taken place on a Saturday and everything had to be in readiness by the time the minister rose in the House of Commons at 11:00 a.m. on Tuesday, 13 October, to announce the agreement.

For example the following tasks had to be done between 10 and 13 October:

Saturday, 10 October
1 Deliver memorandum to the under-secretary covering the *aide-mémoire* to be given to Ambassador Hsueh on Sunday morning;
2 Obtain the minister's signature on note to Ambassador Hsueh and telegram to Nationalist Consul General in Vancouver;
3 Return signed note to Far Eastern Affairs for delivery to the department;
4 Deliver telegram to RCMP for dispatch to RCMP Vancouver;
5 Inform Washington and Rome agreement has been reached;
6 Authorize Tokyo to inform Japanese at 1500 hours Tokyo time, 13 October;
7 Authorize Ambassador Campbell to inform NATO colleagues at 0900 Brussels time, 13 October;
8 Mr Côté to invite Ambassador Hsueh to call on the under-secretary at 1000, 11 *October.*

Sunday, 11 October
1 Under-secretary to receive Ambassador Hsueh at 1000 to break news, and give him *aide-mémoire;*
2 The minister may invite Hsueh to lunch or farewell interview on 12 *October.*

Monday, 12 October
1 The minister may receive Hsueh for lunch or farewell interview;
2 Co-ordination Division to prepare messages for dispatch to provinces, 1000 Ottawa time, 13 October;
3 Under-secretary or Co-ordination Division to telephone Premier Bennett or senior provincial (British Columbia) officials to warn of what will be announced the next day.

Tuesday, 13 October
1 RCMP to inform Nationalist Consul General in Vancouver at 1045 Ottawa time;

2 Department to collect note from Far Eastern Division at 1000 for delivery to Ambassador Hsueh at 1045;
3 Texts delivered to translators in Office of Secretary of State by 1000;
4 Dispatch notifications to all departments and agencies;
5 Co-ordination Division to dispatch telegrams to provincial governments at 1000;
6 The minister makes statement to House at 1100;
7 Inform all posts of the minister's statement as soon as it is delivered;
8 Authorize posts that received it to make use of questionnaire;
9 Obtain first draft of Hansard and repeat it to selected posts.

There were certain friendly governments to be informed but, above all, the Nationalist ambassador, Hsueh Yu-chi, then in Ottawa, had to be informed of what was in store. By what must have seemed, to Ambassador Hsueh, as something more than an unhappy coincidence, the agreement was signed on the national holiday of Nationalist China. There had been some concern over who should attend the reception being given by the ambassador, considering the event that had taken place earlier in the day. Tenth October was the national day of the ROC, and Ambassador Hsueh had invited the Canadian government to attend both a film showing on the evening of the tenth and an afternoon *coupe de champagne*. The department recommended that Canadian participation be 'minimal,' because, 'too great an attendance at this juncture might be misunderstood.' The department recommended four of its officials attend, including the assistant under-secretary responsible for the China area, the chief of protocol, the head of Far Eastern Division (Mr Andrew), and the China desk officer. Apparently, only the chief of protocol attended. In the end, it fell to the chief of protocol, Jean Côté, to deliver the message that Hsueh must have recognized for what it was. He was asked to come to the East Block the next morning, Sunday, to the office of A.E. Ritchie, the under-secretary of state for external affairs, who wished to speak to him.

As part of the contingency thinking, it had been decided that after the agreement became effective there should be no further contact between DEA and the former Chinese embassy. However, it was recognized that at least until the Nationalist diplomats had physically departed from Canada, there would continue to be need for some sort of contact. It was accordingly decided that a special one-man protocol office would be set up, in the shape of J.A. McCordick.

On the morning of Sunday, 11 October, McCordick met the Nationalist ambassador at the door of the East Block and brought him to the office of the under-secretary where Ritchie, accompanied by the head of the Far

Eastern Division, awaited him. The ambassador, although obviously nervous, was nevertheless well prepared for the message he was to receive. It took the form of an *aide-mémoire*; it was addressed to no one, dated but unsigned, and on plain uncrested paper. When the under-secretary had read it to him, the ambassador responded with great dignity to the effect that he deeply regretted the action of the Canadian government which he regarded as a serious mistake. The under-secretary said in return that Ambassador Hsueh had, throughout the long process of negotiation, behaved with great dignity and propriety and that all concerned had appreciated and respected him for it. The ambassador thanked the department for the consideration that had been shown to him personally during the time of the negotiation.

At the same meeting, the ambassador was invited to have lunch with the secretary of state for External Affairs the next day, the day before the withdrawal of recognition was to become effective. It was the custom of Mitchell Sharp to offer lunch to departing ambassadors and he thought it important not to make an exception in this case.

Of all the preparations for the withdrawal of recognition from the Nationalist government, the drafting of this *aide-mémoire* presented the greatest difficulties. Up until then, Canada had declared war, broken relations, and withdrawn missions, but there was no record showing how to go about changing recognition from one government to another. It was not, of course, a matter of recognizing China, the state, but rather of saying that Canada would henceforth regard a different government of China as the rightful one. Fortunately, there was no Canadian embassy in Taipei to have to be considered.

A number of issues concerned the Canadian government. First, would the Nationalists leave quietly, without making a fuss? When they had been 'derecognized' by the French in 1964, they had at first refused to leave and caused the French great embarassment. While it seemed that the Nationalists were willing to leave Canada without incident, no one could be sure. For example, the ambassador could have chosen to deliver an angry public response to Canada's intended course of action. He could have declined the minister's invitation to lunch; he could have found various ways to embarrass the Canadian government. As it turned out, none of this happened. The Nationalists chose not to make an issue of their 'de-recognition' by Canada.

Second, the ambassador asked that if the Stockholm talks resulted in establishment of diplomatic relations between Canada and the PRC, the ROC could keep a representative stationed in Canada in a 'private' capacity to take care of consular matters such as the issuance of visas and 'related questions.' Reference was made to the British and French examples, where ROC affairs were represented by individuals and organizations who did not 'directly' represent the ROC. Should Canada agree to the Nationalist ambassador's request? The department, in consultation with the British and French, concluded that these arrangements were not officially sanctioned by either the British or the French governments. Charlie Wang, in Britain, was a resident alien with a Nationalist passport, who looked into visa and other related questions, prepared investment reports, and facilitated commercial matters. The 'Free China Information Centre.' which he headed, had no official status whatsoever. The Canadian government quickly concluded that it would not agree to the ambassador's request since it had no intention of encouraging the ROC, or of creating any problems with the about-to-be-recognized PRC government.

Third, should the Nationalists be asked to withdraw their press representatives from Canada? The Canadian government concluded that it would be difficult to insist on the departure of the representative of the Taiwan Central News Agency, but that his presence in Ottawa after recognition would cause Canada many headaches. As it turned out, they were right in their assessment. For years afterwards, the PRC sought to remove ROC correspondents from the Ottawa Press Gallery to no avail, and their continued presence was a sore spot in Canadian-PRC relations.

Finally, how could the official Nationalist presence be smoothly removed from Canada after recognition of the PRC? The appointment of J.A. McCordick, as head of a special one-man task force, was designed to solve such problems as what to do about the ROC diplomats' children in the midst of their school year, how to remove and/or dispose of Nationalist files and property, and how in future to facilitate the re-entry to Canada of Canadian residents holding Nationalist passports.

The most obvious source of information on such matters should have been the Vienna Convention on Diplomatic Privileges and Immunities which had entered into force for Canada in June 1966. The best help the legal adviser could provide was that Article 39(2) of the Convention applied to this circumstance. That paragraph reads: 'When the functions of a person enjoying privileges and immunities have come to an end, such privileges and immunities shall normally cease at the moment when he leaves the country, or on expiry of a reasonable period in which to do so, but shall subsist until that time, even in case of an armed conflict. However, with respect to acts performed by such a person in the exercise of his functions as a member of the mission, immunity shall continue to subsist.'

The problem then became one of determining what would be 'a reasonable period' for the Nationalist embassy personnel to wind up their affairs.

Satow's Guide to Diplomatic Practice, the great English-language authority on the subject, was equally unhelpful. The department's legal advisers were draconian in some respects and their advice created visions of the Canadian government having to sequester the ambassadorial limousine, the embassy bank account, and even its files, to be handed over to the new Chinese diplomats on their arrival. After the event, however, it became quite obvious that Hsueh and his colleagues had disposed of all of his government's property in Canada before the fateful hour when recognition was withdrawn from them.

When France and the PRC established diplomatic relations in 1964, the Nationalist government at first attempted to keep the embassy property in ROC hands by transferring title to its UNESCO delegation in Paris. While there was no similar agency of the ROC government located in Canada to whom the Nationalists could transfer title of their embassy and consulate properties, still it was conceivable that they might decide to sell these properties to a 'friendly' organization or individual. This would be calculated to cause the Canadians great embarrassment when the PRC representatives arrived to take over their duties. In January 1969, in an internal memo, the department noted that Canada did not have any legal means of preventing the disposition of these properties by the ROC, or of nullifying their sale. Would the new PRC government demand title of the properties, even if they had been sold? Since the Nationalist embassy in Ottawa formerly had been Sir Robert Borden's residence, could it be declared a historic building, thus preventing its sale by the Nationalists? In the end the Nationalists solved the problem by choosing not to embarrass Canada. They sold their properties to a third party, who then leased the buildings back to the ROC for the duration of their official term in Canada. When representatives of the PRC arrived in Ottawa in 1971, there was no wrangle over property matters, but there were also no premises for them to occupy. They began their stay by leasing space in an Ottawa apartment hotel.

The best information available and the most sensible interpretation of it that could be worked out were incorporated in the *aide-mémoire* read and presented to Mr Hsueh by Mr Ritchie in his office that Sunday morning. The *aide-mémoire* reads, in part:

> At 11:00 a.m. on October 13, 1970, the Secretary of State for
> External Affairs will announce to the House of Commons that the
> Canadian Government and the Government of the People's
> Republic of China have extended mutual recognition and have
> agreed to the establishment of diplomatic relations. The
> Ambassador of the Republic of China will be informed officially and

formally of the Canadian Government's intention just prior to this announcement, as will the Republic of China's Consul General in Vancouver.

As of 11:00 a.m. October 13, 1970, the Canadian Government will cease to recognize the Government of the Republic of China, and that government's Ambassador in Ottawa will cease to be regarded as the Chinese Ambassador to Canada. He is requested, therefore, to arrange for the closure of his Embassy and of his government's Consulate General in Vancouver and the withdrawal from Canada of their non-Canadian personnel within a reasonable period of time. It is considered that a reasonable period of time will be two weeks for the termination of the Embassy's official business plus two further weeks for the completion of personal arrangements by the Ambassador and Chinese members of his Embassy.

After the withdrawal of recognition by the Canadian Government of the Government of the Republic of China, there can be no further formal relations between them. It is recognized, however, that the Ambassador and his Embassy will require assistance in the termination of their activities in Canada. To facilitate the provision of this assistance, Mr. J.A. McCordick is being attached to the Protocol Division of the Department of External Affairs to act as the sole contact between the Embassy and the Canadian Government. All requests and replies from their side must be channeled through him. All departments and agencies of the Canadian Government will be made aware of these arrangements.

In accordance with normal diplomatic practice, the Canadian Government must consider all property in Canada identified as belonging to the Government of China as being property of the Chinese Government which is recognized by it at the time. When recognition is extended to the Government of the People's Republic of China, therefore, the Canadian Government must regard anything registered with it, its agents, the governments of the Provinces, or their agents as belonging to the Government of China as being the property of the People's Republic of China, and will take steps as may be necessary to protect its ownership.

During the two weeks provided for the termination of the Embassy's official business, the Ambassador, and the members of his staff entitled to them, will continue to enjoy unconditionally the normal diplomatic immunities and privileges, so long as they remain in Canada and so long as they have not chosen to seek to change their status with the Department of Manpower and Immigration....

The remainder of the *aide-mémoire* deals with the matter of how members of the embassy staff wishing to remain in Canada beyond the 'reasonable period' provided for could do so.

All this had taken place during the weekend on which Pierre Laporte, Quebec's Minister of Labour, had been kidnapped – later to be murdered. Many of the documents signed by Sharp were brought to him in the Operations Room from which the FLQ crisis was being managed. The lunch given to Hsueh by Sharp, on Monday the 12th, took place at the Restaurant Berger in Hull. The occasion was not, by its nature, a very gay one. The mood was not brightened by the presence of armed soldiers or by a restaurant staff augmented by policemen. It was, however, almost cordial reflecting the mutual respect of the two principals involved. (In an interview in 1986 with the editors of this volume, Mitchell Sharp recalled that while the circumstances were awkward for both participants, the lunch proceeded amicably. Sharp observed that the FLQ crisis added an almost surreal aspect to Ambassador Hsueh's farewell meal.)

On the morning of Tuesday, 13 October, a protocol officer was dispatched to the Chinese embassy to deliver the note by which Sharp formally informed Hsueh that with the announcement of Canada's recognition of the government of the People's Republic of China, 'Canada will cease to recognize Your Excellency's government, and you will cease to be regarded as the Chinese Ambassador to Canada.' The note went on: 'I trust, Excellency, that you will arrange to close your embassy and your government's Consulate-General in Vancouver and withdraw their non-Canadian personnel from Canada within a reasonable period of time.'

Arrangements had also been made to have a similar note delivered to the Nationalist consulate-general in Vancouver. It was later learned that Hsueh Yu-chi had crossed from Canada into the United States before Sharp rose in his place in the House to make his announcement. In return, the Nationalists delivered their own statement on 13 October 1970:

> The Communist Chinese regime was condemned by the United Nations in 1951 for its participation in the Korean conflict. It started a so-called Cultural Revolution in 1965 with the aim of uprooting traditional Chinese culture and this has led to the present disturbances in continental China.
>
> The Canadian government, ignoring its former friendship with the Chinese Republic and the repeated appeals of most of the free countries of Asia and in the Pacific area, started talks with the Communist Chinese at the beginning of 1969. It is regrettable that the Canadian government should announce finally the establish

of diplomatic relations with the Communist Chinese regime which represents a major threat to peace and security in this world. By lending a hand to the Communist Chinese regime when it is about to fall, the Canadian government has not shown much shrewdness. By this same act, the Canadian government has caused serious damage to the rights and interests of the Chinese Republic.

Therefore, the Canadian government will be responsible for all the consequences that may derive after this decline. The government of the Chinese Republic is convinced that the break in diplomatic relations between both countries does not impair the friendship that exists between the people of the two countries.

Again in contingency planning, it had been considered important that all branches of the government should also be aware of the new state of affairs. Accordingly, letters were sent out, also on 13 October, from A.E. Ritchie, the under-secretary, to deputy ministers of departments which might be involved in some aspect of Canada's foreign operations. The letter reported the change in the recognized government of China and said that Canadian and Chinese embassies will be opened in Peking and Ottawa in the near future. It noted that there should be no further contact with the Nationalist embassy or the consulate general in Vancouver. Enquiries were to be referred to McCordick's special protocol office. The letter concludes with a statement on the nature of any future relations with Taiwan: 'While we wish the break in our relations with the Nationalist Chinese to appear as complete as possible, it is clear that we cannot and will not wish to sever all contacts with them. It is intended to create in the very near future, an interdepartmental body made up of representatives of departments and agencies with continuing interests in Taiwan to study and coordinate future unofficial relations with the Taiwanese.' Departments interested were invited to get in touch with McCordick.

The final piece of contingency work was the preparation of a statement that the minister might use in the House of Commons in response to questioning after making his announcement. It was, in fact, used in replying to Robert Stanfield, then leader of the opposition, who expressed the view that while he could see the arguments in favour of entering into relations with the government in Peking, he questioned the government's decision to break with Taiwan.

The government's position as stated by Sharp was that 'There is no disagreement between the Canadian Government and the authorities in Taipeh on the impossibility of continuing diplomatic relations after the Government of Peking is recognized as the Government of China. Both

Peking and Taipeh assert that it is not possible to recognize simultaneously more than one government as the Government of China. Accordingly, the authorities on Taiwan and the Canadian Government have each taken steps to terminate formal diplomatic relations as of the time of the announcement of our recognition of the Government of the People's Republic of China.' Mr Stanfield insisted, however, that he would have preferred to have left the decision up to Taiwan and for its leaders to have accepted the responsibility for making the break.

Although the United States, somewhat later, did manage to have relations with both governments, the withdrawal of recognition from Taiwan was the other side of the recognition coin for Canada. From the beginning of the negotiation, this had been reiterated by the Chinese as an unalterable condition of recognition. No one can say for sure that a 'two-Chinas' solution could not have been negotiated, but some indication might be found in the fact that it took, effectively, twenty months of negotiation merely to shelve the question of the status of Taiwan. As it was, the break with Taiwan, although probably implicit in the establishment of relations with Peking, was, nevertheless, an event in its own right.

After recognition, 'the Taiwan issue' did not disappear as a factor in Canadian-PRC relations. The PRC regularly protested to the Canadian government whenever it detected any potential softening in the Canadian official position on Taiwan. In 1976, the Trudeau government took a strong stand, preventing the participation of Taiwan in the Montreal Olympics. More recently, in the period of China's 'Open Door Policy' in the 1980s, China has tolerated closer relations between Taiwan and countries with whom the PRC has diplomatic relations. In 1986, Canada opened a Chamber of Commerce trade office in Taiwan. The office, which does not perform direct consular functions and is not an official Canadian government office, is, in good part, however, funded from government sources. In a 1987 interview which one of the editors of this volume had in the Ministry of Foreign Affairs in Peking, senior Chinese officials acknowledged their awareness of these arrangements and the Canadian government's arm's length involvement in them, saying that 'the Taiwan situation in 1987 is rather different than the one in 1970.'

Contributors

Paul Evans. Associate Professor, Department of Political Science, York University. Author of *John Fairbank and the American Understanding of Modern China* (New York: Basil Blackwell 1988) and articles on Sino-Canadian relations and the international politics of Eastern Asia.

B. Michael Frolic. Professor, Department of Political Science, York University. Author of *Mao's People* (Cambridge: Harvard University Press 1982) and numerous works on Chinese and Soviet politics.

Arthur Andrew. He headed the Canadian delegation at the Stockholm negotiations for fourteen months. After retiring from the Department of External Affairs in 1979, he taught at King's College in Halifax; he is now living in Chester, Nova Scotia.

Stephen Beecroft. Recently completed his DPhil at Cambridge University. His thesis was entitled 'Walking the Tightrope: Canadian China Policy, 1948–1957.' He now lives in London, England, where, he is international adviser, Barclay De Zoet Wedd.

John English. Professor, Department of History, University of Waterloo. His most recent book is *Shadow of Heaven: The Life of Lester Pearson, vol. I, 1897–1948* (Toronto: Lester and Orpen Dennys 1989).

Brian Evans. Professor, Department of History, and Associate Vice-President for International Affairs, University of Alberta. He was formerly the counsellor in the Canadian Embassy in Peking (1973–4). He writes on Canadian–East Asian relations and the diplomatic history of southwest China.

Patrick Kyba. Professor, Department of Political Studies, Guelph University.

Author of *Alvin: A Biography of the Honourable Alvin Hamilton, P.C.* (Regina: Canadian Plains Research Centre 1989).

Janet Lum. Assistant Professor, Department of Political Science, Ryerson Polytechnical Institute. Her principal areas of interest are contemporary China and organization theory.

Peter Mitchell. Associate Professor, Department of History and Humanities Division, York University. He earlier served as the first secretary (scientific and cultural affairs) in the Canadian embassy in Peking (1977–9). His research now focuses on the connection between the mission movement, educational changes, and the rural question in early-twentieth-century China.

Don Page. Formerly with the Historical Division and the Policy Development Bureau, Department of External Affairs, Ottawa. He is now the Vice-President for Academic Affairs at Trinity Western University in Langley, British Columbia. He has published extensively on Canadian foreign policy.

Norman St Amour. Currently completing his doctoral dissertation in the History Department at the University of Virginia. His thesis is entitled, 'A Colossus and a Conundrum: Canadian-American Policy Interaction and the Recognition of the PRC.'

Index

Abbott, D.C. 50, 52, 66, 79
Acheson, Dean 136
Africa 85, 88, 90, 92–3, 99, 111, 114, 181
Agnew, Gordon 27, 38
aid and developmental assistance 12, 24, 27, 38
Aid-to-China Fund 30
Albanian resolution (at U.N.) 92, 94–7, 99, 101, 114–15, 118–21, 142–4, 193, 205
Aldred, Joel 219
Allen, Stewart 26, 37–8
Andrew, Arthur xi, 11, 214–15, 241–52; ambassador to Sweden 198–203, 205; head of Far Eastern Division of DEA 243, 245–6
Anglican Church of Canada: mission in Honan 31–2, 150
Angus, H.F. 7, 13, 34, 37
Armstrong, A.E. 22, 35, 39–40
Asia Pacific countries, relations with PRC 44, 83, 93–4, 108–11, 114, 116, 139–40, 192, 221, 224–5, 250

atom bomb 123, 153; exploded by PRC 91, 96, 106, 111
atomic energy 76
Australia 11, 13, 57, 59, 62, 70, 79, 87, 135, 138, 151, 169–70, 177, 214

Bandung conferences 93, 114
Banff Conference on World Affairs 95, 143, 158
Barnett, A. Doak 116, 195
Belgium 52, 57, 59, 62, 72, 83, 91–2, 111, 113, 120, 201, 244
Bell, Gerald 26–7
Bennett, R.B. 20
Bennett, William 244
Bethune, Norman 32, 40, 155, 166, 203, 212–13
Bevin, Ernest 49, 79
Blackmore, John 153
Borden, Sir Robert 18, 248
Bowles, Newton E. 145
Bowles, R.P. 134
Boxer Indemnity Fund 22, 24
Brennan, Brian 162

Britain 29, 65, 135; recognition of PRC (1949) 44, 47, 48–51, 56, 246–7; and China seat in U.N. 78–9, 83–4; influence on Canadian policy 8, 18, 21–5, 28, 35, 44, 54, 76–7, 153, 177
British Commonwealth: Canadian relations with 29–30, 38, 61, 154, 177; and recognition of PRC 44, 49–50, 52, 79
Brown, Margaret 26, 38
Bundy, William 117, 119–20, 141, 195
Butterworth, W.W. 141–2

cabinet: role in formulating foreign policy 4, 8, 10, 45, 50–3, 63–4, 76–8, 88–9, 100–1, 136, 170–8, 196–8, 211
Cadieux, Marcel 90–1, 95, 97, 105
Cahan incident 18, 34
Campbell, Peter 69, 71–2, 104, 244
Canadian Congress of Labour 228
'Canadian formula' (for recognition of PRC) 102, 194–8, 202–9, 241–2
Canadian Pacific Railway 19
Canadian Wheat Board. *See* Wheat Board (Canadian)
Canton 26, 31, 189
capitation tax 19–20
Carscallen, Charles 134
Carter, Jimmy (U.S. president 1976–80): establishment of diplomatic relations with China 12, 163, 211, 252
Casey, Richard 57, 138
Chen Li-fu 151
Chen Yi 93, 114
Chiang Kai-shek 27, 30, 44–8, 69, 108, 111, 116–18, 122–3, 150–1, 153–4, 157, 238; 'Chiang gang' 88, 200, 206, 233

Chiang Kai-shek, Mme 24, 27, 36, 151, 227
China, Republic of. *Before 1949, see* Kuomintang. *After 1949, see* Taiwan (Republic of China)
China lobby (U.S.) 53, 82, 116
China policies. *See* one-China policy; two-Chinas policy; one-China, one-Taiwan policy; no-China policy
China Resources Company 170–1
China seat (in U.N.): general 49–51, 54–5, 60, 66, 73–102, 106, 108–21, 137, 140–4, 190–3, 196, 205, 224; in General Assembly 74–7, 87, 90, 109; on Security Council 73–4, 76–8, 86–7, 90, 96, 119; in subsidiary committees 50–1, 75–81, 84, 103
Chinese Benevolent Association 226
Chinese Canadians: students 22–4, 30, 36; in Vancouver 218, 220, 224, 226; in Toronto 217–19, 224, 226–38; community organizations 217–20, 224, 227–33, 238; Christian churches 228, 231–2; school 231–2; clan associations 230–2, 236, 239. *See also* Capitation tax; Chinese Exclusion Act
Chinese Community Centre 218–40
Chinese Exclusion Act 20, 29–30, 32, 36, 39, 227–8
Chinese Freemasons 227, 230
Chinese Labour Corps 18, 34
Chinese language press in Canada 220, 229–30, 235; *Shing Wah* 218–19, 229–30, 235–7; *Shang Bao* 230, 232–3, 235–6; *Hung Chung She Bo* (*Chinese Times*) 230, 235
Chinese Protection Federation 227, 238
Chinese War Relief Fund 24, 26, 36

Chinese Welfare Society 232, 234
Chong Ying 219–20, 227, 231, 235
Chou En-lai 141, 151, 156, 160–1, 166; and Chinese foreign affairs 56, 58, 74, 77, 103, 157, 179–81, 201, 206
Christie, Loring 18
Churchill, Winston 23, 49
civil war in China 9, 27, 189, 221–2, 226; effect on Canadian policy 7, 17, 29–32, 44–8, 73, 136, 151–4; effect on Canadian missionaries 27, 30–2, 39, 151–3
Claxton, Brooke 53
Cleveland, Harlan 112
Cold War 3, 6, 10, 12, 43, 46, 106, 108, 153, 174, 230
Collins, Ralph 26, 33, 150, 214–15, 244
Colombo Conference 38, 49, 69
Colombo Plan 177
Committee of One Million 82, 116
Congo 88, 92
Conservative party. *See* Progressive Conservative party of Canada
containment and isolation of PRC: policy of 3, 54–5, 190; Canadian support for 3, 64, 66, 138; Canadian attempts to end 11–13, 55, 66, 68–9, 89, 101–2, 106–7, 110, 112, 123, 136–9, 143–4, 212–13; U.S. support for 54–5, 64, 89, 96, 106, 112, 116, 137–9, 155; U.S. attempts to end 68, 116, 118; 'containment without isolation' 116, 118, 195
Copland, Bruce 26, 37
Côté, Jean 244–5
Cuba 197
cultural exchanges 209, 219–20, 229, 232

Cultural Revolution 118, 157, 160, 181, 222, 224, 226, 250; influence on Chinese policy 140, 157, 192, 196, 201; influence on Canadian China policy 97, 121, 140, 144, 196
Cunningham, Gladys 26

Davis, T.C. (ambassador) 29–30, 46–8, 69
declaratory resolution (in U.N.) 90–3, 110–13, 139–42
Department of Agriculture 52, 169–70. *See also* Hamilton
Department of External Affairs (DEA) Divisions: American 61, 195; American and Far Eastern 48, 70, 76–7, 102, 196; Commonwealth 61, 72; Co-ordination 244; Economic 61, 91, 105, 110; European 77; Far Eastern 58, 60–1, 81, 83, 86, 90, 95, 104–5, 110, 155, 196, 241–6; Legal 66, 77, 86, 196, 243, 247–8; Protocol 245, 249; United Nations 61–2, 76–7, 102, 104, 196
Department of Finance 50, 170–1, 195–7
Department of Immigration 20, 22, 219, 228
Department of Industry, Trade and Commerce 196–7, 209, 214; Department of Trade and Commerce 53, 168–9, 178
Department of Manpower and Immigration 249
de-recognition of Taiwan (ROC): by Canada 4, 11–12, 51, 55, 66, 82, 191–211, 240–52; possibility of relations after de-recognition 4, 68, 197–8, 204–5, 211, 241, 245–52; in U.N. 55, 73–7, 82, 98, 110, 114, 142–3; protocol of severing

relations 11–12, 55, 68, 200, 209, 241, 244–52
Dickinson, F. 27, 38
Diefenbaker, John: prime minister (1957–63) 10, 60, 65–71, 85–9, 104, 168–78, 184, 218–19, 228–9; leader of opposition 56, 138, 143, 156, 158, 197–9, 224; relations with Eisenhower 85, 172–3; relations with Kennedy 9, 86–7, 173–4
domino thesis 64
Drew, George 56, 153
Dulles, John Foster 81–2, 104, 106, 108, 116, 134, 138, 156
Duplessis, Maurice 52

Edmonds, Robert 201–2, 214
educational exchanges 12, 24, 36, 235
Eisenhower, Dwight (U.S. president 1952–60) 54–5, 57–67, 81–5, 106, 138, 172; relations with St Laurent 84; relations with Diefenbaker 85, 172–3
embassies
– Canadian: in Chungking 23, 26–8, 46, 151; in Nanking 29–30, 46, 48, 50, 148, 151–5; Peking, proposed 50–2, 152, 154; in Peking, established 209; in Washington 61, 80, 84, 92, 96, 109, 111–13, 116, 140, 195, 198, 244; in Stockholm 198, 200–2, 243
– PRC embassy in Ottawa 193, 215, 222, 225–6, 233, 248
– Taiwan (ROC): embassy in Ottawa 11–12, 34–5, 88, 198, 219, 244–51; consulate in Vancouver 244, 248–51
– U.S. embassy in Ottawa 82, 117

Endicott, James G. 39, 134, 136, 145, 150–1, 153, 155–6, 164
Endicott, Mary Austin 134, 144
export credits 182
Export Credits Act 29
Export Credits Insurance Corporation 175

Faibish, Roy 176
Fairbank, John King 33, 116
Far Eastern Commission 50, 75–6, 136
Faris, Don 27, 38, 39
Feinberg, Abraham 228
Flavelle, Joseph 33
Fleming, Donald 170–1, 173, 175
food shortages in China 169, 178–9
Foon Sien 226
France 11, 22, 29, 52, 63, 72, 77, 195, 202; recognition of PRC 89–90, 109–10, 139, 194–5, 206, 246–8
Free China 11. See also Taiwan (ROC)
Friends Ambulance Service 27
Fulbright, J. William 116, 158, 180

Galbraith, John Kenneth 156, 159
Gardiner, James 52, 78
GATT negotiations 181–2
Geneva discussions 56–9, 83, 148, 156–7
George, Walter 58
Ghana 99
Globe and Mail 218–20, 229, 231; Peking bureau 4
Goldberg, Arthur 114–15, 117, 120–1, 141
'Golden age' (of DEA) 4–5, 17–18, 28–9, 139, 163
Goldwater, Barry 180

Index 259

Gordon, Walter 138–9
grain sales to PRC 4, 10, 157, 168–78, 180–2, 184
Great Leap Forward 179
Green, Howard (secretary of state for external affairs) 86–8, 170–3, 176

Hamilton, Alvin (minister of agriculture) xi, 10, 212; relations with Diefenbaker 168, 171, 175–6, 178; threatens to resign from cabinet 171–2; attempts to influence U.S. policy 173, 179–82; meeting with Kennedy 173; 'peace through trade' 173–5, 179–83; negotiates grain sales to PRC 168–72, 176–8, 182–3; advises PRC on export markets 172, 177–81; international influence 179–82; and GATT negotiations 181–2; trips to China 179–82
Harkness, Douglas 168
Harriman, Averell 156, 159
Harris, Richard 162
Harris, Walter 228
Head, Ivan 190, 210, 213–14, 216
Hébert, Jacques 189
Heeney, Arnold D.P. 69, 74, 80, 102–3, 154
Hickerson, Jack 80, 103
Higgitt, W.L. 222
Hilsman, Roger 108–9
Hoffman, C.M. 37
Holmes, John Wendell v, 4, 6, 60, 68, 69, 71–2, 102
Hong Kong 19, 26, 35, 37, 44, 113, 169, 171–2, 177–9, 189, 228–9, 235
Howe, C.D. 53, 136
Hsu Hsu-hsi 218

Hsueh Yu-chi 198, 244–50
Huang Hua 152, 159, 165–6
Hume, Steve 161
Hungary 60, 77

Ignatieff, George 74, 119–21
'important question' (resolutions at U.N.) 85–9, 92, 98–100, 113, 115, 118, 121, 140, 142, 205
India: Canadian relations with 34, 49, 59, 72, 74, 156, 159, 166, 176–8; recognition of PRC 50, 54, 61–2; and representation of PRC in U.N. 79, 83–5; Sino-Indian border conflict 10, 63, 67, 85, 176–7
Indochina. See Vietnam War; Southeast Asia
Indonesia 67, 74, 93, 140
International Bank of Reconstruction 78
International Monetary Fund 78
Italy 196, 201, 215, 244; in U.N. 80, 91–3, 96, 98, 111, 113, 120

Japan 50, 72, 108, 123, 156, 195–6, 237; Canadian relations with 5, 14, 18–19, 23–6, 30, 135–6, 152–3, 178, 214, 244; Gentlemen's Agreement 20, 34, 152; missionaries in 25, 34, 37, 134, 151; boycott of Japanese goods 25, 37; Sino-Japanese conflict 18–20, 23–8, 151, 153, 156, 227; Anglo-Japanese Alliance 18, 152; Japan at U.N. 76, 87; Japanese relations with U.S. 23, 25
Javits, Jacob 116
Jewish community in Canada 228, 238
Johnson, Lyndon (U.S. president

1963-8) 8-9, 68-9, 89-97, 108-23, 139-44, 157-9, 163, 180-1, 189, 190, 192-5, 197, 222; relations with Pearson 117, 119, 141-3
Joint Committee on Trade and Economic Matters 172-3
Joint Intelligence Committee 48
Jung, Douglas 218

Katzenbach, Nicholas 120
Keenleyside, Hugh 27, 32-3, 36
Kennedy, Edward 158
Kennedy, John F. (U.S. president 1960-3) 9, 68-9, 85-8, 106-8, 172-4, 184
Kettle, John 159
Kiely, John 161
Kilborn, Leslie 26-7, 38
King, George K. 39, 40
King, W.L. Mackenzie (prime minister 1935-47) 17-20, 22-5, 28-30, 34-5, 44, 135-6, 151-3, 227
Kissinger, Henry 157, 215
Korean War 5-7, 53-5; outbreak of 28, 52-3, 78, 154; end of 55-7, 67, 81-2, 137, 156; prisoners of war 57, 82; PRC condemned as aggressor 54, 78, 80, 100, 114, 154-5, 220, 250; effect on Canadian China policy 14, 28, 31, 43, 52-7, 61, 63-4, 68, 78-82, 100, 136-8, 154-6, 174, 220; effect on U.N. 54-5, 78-82, 93, 114, 155, 250
Kraslow, David 159
Kuomintang (Nationalists, KMT): government of China (before 1949) 39, 44, 51, 149-52; retreat to Taiwan 11-12, 45, 48
- loans to 29-30, 44, 136; reparations for loans to 50-1, 66, 203-4, 209, 211
- Canadian reaction to: anti-KMT ('losing the civil war') 3, 29-31, 45-7, 54-5, 76, 152; pro-KMT ('Free China') 11, 23-4, 27-8, 31, 46, 85
- political activity among Chinese Canadians 218, 221, 225-7, 229-31, 234, 247

Landon, Alf 181
Laporte, Pierre 250
League of Nations 18, 34, 35
Lee, Y.S. 231
Leger, Jules 59, 62, 69, 104
Liberal party of Canada 11, 45, 60, 63, 66-7, 89, 95-6, 106, 139-40, 143, 151, 189, 233
Liu Chi-tsai 199-200
Liu Shi-shun 23
Lower, Arthur R.M. 13, 19, 22, 32
Lynch, Charles 159

Ma, Y.C. 222
Mackay, George Leslie 155, 165-6
Mackenzie, A.R. 57
Malaysia 67
Manchuria 31, 47. See also Japan: Sino-Japanese conflict
Mao Tse-tung 47, 161, 203-4, 220, 224
Mark, E.C. 227, 231
Marler, Herbert 19, 36
Marshall Plan 45
Martin, Paul (secretary of state for external affairs) xi, 8-9, 52, 68-9, 71, 89-94, 96-7, 101, 104-5, 107-9, 111-19, 120-2, 139, 141, 143, 156
Massey, Chester 33

Maybee, Jack xi, 69–72
McCarthyism 53, 106, 153, 156, 162
McClure, Dr Robert 25, 27, 37, 38
McCordick, J.A. 245, 247, 249, 251
McNamara, W.C. 169, 171–2
Meagher, Margaret 205, 209, 215, 242–3
Menzies, Arthur ix, 33, 40, 48, 60, 69–72, 103, 136, 150
Menzies, Merril 174
Menzies, Robert 57
Michener, Roland 228
Ming Sung Company 29, 44, 66, 203
Ministry of Foreign Affairs (PRC) 52, 74, 201, 215, 252
missionaries
– in China: work 4, 17, 20–1, 30–3, 34, 149, 152–4, 220; freedom of religion in PRC 161, 231; influence on Canadian public opinion 8, 17, 20–1, 24–5, 28, 31–3, 46, 100, 133–5, 152–3, 220; influence on Canadian China policy 7–8, 18, 20–8, 30–3, 36, 39, 46, 152–3; relations with Canadian embassy 26–7, 151
– in India 34
– in Japan 25, 34, 37, 134, 151
– in Korea 34
– in Taiwan 7, 24, 155, 165–6
missionaries' children ('Mish Kids') 7, 31, 33, 150. *See also* Collins; Edmonds; Endicott; McClure; Menzies; Norman; Outerbridge; Ronning; Small
Molotov, Vyacheslav 138
Morton, W.L. 28
Mosher, A.R. 228
mutual aid agreements 23, 136

Nanking 29–30, 39, 46, 48, 50–2, 74, 151, 153–4, 157, 203
National Development Programme 175, 181
National Farmers Union 174–6
Nationalist government of China. *Before 1949, see* Kuomintang. *After 1949, see* Taiwan (Republic of China)
Nehru, Pandit 49, 62, 72, 83, 137, 156, 176
Netherlands 52, 76, 135
New China News Agency 224
new members initiative (at U.N.) 59, 62, 73, 83–4, 89
New York Times 74, 154, 157, 160–2, 224
New Zealand 57, 62, 70, 79, 120, 135, 166
Nixon, Richard (U.S. president 1968–74) 11, 99–100, 160–1, 164, 181, 199–201, 205, 210–11, 215, 222, 228
no-China policy 155
Norman, Herbert 136, 156
North Atlantic Treaty Organization 29, 44, 58, 64, 86, 89–90, 94, 107, 109, 138, 172, 244
North Atlantic Triangle 22–3, 29, 44–5
Norway 156, 166. *See also* Ronning
Nossal, Frederick 159
nuclear weapons. *See* atom bomb

Odlum, Victor W. (ambassador) 23, 26–30, 46, 69, 136, 151, 153–4, 165
one-China, one-Taiwan policy (at U.N.) 90–3, 108, 110–13, 119–20, 139–43, 191–2; Canadian support for 88, 90–3, 98, 108, 110–13, 119, 139–43, 192–3; Canadian rejection of 86, 113, 119–20, 140, 142, 194, 196, 199, 202, 204–7; U.S. support

262 Index

for 12, 141, 194-5, 199; U.S.
rejection of 110-13, 119, 140,
142-3; rejected by PRC 114, 142-3,
191-3, 196, 199-202, 204, 206-7;
rejected by Taiwan (ROC) 91,
111-13, 120, 142-3, 194-5, 198,
204, 206-8
one-China policy (at U.N.) 75-7, 79,
81, 99, 115, 119, 191; Canadian
support for 12, 99, 155, 191, 194,
197, 200, 202, 208-9; U.S. reaction
to 12, 194, 202; PRC insistence on
74, 77, 93, 104, 200, 205-9
Open Door policy (PRC) 252
Outerbridge, Howard 37
Overseas Chinese Anti-Communist
National Salvation Covenant
Movement 226

Pacific Council 135
Pakistan 79
Panmunjom negotiations 82
Parliament of Canada 5, 10, 56, 60,
63, 80, 100, 160, 169, 172, 176,
181-2, 199, 201, 208, 215, 227,
244-5, 250-1
Patterson, George S. 26
Pearl Harbor 23, 25, 153
Pearson, Lester B.: childhood and
education 33, 133-5; personal
views of Canadian foreign policy
8-9, 54-5, 61, 74, 121-3, 134-8,
144, 189-90; views of communism
9, 68, 107, 157-8
– in DEA: under-secretary of state for
external affairs 28; ambassador to
U.S. 135-6; secretary of state for
external affairs 8-9, 43, 49-63,
74, 77-84, 101, 136-8, 156;
meeting with Eisenhower 84;

relations with St Laurent 8, 49-50,
53, 56, 58, 84, 101, 137-9;
relations with cabinet 50-3, 56,
63-4, 77-9, 136
– prime minister (1963-8) 6, 8-9,
67-9, 89-98, 106-23, 139-44,
156-7, 163, 190; influence of U.S.
on 68-9, 89-94, 96-7, 106-14,
116-23, 139-42; economic
influence 91-2, 139; relations with
Johnson 109, 112, 115-19, 140-3;
Canadian attempts to influence U.S.
policy 68, 90-7, 107-13, 115-23,
139-44
Peking Opera tour of Canada
219-20, 229, 232
Pentagon Papers 141, 160, 162
Presbyterian Church in Canada:
North Honan mission, *see* United
Church of Canada, North Honan
mission; Taiwan mission 7, 24, 155,
165-6; Chinese Presbyterian
church 228, 231-2
prisoners of war: Hong Kong 26, 37,
44; Korea 57, 82
Privy Council Office 6-7
Progressive Conservative party of
Canada 10, 52, 56, 60, 66-7, 77,
81, 85, 138, 153, 179, 182, 198, 218,
225, 228
public opinion
– Canadian, re PRC: general 54-6,
81, 86, 89, 100; divided 5-6, 31-2,
63, 158-9; anti-communist 11, 32,
52, 54, 56, 65, 79, 81, 86, 100,
152-3, 156, 159, 161-2, 171,
174-7, 193, 219-27, 229, 239;
sympathetic to PRC 46, 62, 100,
103-4, 119, 157-9, 162, 175,
189-90

– influence on Canadian China policy: general 5–8, 11–13, 63, 100–1, 103–4, 214; King 19–21, 23–5, 28, 31–3, 152–3, 227; St Laurent 45–6, 52, 54–6, 59, 76, 78, 83, 138, 140, 153–6, 190, 227–8; Diefenbaker 138, 157, 171, 174–7, 218–20, 228; Pearson 68, 86, 88–9, 92, 112, 115, 119, 121–3, 143, 158–9; Trudeau 191, 193, 198, 211, 220, 222–5, 232–3
– United States 6, 55, 64; anti-communist 53–4, 68, 152–4, 180, 195; sympathetic to PRC 68, 157–9, 162, 164, 195
public opinion polls 63, 81, 86, 90

Quebec 31, 52, 56, 63, 68, 173, 212, 250, 252
Quemoy 57. *See also* Taiwan Straits
quiet diplomacy 9–12, 64, 101, 121–3

Rankin, Bruce 50, 69
Red Cross 24, 26
Reid, Escott 20, 62, 69–71, 76–7, 100, 102–5, 122, 136
Republic of China. *Before 1949, see* Kuomintang. *After 1949, see* Taiwan (ROC)
Ritchie, A.E. 91, 96, 113, 116, 119–20, 244–6, 248, 251
Ritchie, Charles 105, 109, 111–12, 140
Roberts, Peter 113
Robertson, Norman 28–30, 67, 69, 86, 104, 107, 171
Robinson, Basil 60, 72
Rogers, R.L. 69, 71–2
Roman Catholic church: missionaries 17, 20, 31–2, 34, 35, 57, 220; anti-communism of 32, 52, 56, 97, 104, 138; Chinese Catholic Centre 232
Ronning, Audrey, *See* Topping, Audrey
Ronning, Chester 9–10, 68, 122, 148–67, 212; missionary educator 30, 33, 62, 148–50, 152, 155–6; left-wing politics of 10, 62, 136, 150–1, 156, 158; view of China policy 9–10, 30, 46, 48, 152, 154–64, 212; recruitment into DEA 62, 148, 151, 154; relations with DEA 10, 70, 136, 154–8, 163–4; counsellor of Chungking embassy 30, 46, 48, 70, 151; chargé d'affaires of Nanking embassy 30, 51–2, 70, 77–8, 148, 151–2, 154–5, 159; at U.N. 68, 148, 155–6; ambassador to Norway 154–6; high commissioner to India 84, 104, 148, 156, 159, 176; negotiates at Geneva 56, 148, 156–7, 159; emissary to Hanoi 94, 115, 141–2, 148, 155, 157–9, 162–3; anti-Vietnam War speaker 157–60, 162, 185; influence on U.S. 10, 122, 156–8, 160–4; influence on Canadian policy 156–64; return visits to China 157, 160–3
Roosevelt, F.D. (U.S. president 1932–45) 23, 25
Rostow, Walter 109
Rowell, Newton W. 20, 133, 145
Royal Canadian Mounted Police 222, 226, 228–9, 234, 244
Rusk, Dean 9, 90–2, 94, 96, 98, 101, 103, 108–21, 123, 139–43, 155–7, 159
Ryan, Perry 219

St Laurent, Louis: secretary of state for external affairs 28–9; prime minister (1947–57) 8, 43–65, 73–9, 84, 100–1, 136–8, 154–6; effect of Korean War on 8, 43, 52–7, 61, 63–4, 78–80, 100, 136–7, 154–6; Taiwan policy 45–7, 54–5, 57–8, 63–4, 73–9, 81–3; relations with Eisenhower, 54, 64, 81–4; Canadian attempts to influence U.S. policy 43, 50, 53, 55, 57–60, 64–5, 101, 136–8, 156
Scarboro Foreign Mission Society 34
Seaborn, Blair 214
Seetow, Y.C. 229
Shanghai 19, 26, 29, 35, 50, 74
Shanghai communiqué 161
Shantung Christian University 21, 36. *See also* United Church of Canada, North Honan mission
Sharp, Mitchell (secretary of state for external affairs) xi, 11, 98, 101, 190, 193–9, 201, 204–5, 207–11, 220, 222–3, 232, 242–6, 248, 250
Sinkiang 47
Sino-Japanese conflict. *See* Japan; Manchuria
Sisco, Joseph 117, 120, 141
Skelton, O.D. 18, 35
Small, John 33, 150, 183
Smith, Sidney (secretary of state for external affairs) 60, 66–7, 85
Social Credit party of Canada 81, 153
Soong, T.V. 135
South Africa 70, 79
Southeast Asia, effect of PRC on 44, 48, 63–4, 66–7, 108–10, 114, 122–3, 137, 140, 157, 195
Southeast Asia Treaty Organization 64

Soviet Union 59, 171; Sino-Soviet relations 46–9, 66–7, 81–2, 106, 138–9, 143, 152–3, 180, 201, 206; in U.N. 74, 79, 85, 88, 113; boycott of U.N. 50, 76–8, 102
Soward, E.H. 161
Spaak, Paul-Henri 57
'special relationship': Sino-Canadian 5, 210–13; India-Canada 62, 176–7
Stalin, Josef 137
Stanfield, Robert 251
Stevens, H.H. 20, 35
Stevenson, Adlai 87
Stockholm negotiations 11, 98–9, 198–210, 223–5, 241; agenda 198–202, 241; face-to-face meetings 200–9; Chinese 'three constant principles' 98, 200–4, 206, 209, 216; Canadian practicalities 202–4, 209, 216; joint communiqué signed 209, 242–3
Stollery, Peter 237
study committee resolutions (at U.N.) 79–80, 87–8, 93–4, 96–8, 112, 118, 120–1
Suez crisis 60
Sun Yat-sen 149, 229, 236
Swanson, R.F. 162

Taipei 7, 11, 246, 252
Taiwan (Republic of China, ROC): establishment of 11, 30, 45–8, 54, 151, 155; relations with PRC 54, 79, 250–1 (*see also* territorial claims); reaction to PRC nuclear test 91, 111; U.S. support for 47, 54–5, 58, 66, 73, 76–9, 81–8, 108–11, 113–14, 116–20, 122–3, 136, 138, 140–3, 190, 193–5, 198–9, 207, 211;

Taiwan problem in U.S. foreign policy 48, 54, 79, 82–4, 109–11, 113–14, 119–20, 195; in U.N. 51, 73–7, 83, 85–8, 90–2, 94–5, 98, 108–20, 139–43, 191–3, 205; on Security Council 73–4, 77, 87, 90, 119; threatens to leave U.N. 55, 81–2, 117, 119
– relations with Canada 4, 6, 11–12, 45–8, 51, 73–8, 81–8, 90–1, 94–6, 98, 108–10, 139–43, 193–211, 219, 223, 241–52; unofficial relations 4, 7, 155, 197, 204–5, 211, 218–22, 225, 246–7; trade 4, 155, 178, 193, 196–7, 205, 252; ROC political activity in Canada 219–27, 229–30, 235–6, 247; Central News Agency 247; ROC reaction to Canadian recognition of PRC 198, 220–1, 246–7, 250–1; Canadian support for ROC 54, 64–8, 78, 81–3, 85–8, 94–6, 108–14, 117–20, 123, 139–40, 191–8, 210, 218–19; Taiwan problem in Canadian relations with U.S. 54–5, 68, 78, 81–3, 85–8
Taiwan Island 7, 14, 24, 45, 155, 165–6
Taiwan Relations Act 12, 211, 252
Taiwan Straits 57–8, 63–4, 68, 79, 85, 138
Taylor, Charles 161
territorial claims: PRC claim to Taiwan 54, 74–5, 90, 114, 191, 197–204, 206–9, 242; ROC claim to mainland 75, 83, 87, 90, 117, 122–3, 157, 159, 191, 199, 221–3; Canadian refusal to comment on PRC claims 90, 197–242

Thailand 108, 123
Third World 181–2
Thomson, James C, Jr 118
Tiananmen Square incident 5, 12
Tibet 62, 220
Tito-in-Asia thesis 47–8
Topping, Audrey Ronning 154, 157, 160
Topping, Seymour 157, 160
trade, Canadian, with China: potential 5–6, 12, 18–20, 48, 53, 66–8, 106, 111, 113, 139, 193, 196, 200, 213, 222; actual 10, 29, 44, 60, 67, 85, 191–2, 223–4
trade offices, Canadian 192, 196; Shanghai 19, 29, 74; Hong Kong 113, 177; Nanking 29; Peking 113–14; Taipei 252
Treasury Board 171
Trudeau, Pierre E. (prime minister 1968–79 and 1980–5) 8, 10–12, 96–101, 120–1, 159–63, 182, 189–213, 215, 218, 220–4, 233–4, 248–9, 252; U.N. policy 11, 98–102, 144, 190–3, 196, 204–5, 224, 233; China policy 8, 10–13, 98–101, 159, 182, 189–213, 218, 220–5, 231–4, 241–52; May 1968 policy statement 98, 191–4, 220, 234; Taiwan policy 11–12, 98–9, 159, 190–211, 218, 221–5
Truman, Harry (U.S. president 1945–52) 53, 54, 76, 78, 80, 106; view of communism 47, 53–4, 152, 155–6; U.N. policy 54–5, 76–81; China policy 44–5, 47–50, 54–5, 74, 106, 136–7, 151, 154–6; Taiwan policy 47, 54, 73, 78, 136; influence on Canadian policy 49–50, 53–5, 78–80, 136–7, 151,

153; Canadian attempts to influence U.S. policy 52, 76–81, 136–7, 153–6
Tsiang, T.F. 73
Tung Pi-wu 151
two-Chinas policy (at U.N.) 77, 82, 86–95, 98–9, 108–9, 112, 116–20, 140–3, 191–3; interim two-Chinas policy 82, 95–7; Canadian support for 54, 58, 77, 82, 86–92, 94–7, 108–9, 112, 117–18, 121, 193; Canadian rejection of 98–9, 118, 120–1, 140, 196, 199, 203–6, 208; French support for 89–90, 109–10; U.S. support for 58, 86–7, 117–18; U.S. rejection of 82, 87–92, 94–7, 108–9, 118–20; rejected by PRC 54, 77, 82, 86, 93, 98, 110, 114–15, 191–4, 196, 199, 204, 206, 208; rejected by Taiwan 54, 77, 87–8, 91, 110, 116–18, 142–3, 194, 252

UNESCO 76–7, 84, 248
UNICEF 75, 103
United Church of Canada 21–2, 25, 27, 31, 34, 150, 231–2; North Honan mission 22, 25, 27, 31, 34, 150; West China mission 21, 26–7, 37, 133–4; Chinese United Church 231–2
United Nations: sets qualifications for ('earning') membership 54–5, 63–4, 66–7, 74–5, 80, 82, 85–6, 91–4, 96, 108–10, 112–14, 118, 136–8, 143, 224; 'universality' principle 88–9, 94, 114, 139–40
– General Assembly, debates: Fourth (1949) 49; Fifth (1950) 74, 76, 79–80; Sixth (1951) 54, 80; Ninth (1954) 82; Tenth (1955) 59, 83–4; Thirteenth (1958) 85; Fifteenth (1960) 85; Sixteenth (1961) 88; Nineteenth (1964) 90–3, 110–13; Twentieth (1965) 93, 112, 114–15; Twenty-first (1966) 97, 105, 117–21, 190, 193; Twenty-third (1968) 98, 196; Twenty-fourth (1969) 205; Twenty-fifth (1970) 99, 224; Twenty-sixth (1971) 100
– Secretary General 75, 77
– subsidiary committees: Economic and Social Committee 75, 80; Trusteeship Council 77; Ten Member Committee on Disarmament 85; peacekeeping operations 113; International Commission for Supervision and Control 107
– and Canada: support for U.N. 29–30, 44, 55, 69, 73, 99–102, 123, 136–44, 155–7; Canada on Security Council 73–4; permanent delegation New York 61, 73, 78, 84–5, 92–3, 97, 102, 114–15, 120–1, 155
– and People's Republic of China (PRC): representation in, general 3, 8, 11, 73–102, 106–21, 191–3; PRC demands representation 54, 74–5, 77, 114, 200–1, 204–5, 207; hostility to U.N. 77, 93, 114, 122; Canadian support for PRC in U.N. 51, 54, 66, 76–80, 82–3, 86–102, 108–21, 123, 137, 140–4, 155–6, 190–3, 201, 204–5; opposition to 50, 59–62, 74–6, 78–85, 88, 91, 94, 111, 136–40, 224; linked to Canadian bilateral recognition of PRC 51, 55, 67–9, 74–7, 82, 84, 89, 95–9, 101–2, 108, 115, 121, 196, 200, 204, 224; representation accomplished 100, 102, 159

– and Taiwan (ROC). *See* Taiwan (ROC), in U.N.; United States and Taiwan, support for ROC in U.N.
United Nations Relief and Reconstruction Agency (UNRRA) 26–7, 30
United States: Congress 197; House Committee on Foreign Affairs 116–17; Senate 58, 80, 116; Senate Foreign Relations Committee 116, 158, 180; Central Intelligence Agency 117; State Department, *see individual presidents*; Treasury Department 173–4
– and China (PRC): role of PRC in U.S. Pacific policy 54, 64–5, 93–4, 106–10, 114–19, 122–3, 136–8; opposition to PRC in U.N. 50, 59–62, 64, 78–85, 87–100, 106, 108–14, 118–23, 136–40, 142–4, 155, 190, 193; support for PRC in U.N. 58, 77, 83, 85–7, 94, 97, 99, 101, 108, 115–18, 141–2, 205; hostility to PRC, general 6, 8–11, 53, 59–60, 81–2, 90–2, 96, 100, 106, 114–15, 118–21, 154–6, 173–4, 195, 210; PRC as international aggressor 54–5, 57, 68–9, 78–81, 91–2, 96, 108–13, 119–20, 136–43, 193; 'moderation' of U.S. views 57–8, 68, 83, 93–4, 101, 106–8, 117–18, 173, 180–1; policy reviews 58, 87, 106, 108–9, 115–18, 141; establishment of diplomatic relations with PRC 12, 163, 211, 252
– and Taiwan (ROC): diplomatic relations 11–12, 47, 87, 108, 116–17, 211, 252; U.S. support for 54, 57–8, 64, 66, 68, 79, 82, 90–1, 94, 108–15, 118–20, 122–3, 136–8, 195; U.S. disputes ROC territorial claims 86–7, 116–17, 122, 157–8; support for ROC in U.N. 73, 78, 83, 87–8, 108–12, 116–23, 139–43
– and United Nations: U.S. threats to withdraw 64, 78, 80, 82, 85, 88, 90, 98–9, 144
Universal Postal Union 77, 103

Vatican 223
Vienna Convention on Diplomatic Privileges and Immunities 247
Vietnam War: Gulf of Tonkin Resolution 69, 111; U.S. involvement in 68–9, 89–93, 100, 108–13, 115–16, 121, 123, 139–43, 158–60, 163, 174, 195; Canadian views of 7, 14, 68–9, 92–4, 107, 110, 112, 115, 139–43, 157–60, 163, 193

Wahn, Ian 218
Walker, John R. 159
Wang Tung 204, 242–3
Warsaw Pact 58
Washington Conference 18
West China mission. *See* United Church of Canada
West China University 21, 27
Wheat Board (Canadian) 168, 184; negotiates with PRC 107, 169–71, 177–8, 196–7, 205, 210; and recognition of PRC 196–7, 205, 210, 215
wheat sales to PRC. *See* grain sales
White, Bishop W.C. 32
Wong, B.F. 231
Wong, William C. 229, 231
Woodsworth, Charles J. 13, 19, 34
World War II 23–30, 45–6, 135–6, 151

268   Index

Worthington, Peter 161
Wright, Jerald 108
Wrong, Hume 28, 33, 53, 69, 103, 137

Yao Guang 215, 239–40
Young, Christopher 161

Zhao Ziyang 240